Masculinity in the Making

Masculinity in the Making

Managing the Transition to Manhood

Nicholas D. Young,
Christine N. Michael,
and Elizabeth Jean

ROWMAN & LITTLEFIELD
Lanham • Boulder • New York • London

Published by Rowman & Littlefield
An imprint of The Rowman & Littlefield Publishing Group, Inc.
4501 Forbes Boulevard, Suite 200, Lanham, Maryland 20706
www.rowman.com

6 Tinworth Street, London SE11 5AL, United Kingdom

Copyright © 2020 by Nicholas D. Young, Christine N. Michael, and Elizabeth Jean

All rights reserved. No part of this book may be reproduced in any form or by any electronic or mechanical means, including information storage and retrieval systems, without written permission from the publisher, except by a reviewer who may quote passages in a review.

British Library Cataloguing in Publication Information Available

Library of Congress Cataloging-in-Publication Data Available

ISBN 978-1-4758-5410-7 (cloth: alk. paper)
ISBN 978-1-4758-5412-1 (pbk.: alk. paper)
ISBN 978-1-4758-5413-8 (electronic)

∞™ The paper used in this publication meets the minimum requirements of American National Standard for Information Sciences—Permanence of Paper for Printed Library Materials, ANSI/NISO Z39.48-1992.

Contents

Preface		vii
Acknowledgments		xi
1	Toward A New Psychology of the Contemporary Man	1
2	Psychological Pitfalls: Males and Mental Health Issues	21
3	Manhood in the Making: Social and Cultural Influences on Masculinity in America	55
4	Education for Self-Efficacy: Breaking the Cycle of Male Underachievement in Post-Secondary Education	67
5	Making Their Way into the World: Finding that Just Right Career Fit	103
6	The Myth of Being the Macho Man: Aggression, Competition, Bullying, and Violence in Contemporary Society	125
7	Being Batman: Media Portrayals of Masculine Behavior	137
8	Does Father Know Best? The Many Paths to Contemporary Fatherhood Among Young Males	147
References		171
About the Authors		199

Preface

Masculinity in the Making: Managing the Transition to Manhood is written for everyone who is concerned about the health, education, career path, and well-being of contemporary American males who are transitioning from adolescence to emerging and young adulthood—parents, educators, counselors, educational administrators, student services personnel, higher education faculty, and students studying education, counseling, and psychology. The primary purpose of this book is to describe the developmental challenges that this transition poses and suggest ways that we can support young males as they grow into healthy manhood. While this book places its major emphasis on explicating the societal forces that impact young males' trajectory to adulthood, it also looks at the internal factors that influence this path. The goal is to help readers gain a better understanding of the roles that each of us can play in promoting healthy, prosocial development that resists the pervasive aspects of toxic masculinity.

It has been argued that the traditional rites, rituals, and human supports that historically have taught boys what it means to be a man and have served as markers of leaving behind boyhood and entering the adult world are few and far between in modern American culture. Young males on the threshold of adulthood, therefore, must scramble to find clues as to how to attain masculinity. They are often bereft of mentors and guides, and sometimes of fathers, and so they turn to the media, popular culture, and each other for answers.

Caught in a world in which women appear to have made great strides toward leveling the playing field, and with definitions of masculinity in flux, young males are left wondering how to construct a self that is both "man enough" and yet sensitive enough to meet expectations. Their friendships, connections, dreams, and inner lives are often misunderstood, masked, or dismissed, leaving them vulnerable to isolation, anxiety, sadness, or even depression. It is imperative that we better understand the complexities of fashioning an adult male self in order to help young men navigate the transition to the adult world with confidence and fidelity to their unique talents.

Most of the literature on boys and men in the years since the 1990s—commonly viewed as the birth of true scholarship on "whole men"—has decried the Boy Code and the effects of "toxic masculinity" as well as chronicling the woeful academic failures of boys and adolescents. The downtrend in male academic achievement on college campuses has been recently added to the negative literature on males. While this book definitely does not shy away from these problems, the authors are most interested in both understanding the transition from adolescence to early adulthood from a male perspective as well as suggesting ways to honor males' emotional lives, recognizing their special ways of making meaning, and proposing activities and relationships that positively address their identity needs.

Young males in America are falling behind in both college attendance and graduation. While as recently as the 1970s, males accounted for 58 percent of college students, they now lag behind women (Marcus, 2017). As recently as 2017, females made up 56 percent of the college-going population, reversing a trend in staggering fashion (Marcus, 2017). This reversal occurs during a time period in which well-paying careers require post-secondary education. In 2017 alone, 2.2 million fewer men than women will attend college (Marcus, 2017). With the lower attendance and graduation rates, there is also less of a chance that men will go on to graduate education and complete graduate degrees.

The problem, as most authors see it, begins with boys' earliest educational experiences. Most schools are not geared toward boys' ways of knowing and acting, and boys developmentally are ready for formal schooling later than girls; therefore, many young males are turned off or left behind educationally at a young age. They are designated as special education or other special student statuses in school, have far more disciplinary infractions, are retained, and earn lower GPAs than girls during their time in school. This continues throughout their school years and by middle school, far too many have already ruled out higher education or, even worse, will become dropouts during the critical transition from eighth grade to high school. Males are less likely to see post-secondary education as necessary or worthwhile in their futures.

For those who do attend post-secondary institutions, struggles abound. Unsure of their place on campus and looking for role models and mentors to guide them during their transition away from family and community of origin, the young men search for a sense of place and self within a variety of organizations. The authors explore both the positive and detrimental aspects of relying on institutions such as fraternities, clubs, and organizations to socialize young males into manhood.

The motivation for writing this book comes from several concerns:

- Our recognition that boys and adolescent males are struggling in our schools and colleges, which leads to lower academic achievement and difficulties as they pursue meaningful career paths;
- Our concern that while there are higher rates of college access, males lag behind females in college attendance and persistence to graduation;
- Our awareness that young males are confused about what it means to be a "man" in contemporary society and have few rites, rituals, and guides to help them attain healthy masculinity;
- Our sense that contemporary American society needs to develop healthy rituals and rites of passage to mentor and transition young males into responsible and fulfilling adulthood;
- Our knowledge that young fathers do not have the involvement, skills, and support that they need to provide adequately for their children and children's mothers;
- Our belief that society—via media and other prominent social and cultural influences—displays an unhealthy sense of what it means to be a man in our society;
- Our awareness that mental health issues affect young males, who experience higher rates of risky behavior, substance abuse, and suicide than girls in adolescence and emerging adulthood;
- Our knowledge that males' help-seeking behaviors complicate both academic achievement in college and mental health and well-being; and
- Our understanding that, given the epidemic of mental and emotional health issues that threaten the well-being of young males, the counseling field must develop effective strategies and campaigns to promote better psychological health and address acute mental health problems among males in the adolescent-to-early adult years.

This tome seeks to illuminate the challenges to prosocial male development in contemporary American society, particularly as the trajectory from boyhood to manhood has changed. The authors consider the developmental tasks inherent in the expanded period of late adolescence to early adulthood, with the proposed new stage of "emerging adulthood" and its implications for those in the eighteen through twenty-three-year-old range. This period is viewed both from the standpoint of college attendance as well as direct entry into the world of work. The authors also depict the personal and societal ramifications of fathering children during the aforementioned developmental periods. The challenges and lack of supports facing young fathers lead most young men to be absent from meaningful fatherhood roles, leaving young mothers, society, and the children themselves suffering from their absence.

Special attention is paid to the forces that shape attitudes and behaviors contrary to positive masculinity. The messages that so many young males receive from myriad sources imply that they attain masculinity through power, sexual prowess, domination, and avoidance of anything that smacks of the feminine or being considered "gay." Instead, the authors tease out aspects of education and intervention that can counterbalance the toxic elements at play in society.

Hopefully, the reader will gain a deeper understanding of the educational, relational, and emotional needs of emerging and young adults, as well as of the educational, counseling, and social programs and practices that can be employed to successfully guide their transition to adulthood. The authors seek ways to improve college access and success, provide career guidance and support, develop counseling and academic approaches that are male-friendly, and bolster all aspects of parental skill and involvement among young fathers.

The chapters to follow cover the topics mentioned previously, integrating scholarly studies and practical suggestions and are trans-disciplinary in nature, as they integrate the fields of education, cultural studies, psychology, family relations, and counseling. The goal is to offer best approaches to promote prosocial behavior, boost post-secondary academic access and achievement, support young fathers and their children, and offer ideas for guiding all young males into healthy, "whole" models of masculinity as they transition to adulthood; therefore, this book is organized around chapters that provide a brief review of relevant scholarly literature and research as well as strategies for moving from theory to praxis.

Manhood in the Making: Managing the Transition to Manhood was written by a veteran team of educators and counselors who have worked with young males in a variety of roles and settings during their careers. In their positions in PK–12 and higher education, as counselors, coaches, and parents, they have experienced the joys and challenges of supporting young males. Recently, they have published *The Burden of Being a Boy: The Educational Achievement and Emotional Well-Being in Young Males*, which delves into the critical issues of growing up male in contemporary society.

We believe this book will be a valuable resource for those readers who are invested in helping emerging males achieve their potential through their work in the fields of education, coaching, counseling, or in roles as parents, mentors, or employers. Rather than decrying the current state of manhood in our country, as so many works have done, we strive to inspire all members of our society to join in a celebration of healthy masculinity by helping young men find roles that fit their talents, relationships that support their dreams, and pathways to meaningful membership in the communities that surround them.

Acknowledgments

We would like to give our sincere thanks and appreciation to Sue Clark for editing this book. Her efforts undoubtably made the pages to follow stronger and more reader friendly. She has again outdone herself and is a highly competent and capable editor who we will be forever indebted to. Thank you, Sue, for making our work better.

Chapter One

Toward a New Psychology of the Contemporary Man

James O'Neil (2015), the father of the gender role conflict model and research, stated that "men's lives are not understood by either sex" (p. 12). Recent theories and research, however, have propelled us toward a new and different psychology of men. As O'Neil (2015) noted, it was the feminist movement of the 1970s that prompted the risk of the men's liberation movement; in turn, this movement prompted the genesis of men's studies and theories of a new psychology of men among scholars.

Prior to the mid-1970s only a few serious scholarly articles about men's gender roles had been published. Pleck's (1981) *The Myth of Masculinity* was one of the only books on the topic. These led to the 1990 American Psychological Association's annual meeting in Boston to raise the issue of devoting a specific division to focus on men's psychology, and this came to fruition five years later with the Society for the Psychological Study of Men and Masculinity. A peer-reviewed journal of the same name came out in 2000. By 2014, the psychology of men was formally recognized as an academic discipline in psychology (O'Neil, 2015).

There are still many deficiencies to be found in the applications of this research and theory; for example, O'Neil (2015) raises the unanswered question of how men's social gender roles contribute to problems such as depression, oppression, and violence. O'Neil (2015) also questioned if men fit into the diagnostic criteria that currently exist as well as what the most effective interventions and treatments for boys and men who need counseling are.

For several centuries, lifespan has been conceptualized as a straight-line transition from adolescence to adulthood, with teens essentially stepping into the roles of full adults in terms of career, relationships, and family. Looking back in history, this seamless transition makes sense, given that human life spans were considerably shorter than they are now. As the life span lengthened, developmentalists added stages such as "old age" and "old, old age" to note this expansion of human life.

Emerging adulthood is a new concept that reflects social and economic changes in addition to the lengthened life span. The very thought of asking what makes one an adult is an extremely timely concept; this question would not have existed in earlier history and it does not exist in contemporary cultures in which there are clearly demarcated rites and rituals that denote the passage into adult stages (Cote, 2000).

Prior to the twentieth century, there was little attention paid to life cycle theory. Indeed, there is scant reference to anything resembling life cycle theory until the twentieth century. While there are records that indicate various social roles, rights, and responsibilities of different individuals, with variations based upon one's gender, social class, or age, the idea of psychological adulthood is absent from the scholarly literature (Cote, 2000).

During the twentieth century, there was a dramatic reduction in fertility and mortality rates (Cote, 2000). This resulted in parents having much more time and attention to give to fewer children. With more resources and attention, some have argued that those very children became more closely tied to their parents and that childhood and adolescence were reshaped and lengthened. Cohabitation and higher education pursuits delayed marriage and initial childbearing, and the whole concept of adulthood became segmented into its own substages, depending upon the roles that the young person occupied (Cote, 2000).

THE RISE OF EMERGING ADULTHOOD

In the end of the twentieth century, Clark University professor of psychology Jeffrey Arnett and his team embarked on a qualitative research project, interviewing young individuals whose ages ranged from eighteen to twenty-nine about their life goals, career plans, and life satisfaction. With a diverse group of interviewees' transcripts to comb, Arnett, Kloep, Hendry, and Tanner (2011) came across startlingly similar themes from the participants. This period, it seemed, was experienced as a kind of limbo, with young people acknowledging that they felt stuck in between a departure from their adolescence but an incomplete separation from parents, family, and community of origin (Arnett et al., 2011).

Arnett et al. (2011) found them to be obsessed with personal identity—a task that most developmentalists would have posited as having been finished in adolescence. Sensing that the transition from adolescence to adulthood was not so linear, he coined the phrase "emerging adulthood" to describe a new stage (Arnett, 2017). This phase is a relatively new phenomenon, existing only in the last few decades in this country, and it has been suggested that it was borne out of social and economic factors common among the most developed countries (Arnett & Murray, 2019).

Arnett (2015) defined five distinct features that emerging adults share. The first is that this is a time of identity exploration with a heavy focus on making decisions about relationships, education, and career (Arnett, 2017). It is also a time of instability. Emerging adults make geographic changes, through college or partnerships, travel or job, and this pattern of change doesn't tend to end until families and careers are settled in their thirties.

Arnett (2015) also deems this the age of self-focus and of feeling in between. It is natural that emerging adults focus on the self, as they are preparing to make important choices about their identity, career, and life path before they are more restricted by relationships and jobs; however, despite being free of parents and the constraints of schooling, they report not feeling totally adult (Arnett & Murray, 2019). They know that they should be responsible for themselves but are not always certain how to do so.

The stage also is termed "the age of possibility"—probably the freest time that they will have as adults (Arnett, 2017). The study informants believed that they would live better than their parents had and would be capable of finding a lifelong soul partner. These emerging men have high expectations for their lives, both in terms of meaningful, well-compensated work and satisfying, long-term relationships; however, the realities may well be daunting (Arnett, 2015). Their high expectations may be setting them up for being unhappy in later life.

According to Arnett (2015) the stage of emerging adulthood is linked to key social trends in American society. Whereas a half century ago the median age for marriage was twenty-three years old for men and twenty-one for women, that median age now stands at thirty for males and twenty-eight for females (United States Census Bureau, 2018a). College attendance accounts for a longer period of transition between adolescence and adulthood and was prompted by the GI Bill of Rights for World War II veterans (Young, Michael, & Jean, 2018). While that privilege was overwhelmingly enjoyed by males, now both genders take part. College attendance also accounts for later ages of marriage.

Women now comprise the majority of college undergraduates; and having earned their degrees, a large number hope to have a career that puts their education to use before they marry and start a family. With advanced contraception and the ability to cohabitate—both far less available to previous generations—they have less incentive and are less likely to move directly into formal adult roles. Arnett (2015) also saw young adults overwhelmed by the incredible number of different paths that are available to them. Whereas earlier generations of young people, especially males, might have been automatically assumed to follow in their forebears' footsteps, entering family business, religious occupations, or the military, today the possibilities are much more diverse and accessible.

Arnett (2017) had a degree of sympathy for emerging adults and their struggles and wrote of the real need for expanded societal efforts to support them during the transition into careers and family. He championed this support, in part because he believed it would bear fruit. Given that individuals in their twenties are interested in exploration and change, Arnett (2017) felt that if provided with resources, they are more likely to improve their lives.

Arnett et al. (2011) wrote of the enormous cost both to society and young people themselves if they are not equipped to transition successfully to adulthood. Arnett et al. (2011) tackled the question of why some adolescents are well prepared to make the transition, while others flounder or fail to launch. One factor that appears to impact success is having the right balance of support and encouragement to spread their wings.

Emerging adults who have had helicopter or snowplow parenting struggle to take on tasks of early adulthood and finding their own independent paths as opposed to those who have been nurtured yet nudged along a path toward greater autonomy (Reilly, 2019). When emerging adults go off on their own, those who have endured too many life challenges may have had their reserves compromised and be less able to take on early adult challenges or be burdened by mental health issues as the result of earlier life stressors (Reilly, 2019).

Many emerging adults who struggle to find their early independence have likely faced past challenges that have inhibited their ability to complete developmental tasks of earlier stages, Arnett et al. (2011). This might be the result of early childhood adverse events, poverty, absent or neglectful parenting, historical or societal events such as war or economic depression, or a combination of factors (Collins et al., 2010). The absence of role models, mentors, and other social supports, including extended family, educators, and faith groups, makes failure more likely (Collins, 2010).

Phinney (2003, 2006), well-known for work on ethnic identity formation, wrote about the challenges in emerging adulthood due to different features in ethnic-minority groups. Due to various cultural and economic factors, many adolescents and emerging adults from ethnic-minority groups tend to assume what would be considered adult responsibilities earlier than their majority peers, contributing to the family through income, caring for younger siblings or parents, translating between the world of school and home, and other tasks that may interfere with their own schooling and goal attainment (Phinney, 2006).

During emerging adulthood, ethnic minorities also have the added task of negotiating their individual and cultural identity within the majority culture. Phinney (2006) found this task to be difficult both for native-born and immigrant young people. Balancing the cultural expectations of one's home culture and that of the large majority of society is extremely difficult.

Hamilton and Hamilton (2006) wrote on the difficulty of emerging adulthood for those adolescents and emerging adults who are either priced out of the college market or who don't transition seamlessly into vocational programs. They are consigned to working in low-paying jobs in the secondary labor market and generally move only from one dead-end job to the next for their working life cycle (Hamilton & Hamilton, 2006). Many suffer the effects of the lack of family or role models to help them prepare for a career, and those in low-performing or under-resourced secondary schools rarely have access to the kind of guidance, counseling, or internship or field experiences that more well-heeled students have (Hamilton & Hamilton, 2006). These authors suggest that it is important for American society to be devoted to helping all young individuals become equal members of the primary labor market and have careers that include decent pay, benefits, and opportunities to advance over the career life span.

In addition to the five main features of this stage, there is other developmental work to be done. For many emerging adults, one of the most difficult tasks is renegotiating roles with family. Arnett and Murray (2019) described the ideal transition moving from a point of conflict to that of companionship. The earlier notion of individuation and separation is inaccurate for today's young adults, as they need their families to continue their support but, at the same time, they need to restructure those relationships (Arnett & Murray 2019). Positive relationships with siblings and parents are predictive of better psychological adjustment and overall well-being in emerging adulthood (Arnett & Murray, 2019).

Arnett (2015) also discussed topics of love and sex with his participants and discovered that their world included concerns about intimacy. Meeting possible partners, the "hook up" culture, casual sex fueled by drugs or alcohol—all of these caused concern and often empty feelings as they lacked the qualities of true intimacy. While emerging adults experience higher levels of intimacy and passion than they did in adolescence, they also are more cynical and have a less-idealized picture of what love is (Arnett, 2015). One thing that is unchanged from adolescence is the belief that there is one special person out there meant especially for them and cohabitation is not as frequently a trial run for possible marriage as it is a matter of economic convenience in terms of finances or housing (Arnett et al., 2011).

In this period, says Arnett (2015), young people must find their own moral compass to guide them through decision-making that now takes place despite an absent family or community of origin. If these values have not been inculcated, or if they have been examined and found not to fit any longer, the young adult must seek to define his own ethical and moral codes of conduct (Arnett & Murray, 2019). Emerging adulthood is also a time to explore gender roles and form a tentative acceptance of one's own definition of male or female identity. This may be the first opportunity for LGBTQ+ individuals to safely explore or express their sexuality (Lang, 2018). New sexual feelings result in a false sense of intimacy with others and some emerging adults may struggle with issues involving body image.

Friendships are crucial to bolstering young adults' well-being and smooth transition and also are predictive of young adult competence and psychological adjustment (Way, 2013). Emerging adults are most likely to define their personal connections in terms of friends and are less likely to list family members. Married emerging adults listed their spouses as their closest friends and confidants while for singles of that age group, friends were the primary social support (Arnett et al., 2011).

Emerging adults need to find a wide variety of positive relationships, not just sexual partners—friends, role models, mentors, and affinity groups. Erikson (1968) identified the key developmental task of this period as intimacy versus isolation, noting that without intimate relationships, a young person cannot complete the developmental task at hand and risks being isolated. Isolation can lead to many psychological problems, including depression, low self-esteem, or a lack of a sense of belonging, which Tinto (1993) and others found correlated positively with dropping out of college. Among contemporary emerging adults, Smith (2011a) found that many confused sexual hookups with true relationships.

DELAYED ADULTHOOD

Hymowitz (2008) made the case that twenty- and thirty-year-old males need to "put down the Xbox controller and grow up" (n.p.). Not so long ago, the average mid-twentysomething had achieved most of adulthood's milestones—high school degree, financial independence, marriage, and children. These days, he lingers—happily—in a new hybrid state of semi-hormonal adolescence and responsible self-reliance. Decades in unfolding, this limbo may not seem like news to many; however, it is to the early twenty-first century what adolescence was to the early twentieth, that of a momentous sociological development of profound economic and cultural import (Hymowitz, 2008). Some call this new period "emerging adulthood," others "extended adolescence," while Brooks (2007) called it a "decade of wandering" (n.p.).

Hymowitz (2008) saw contemporary emerging adult males as those who "linger happily [in a hybrid state that is characterized as], semi-hormonal adolescence and responsible self-reliance" (n.p.). The child-man is stuck in this delayed adolescence, in part, due to a current pop culture that encourages him to do so (Hymowitz, 2008). Television, and particularly the gaming industry, target these young men and work to lure them into an addiction to these forms of entertainment that eventually become a substitute for real life and all its responsibilities.

The lengthened path to adulthood, Arnett believed (2015), puts emerging adults in no rush to get married or start a family. Because they do not have these economic responsibilities, such adults—particularly males—define their semi-adulthood as not feeling as though there is any rush to get married or have children. They are content with improving their career and waiting for everything else to fall into place. One of Arnett's (as cited in Neighmond, 2007) informants described his semi-adulthood as including "a roommate down at school. I feel independent in that way. I have to make sure my rent gets paid and I buy my own groceries, take care of my car, feel like I have adult relationships. I'm responsible for getting my work turned in and staying on top of things, so in that way, I do" (n.p.).

For this emerging adult, dependence on his family for some contributions to his living expenses, plus the loans he has taken out and his admitted lack of financial knowledge prevent him from seeing himself as a full-fledged adult (Neighmond, 2007). These comments were echoed by unmarried college students and their parents who were surveyed by a team of researchers at Brigham Young University. The parents were asked whether they considered their child—eighteen to twenty-six years old—to have achieved adulthood or not, and over 80 percent said no (Willoughby, Olson, Carroll, Nelson, & Miller, 2012). Of this group, the children had financial ties to their parents and also maintained a high degree of emotional attachment (Willoughby et al., 2012).

For the children, this provided an emotional security net and for the parents, it continued relationships forged in childhood and adolescence (Willoughby et al., 2012). For many parents, their children were considered to be friends with whom they could talk about almost anything. Children viewed their parents as safety nets for as long as they remain alive. A 2006 survey reported that 80 percent of young individuals had talked with their parents within a day and 75 percent see their parents weekly (Taylor, Funk, Craighill, & Kennedy, 2006).

Hymowitz (2008) pointed out that while young males seem in no rush to enter adulthood, there are legions of young females in the same age group frustrated by their limbo. These same women are, in fact, hyper-achieving in their educational pursuits, their jobs, and their social lives, which seem packed full of traveling and connecting with friends (Hymowitz, 2008). Their male counterparts are more likely to "hang out in a playground of drinking, hooking up, playing Halo 3, and, in many cases, underachieving" (n.p.). Media and other sales executives have found a market niche among the growing legions of emerging adult males who are free from bills related to marriage, home ownership, and childrearing (Hymowitz, 2008). While in 1970, 69 percent of this population was married, young males in 2000 tied the knot at only a rate of 33 percent, and in 2015 that rate was around 22 percent (Hymowitz, 2008; Yau, 2017). Free time and more money make this a very lucrative market for advertisers and salespeople.

Hymowitz (2008) chronicled the rise of men's magazines, lingerie events, the marketing of skateboards, tech products, video games, and entertainment that captures a somewhat disturbing side of toxic masculinity at this age. "Frat Pack" movies and comedians have plenty of "stupid fun"; [however, other forms of entertainment include] "low-level sadism for child-man viewers" (Hymowitz, 2008, n.p.). Emerging adult males spend more time gaming than do twelve to seventeen-year-olds (Hymowitz, 2008).

Young males have an overdependence on the internet, including those cites that cater particularly to males (Naskar, Victor, Nath, & Sengupta, 2016). Some, again, are humorous or news providers, while others cross the line into anti-female rhetoric. Some of these sites are misogynistic in nature and those who use them regularly pride themselves on lambasting women over their "numerous" flaws and foibles (Southern Poverty Law Center, 2012). Young women of the same age seem to link the words "immaturity" and "men" in their chat rooms and talk about the Peter Pan Syndrome and "Mr. Not Readys." The gender gap in readiness for entering adulthood seems stark, if you are to believe Hymowitz (2008).

If young males are lost or are reacting to feminism in backlash mode, they are also suffering emotionally and psychologically as their world changes. They are not forced by society to toe the line, settle down, go to war, and do what for centuries has turned adolescents into men—marry and father children as well as take on roles in one's community. The contemporary emerging adult male, Hymowitz (2008) argued, remains immature because he can be and because he is encouraged to be by popular culture; "there's no denying the lesson of today's media marketplace: give young men a choice between serious drama, on the one hand, and Victoria's Secret models, battling cyborgs, exploding toilets, and the NFL on the other, and it's the models, cyborgs, toilets and football by a mile" (p. 4).

Smith (2011a), in his exploration of the "dark side" of emerging adulthood, related the substance abuse of young males in this age demographic as a futile attempt to locate happiness and to become connected socially. For the emerging adult interviewees, this activity permitted them to feel a false sense of happiness. While for some, their intoxication allowed them to make social connections they might have felt too awkward to attempt, others used substance abuse to chase the blues or boredom or to manage their stress (Smith, 2011a). This was a more common theme among emerging adults who were not enrolled in college or engaged in specific career training. Smith (2011a) commented that such individuals are not only economically fragile but generally have more mental health issues and fewer resources to treat them.

Smith (2011a) was interested in why intoxication was such a seminal part of emerging adulthood and cited the statistic that 47 percent of emerging adults have engaged in binge drinking over the past two weeks. Traveling through adolescence and into emerging adulthood, the number of those individuals becoming smokers, drug users, and serious drinkers increases dramatically. Linked to being social and to releasing their inhibitions, emerging adults—especially those in college—tend to normalize their behavior, believing that "everyone" is doing it.

One disturbing outcome of Smith's (2011a) study was that emerging adults believed that they would be able to quit these behaviors once they emerged in later life and were ready to get serious. The effortless off-ramp from partying behavior did not appear for so many; yet the general belief of the age group is that their before-and-after emerging adulthood selves were somehow sealed off and unobtainable (Smith, 2011a). Fortunately, the end of emerging adulthood seemed to be accompanied by some sort of natural closure or at least a scaling back of destructive actions (Smith, 2011a). It seemed that the informants recognized that they were not able to hold down jobs, pass a drug test, be a present partner, or care for children and keep up the same level of partying (Smith, 2011a). Some also raised pragmatic concerns about possible long-term physical and mental damage they were causing themselves (Smith, 2011a).

Sometimes a life transition brought about a concurrent change and many of Smith's (2011a) informants reported simply growing tired of this lifestyle; while still others experienced religious or spiritual awakenings. Regardless of their motivations for change, they began to exit what they had once considered to be mainstream behavior and moved into a more temperate lifestyle that they saw as the hallmark of adulthood.

Smith (2011a) uncovered what he called the "shadow side of sexual liberation" in his study, remarking that while emerging adults inherited the legacy of the sexual revolution of the 1960s and 1970s, they were not necessarily liberated from struggles over their own sexual identity, behavior, and values. Sexual freedom, in many cases, led to making poor relational choices and the resulting ruptures in these false relationships plunged many into negative emotions, confusion, and uncertainty about how to proceed in their future sexual encounters (Smith, 2011a).

Emerging adult culture, it appeared to Smith (2011a), was one of hooking up, which is different from either dating or friendship and it boiled down to various forms of sexual behavior between strangers or those who were acquaintances. Many of the informants regretted their decisions later, as they resulted in such things as unwanted pregnancy, abortion, STDs, shame, or strained relationships (Smith, 2011a). Females, far more so than males, seemed to suffer the negative effects of this culture.

Smith (2011a) also found that many emerging adults were traumatized by ruptures in relationships, especially those that were sexually involved or involved cohabitation. Many admitted to being depressed, using substances, or seeking casual sex as ways to dull their considerable psychological pain (Smith, 2011a). For young men who were not prone to understanding or admitting to such pain, seeking help when it was warranted rarely occurred. They viewed their pain and isolation as something to be overcome by a kind of grit or hunkering down because they believed that was what men were supposed to do (Smith, 2011a).

Smith's (2011a) research reported that "65% of emerging adults found shopping and buying things to give them pleasure, 54% said that being able to buy more things would make them happier, and 47% equated what they own with how well they are succeeding in life" (p. 70). Rather than seeing money as a means to stimulate the economy, improve one's self, or help others, these young adults saw money in individualistic ways. Among young males, electronics, video games and other forms of entertainment, gear and other material possessions were important and mass consumerism was not an issue for them (Smith, 2011a).

Expressed visions of ideal lifestyles included being materially and financially comfortable. No debt, cars, homes and vacation places, trips, and being able to send kids to good schools combined for a happy lifestyle; while their focus on materialistic lifestyles. Their belief that

> recently invented, high-tech communication and entertainment gadgets—like IPhones, laptops, high speed internet, and big-screen televisions—as basic essentials in life [are byproducts of socialization and the] mirroring back to the older adult world, to mainstream society and culture, what has been modeled for them and what they have been taught. (Smith, 2011a, p. 108)

These findings make it difficult for many emerging adults to delay gratification by taking on debt for college or other postsecondary training. This is particularly true among young males. Taking on paying jobs right out of high school allows them the income to make some of these purchases, even though they trade off better paying and more secure future jobs. As is sadly true, these young men rarely pay their fair share for children they have sired, leaving legions of young mothers to carry the economic burden of raising them alone or with state aid.

Oesterle, Hawkins, Hill, and Bailey (2010) remarked on the difference in young males' and females' pathways to adulthood. They examined the interplay of the role transitions in education, marriage, career, and parenthood in their longitudinal study of the run-up to entering the adult world. The researchers found differences in the timing of transitions, particularly in marriage and childrearing, noting that while there generally is greater gender equality at this time in history in the United States than in any time previously, there still is gender inequality when it comes to responsibility for family roles.

Taking on marriage and/or family formation (which in many cases occurs outside of legal marriage) is seen as the major demarcation for entering adulthood. Oesterle et al. (2010) discovered three distinct pathways: (1) remaining unmarried through age thirty and having limited postsecondary educational involvement (27 percent of women and 26 percent of men); (2) marriage and living with children in the mid-twenties and limited postsecondary involvement (29 percent of women and 32 percent of men); and (3) investment in postsecondary education and postponing family formation (43 percent of women and 42 percent of men).

In the first pathway, women far more so than men, were mothers living with children, taking on the mother role early, usually by age eighteen (Oesterle et al., 2010). While men obviously had fathered children, very few were living with their children or serving as the primary caretaker. They tended to work more blue collar jobs and were more likely to delay actual marriage until age thirty or after (Oesterle et al., 2010).

The second category of moving into marriage and parenting responsibilities also differed. Women became married mothers at a much earlier age and began living with children earlier, 50 percent by twenty-one (Oesterle et al., 2010). While women were more likely to live with children than to get married before thirty, men tended to combine the roles but at a later age.

Women in the third category tended to marry earlier than men and were more likely to live with children. Men, on the other hand, tended to marry later, and to marry before living with children (Oesterle et al., 2010). Having been born to a teenage mother lowered the likelihood of postsecondary engagement for both genders and greatly increased womens' chances of being an unmarried early mother and mens' chances of being on the unmarried-by-thirty pathway (Oesterle et al., 2010).

EASING THE TRANSITION TO ADULTHOOD

Padilla-Walker and Nelson (2017) wrote a book that covers the topic of thriving in emerging adulthood, and they included first-person essays from young individuals. Many of the chapters and essays in this collection illustrate the value of activities that develop a sense of purpose and connections to a world larger than the self, such as service projects, religious missions, university-organized cultural immersion trips, and activities aimed at helping those less fortunate. There is a strong argument made for mandatory national service and other opportunities for meaningful exposure for those who do not have the resources to do so. Meaningful service activities, Padilla-Walker and Nelson (2017) argued, support personal development, cultural awareness, problem-solving skills, and civic engagement.

Bronk and Baumsteiger (2017) located the role of purpose as critical in emerging adults' development, viewing it as a powerful construct that can lead them to discover their own aspirations and values. A coherent identity cannot be formed without purpose development (Bronk & Baumsteiger, 2017). This is because purpose development helps them find answers to the important life questions such as "Who do I want to become?" and "What do I hope to accomplish in life?" Being able to answer these questions leads one to a positive sense of self efficacy.

Purpose can be the glue that holds the young adult's life together as he weathers the onslaught of societal messages about what he should be or could be. It can diminish feelings of being overwhelmed or uncertain; it can organize the structure of one's days and lessen psychic disease (Bronk & Baumsteiger, 2017). Having a clear sense of purpose is more likely to provide an emerging adult with appropriate peers who are like-minded and with a social network of others (Bronk & Baumsteiger, 2017).

Purpose development grows organically out of quality career development education and activities, particularly assets-identification and other strengths-based approaches. This is particularly critical for non-college-bound youth and those with limited resources. The manner in which an employee approaches his work is far more important than the job itself when searching for meaning and purpose in that domain (Bronk & Baumsteiger, 2017).

Matsuba, Alisat, and Pratt (2017) explored the role that activism could play in this age group, highlighting that as individuals mature in the development of their adult identity, they become more politically liberal and more willing to take part in support of issues that are larger than themselves. Erikson (1968) saw in his notion of generativity—the desire to give to future generations, to leave the world a better place after one is gone—the commitment to a kind of social activism, whether on a large or small scale. Being engaged in meaningful advocacy provides emerging adults with a sense of belonging, positive identity, and a "family" of other individuals who share similar values; however, Smith (2011a) found that

> whatever any popular culture or political observers have had to say about the political interests of emerging adults, we—without joy—can set the record straight here: almost all emerging adults today are either apathetic, uninformed, distrustful, disempowered, or, at most, only marginally interested when it comes to political and public life. (p. 225)

ELUSIVE MASCULINITY

Male development, Pittman (1993) wrote, is further confounded by the fact that "masculinity," a culturally constructed concept, is elusive and "an artificial state, a challenge to be overcome, a prize to be won by fierce struggle" (p. xiv). Gilmore (1990) agreed after he examined the ways in which boys become men in various cultures. Gilmore (1990) tried to define what it takes to be a man, what the puberty rituals attempt to instill in boys. "To be a man in most of the societies that we have looked at, one must impregnate women, protect dependents from danger, and provision kith and kin . . . Manhood is a kind of male procreation; its heroic quality lies in its self-direction and discipline, its absolute self-reliance" (p. xiv).

According to Pittman (1993), "masculinity is a group activity . . . [an] invisible male chorus [made up of] all the other guys" (p. xvi) who either applaud a man's successive approximations toward achieving manhood or jeer him if he is less than successful. The chorus is comprised of a huge cadre of men—real and mythical—who urge the man to abandon the less-than-masculine parts of himself and censure him harshly if he is unwilling to do so. It is no wonder that the Fox tribe of Iowa "considers being a real man The Big Impossible. No man who sets out to achieve total masculinity can ever be man enough" (Gilmore, 1993, p. xiv).

To make matters worse, masculinity is a generational, as well as cultural, concept. Therefore, a young man cannot inherit an historical sense of what being a man entails. Perhaps Levant (1995) best summed up the challenge of gender solidification in his comment on the incessant nature of male self-definition:

> In most societies, the tests for manhood are never considered finished; it is impossible for a man to feel that he has found a permanent place in the community of men. He believes that he can always slip back over the line, losing his manhood and suffering shame and disgrace by failing the test. In fact, most

men do slip over that line. The consequences for men of violating sex role norms are quite severe (and a fate worse than death in many societies) and usher in enormous shame. Many a man harbors the feeling that he is alone in his shame, that he alone has egregiously violated the male code, that "all the other guys" are doing just fine, and that if anyone knew his secret, he would be completely ostracized. (p. 244)

Boon (2005) updated the notion of men's struggles to live up to the "mythic figuration of the hero [that] thrives in contemporary American culture" (p. 1). Men are confronted with a paradox—either reject the traditional images of the masculine hero and be considered "less than a man," or accept "the testosterone-based behaviors that define the hero figure and pursue the impossible acquisition of superhuman qualities, a goal that by its nature must result in failure" (Boon, 2005, p. 1).

The mythic hero, according to Boon (2005), must go above and beyond, transcending the standards of the mere mortal. Such heroes hark back to the Greeks, who relied on the notion of heroes to infuse the characteristics of the Gods in humans on earth and suggested to humans the possibility of transcendence (Boon, 2005). The latter part of the twentieth century was marked by the decline of influence from "meta-narratives" with "narrative function . . . losing its functors, its great heroes, its great dangers, its great voyages, its great goal" (Boon, 2005, p. 2).

Post-September 11, 2001, American society needed heroes more than ever, and those heroes rose up in the images of firefighters, police officers, the military, and rescue workers—traditional men (Boon, 2005). Yet there is danger in such hero worship because heroes become "an idealized reference group . . . an important marker of identity" (Porpora, 1996, p. 211). Moreover, such heroes cannot be criticized, nor their actions scrutinized, because to function properly in society, they must be idealized. Boon (2005) offered such examples as the public's unwillingness to accept that looting, stealing, and racist action existed after such events as 9/11 and the aftermath of Hurricane Katrina, and that the heroic men who were the rescuers were some of the same individuals who perpetrated these crimes. Such idealized figures do "not occupy the social space of genuine male experience [and thus, mortal men] are always and necessarily inadequate embodiments of the hero figuration" (Boon, 2005, p. 3).

Society embraces male heroes that live by the ancient codes of bravery and violence, and as such "there is little difference between Odysseus slaughtering suitors in the Odyssey to regain his wife and Bruce Willis in [the movie] *Die Hard* slaughtering terrorists to regain his wife . . . [therefore] masculine behaviors that have been openly condemned are still rewarded" (Boon, 2005, p. 6). This produces a set of contradictory images for men to aspire to in what

Sheehy (1999) called "the sensitive New Age guy." Boon (2005) argued that "sexy" wins out. Citing Palahniuk's 1996 novel, *Fight Club*, Boon (2005) noted that despite society's politically correct statements about wanting more sensitive males, such men still are seen as effeminate (Boon, 2005). In a 1976 study by Michaelson and Aaland (cited in Boon, 2005), "men are perceived as masculine when they exhibit agency . . . [and sensitivity was admired] only when coupled with control" (p. 6). It is an extremely difficult tightrope to walk, one which, Boon (2005) argued, is essentially a no-win situation as "they either embrace the mythic figure of the hero, which they inevitably fail to embody . . . or they reject the mythic figuration of the hero and thus fail to embody the culturally coded definition of a man" (p. 7).

RELATIONAL ASPECTS OF MASCULINITY

Bergman (1995) believed that both men and women desire connections with others and are motivated toward self-in-connection; however, men's socialization makes fulfilling such a desire more complex. The first step in "becoming a man" actually consists of disrupting relationship, through disconnection from the mother. In his summary of "self-out-of-relation" or "self-partly-in-relation," Bergman (1995) crystallized the dilemma facing men:

> Motivated by sex and aggression, development means learning to be a separate, strikingly impermeable, and static self. A strong identity is necessary for a mature relationship. What is a mature relationship? It may be a deep attachment between self and object, or self and other, it may even be an "intimacy"—a sense of closeness—but it is an intimacy framed by never losing touch with this strong clear vision of self . . . it is not a mutuality. (p. 71)

Boys' and girls' primary experience of connection and mutual responsiveness, Bergman (1995) wrote, is similar in the first few years of life; yet the disconnection from mother that occurs as part of male socialization is not about breaking from the mother per se, but a turning away from the relational mode altogether. This sets the stage for future conflicts when dealing with mutually empathic relationships. The young boy sees that he must differentiate himself from his mother in "a kind of declaration of maleness" (Bergman, 1995, p. 74).

Difference becomes synonymous with comparison, and "comparison implies better than or worse than and can lead to the idea of one person having power over another" (Bergman, 1995, p. 74). The real danger, Bergman argues, is that if the boy's conflict over difference cannot be addressed satisfactorily, "the door is opened for the disparagement of mother, and of the relationship with mother, and even of relationship itself" (p. 75).

Men may be prone to developing what Bergman (1995) called "relational dread." Such dread makes men want "to avoid things relationally" (Bergman, 1995, p. 81), while their female partners seek resolution and understanding through the medium of the relational process. While conducting his mixed gender workshops, Bergman (1995) noticed an awkward "dance" between male and female partners. It is not, Bergman (1995) noted, that men do not listen to their partners (they do), nor that they don't have feelings (they do), nor that they aren't able to express those feelings (they are). But as they move on a slower timetable, trying to sort out the feelings and name them, their female partners, more adept at interacting relationally, pressure them to say what they feel.

Under such pressure, men experience relational dread and become increasingly desirous of escaping this mode of interacting totally. This causes the female partner to become even more insistent. Such tension is caused, not because the man is reminded of his mother, as some theorists would say, but because "one relational style is meeting another, quite different one" (Bergman, 1995, p. 82). Relational dread is experienced in a host of feeling states which include feelings of impending disaster, inadequacy, guilt, incompetence, and shame, and often, paralysis. So even when men desperately want connection, they may become an agent of disconnection by virtue of their lack of skill and comfort in this realm. For women, what happens is baffling; as one of Bergman's (1995) workshop participants describes it.

> When you want to talk about it, they get this glazed look, they look at you like you're a vegetable in a market. When you keep at it, they start to look like you're the enemy. You say, "yoo-hoo, it's me—remember me? Your friend? How did I get to be the enemy? I mean things were fine—what happened?" It makes me feel like a Martian in relation to men. (p. 83)

Summed up, Bergman (1995) described the difference in participants' desires for the workshop outcomes with the fact that men start out with dread "that something might happen" and women with the hope that it might.

One major barrier to men's comfort in the relational mode, Bergman (1995) felt, is their socialization to power. Taught that they both have power and should use it, men are afraid of power, in themselves and in other men. Because they are caught up in a hierarchical power structure, they suffer from constant comparison and fear that they will not measure up. The most powerful, in effect, also can have the most to lose. Believing that "sensitivity to the welfare of others drains power and is hazardous [men struggle with], how to express power in relationship" (Bergman, 1995, p. 79).

Bergman's (1995) observations led him to believe that men genuinely desire both connections with others and connections with self—what Jordan

(1995) called "self-empathy." When they actually enter into a true mutuality, it feels foreign; thus, prompting creeping relational dread. Further, men are socialized to compartmentalize, separating the world of work from the world of home and family in ways that most women are not. This presents a problem because "my women patients have taught me that women want to feel that men are engaged actively and with continuity in the process of relationship" (Jordan, 1995, p. 80). Men in relationships do display a host of positive qualities, according to female partners. Among these are directness, taking action, producing things, dealing with fear, being strategic, and thinking rationally; yet these qualities are not what one generally associates with intimacy and connectedness (Jordan, 1995).

FINAL THOUGHTS

Emerging adulthood—that period from eighteen to twenty-five years of age—is a new developmental stage that was postulated as the result of dramatic social, economic, and life span changes over the past century. Such factors as extended life spans, lower fertility and mortality rates, greater social mobility and social diversity, more access to postsecondary education, changing job markets, an increased likelihood of holding multiple jobs over one's career life span, and simply a greater interest in human beings and their development have driven changes in the way we conceptualize psychological growth and maturation.

Emerging adulthood, like all stage theories, is characterized by a number of specific developmental tasks that must be completed successfully in order for young individuals to launch into adulthood. These tasks center on young people moving away from their families and communities of origin into more self-authored identities. The major emerging adult tasks include forming a more autonomous identity, setting career goals, discovering a sense of purpose, renegotiating family relationships, creating new social networks, and developing a moral compass. For emerging adults who juggle multiple identities, have taken on family responsibilities such as child-rearing early in life, are from marginalized groups, or who have limited resources and social supports, navigating the transition to adulthood may be particularly challenging.

College may be a wonderful launchpad for some emerging adults, yet not all young males thrive there. Those who are not able or who choose not to attend college during emerging adulthood may find their identity and purpose through career and technical education, military service, travel, service projects that benefit others, or apprenticeships or mentored work experiences that give them the skills, attitudes, and aspirations to succeed in work roles in adulthood.

Arnett (2015) and Smith (2011a) portray emerging adulthood as a time of confusion, as well as optimism, with so many emerging adults undergoing the experience of feeling "lost in transition," unsure of their identities, their goals, their moral guidelines, or their paths forward. These uncertainties can unfortunately lead some to risky behaviors that may have short or long-term consequences to their health and well-being.

Young males in this developmental period seem at particular risk for not fulfilling their potential to make a smooth transition to full adulthood. They linger in a kind of delayed adolescence or "neverland" in which they refuse or don't know how to grow into healthy manhood. Fewer of them attend postsecondary education, many have fathered children that they do not adequately support, and there is a large population that passes up the sacrifice of preparing for a later, more fulfilling, secure, and better-paying career for the short-term financial benefits of a job (Carnevale, Hanson, & Fasules, 2018).

Factors such as socialization to toxic masculinity, media, absent fathers, and the failure to convince young males of the necessity of postsecondary education in one form or another, may account for their poor transitioning. More males than females are still living at home and are at least partially dependent upon family for economic survival during emerging adulthood. There seems also to be more role confusion for young males. While contemporary girls are told that they can be anything that they aspire to be, it's not quite clear what young males are supposed to be. Are they the providers, the warriors, the lovers, the present parents, the CEOs, the Iron Johns, or the equal household partners—or all of these?

Emerging adulthood can be an extremely exciting period of life, full of possibilities for personal growth, relationships, career, and civic engagement. Understanding how to help young individuals, especially young males, reap the full benefits of this period and helping them to achieve personally meaningful goals that also prepare them to contribute to society, be good partners, and responsibly parent their children is a current challenge that all who are interested in young males' development must address.

POINTS TO REMEMBER

- Emerging adulthood, a relatively new developmental stage, is comprised of the years from eighteen to twenty-five and is marked by the transition from adolescence into early adulthood.
- Emerging adulthood is made up of five main characteristics: identity explorations, instability, self-focus, feeling in-between, and possibility/optimism.

- How well young individuals navigate the emerging adult transition into adulthood depends upon individual, societal, and family supports.
- Those who struggle with this transition are more likely to fall prey to aspects of the "dark side" of emerging adulthood: substance abuse, false happiness, casual sexual relationships, mental health issues, isolation and loneliness, consumerism, moral confusion, and identity crisis.
- During emerging adulthood, females are more apt to access and complete postsecondary education than are males.
- Successfully navigating emerging adulthood and consolidating a positive identity may be more difficult for youth from minority and marginalized populations.
- Males tend to delay marriage longer than females, especially if they have grown up in single-mother households or had family disruptions during their youth and tend to live with children within the context of marriage.
- There are gender differences in the pathways to adulthood with more females living with children and being their primary caregivers, either married or unmarried during this time period, and far more unmarried females being the primary economic provider for children than young males.

Chapter Two

Psychological Pitfalls
Males and Mental Health Issues

To be a boy in contemporary America is to face a gauntlet of challenges to one's mental and emotional health and well-being. While Amin, Kågesten, Adebayo, and Chandra-Mouli (2018) noted the rightful attention in global health and development initiatives on women and girls, the authors also expressed concern about the need to focus on the mental health and well-being of boys. Entering adolescence, boys are more at risk for hazards to their mortality and morbidity. Among these are greater risks for interpersonal violence, personal injury, substance abuse, sexually transmitted diseases, and other threats to their bodies and minds (Amin et al., 2018). Boys are medicated more often, account for almost all of the school shooters, and are at even higher risk in most categories if they are minority or marginalized youth. Compounding this is the fact that males are less likely to seek early help or treatment. Male behaviors in the health domains have long-lasting and profound consequences both for themselves and their partners (Amin et al., 2018).

Many authors argue that it is the very construction of masculinity norms in our country that put boys and young men at great risk. For these writers, the ways in which boys learn what it means to be a "man" increase the likelihood of engaging in risky behaviors. Gender socialization itself can be a key factor contributing to poor health and well-being. Zakrzewski (2014) decried the type of socialization that equates male maturity with "emotional stoicism, autonomy, and self-sufficiency" (n.p.).

Historically, an interest in boys' and men's psychological and emotional health and well-being sprung up in the 1980s and 1990s with the rise of the men's movement and great dedication on the part of the American Psychological Association and other professional groups to creating separate groups to research and disseminate knowledge about men's development, psychological crises, and effective therapeutic interventions. Some of the seminal studies paved the way for thinking about the genesis of men's problems, beginning in boyhood.

AN EPIDEMIC OF UNWELLNESS

The scope of psychological unwellness among children and adolescents in contemporary America is staggering. Anderson (2016) believed that mental health disorders among children currently affect approximately one fifth of our population and Mahnken (2017) concurred. According to Page and Johnstone (2017), between the years of 2010 and 2015, the number of hospitalizations due to children's committing self-harm increased 50 percent. The percentage of children younger than seventeen who suffered from mood disorders increased by 68 percent during the time span of 1997 to 2011 (Page & Johnstone, 2017).

Of those adults teaching in American schools in 2017, 80 percent saw more stress, panic attacks, and anxiety disorders in their students; statistics show that similar increases in depression, eating disorders, and incidents of self-harm also were noted (Page & Johnstone, 2017). The national suicide hotline, Childline, pegged 2016 as the year with the highest number of youth calls (Page & Johnstone, 2017). Schools also reported that more than a half of their student populations was plagued by significant, diagnosed behavioral, emotional, or learning problems (Adelman & Taylor, 2010).

These estimated numbers translate into around 15 million children and adolescents nationally who should be receiving mental health care; yet only approximately one half actually do (Mahnken, 2017). Boys are notoriously resistant to mental health counseling and interventions and only 7.4 percent of adolescents reported seeing a counselor or therapist during the 2016 calendar year (Mahnken, 2017).

The numbers of children and adolescents with ADHD, conduct disorders, depression, autism, and substance abuse continue to rise, yet fewer families have adequate health insurance to address their children's needs and, more and more often, schools are the last resort in the fight for better health and well-being. There is no doubt that children and adolescents who suffer mental health disorders have their problems compounded, as is reflected in higher rates of substance abuse, dropping out of school, and engagement with the criminal justice system (Mahnken, 2017). As school budgets become stressed, they become less able to serve as de facto mental health clinics, given how short-staffed they are.

It is important to note that there are many life circumstances that cause emotional, social, and behavioral problems for both boys and girls. These include grief, loss, victimization, abuse and neglect, assault, poverty, relationship problems, disabilities, family stress, and transitions (Degges-White & Colon, 2012). There are many developmental challenges for both genders that are simply part of growing up; yet there also are differences in the types of disorders, their expression, and the diagnostic criteria between young males and females.

"MALE" DISORDERS

Another critical element that the therapist must contend with is the fact that psychological conditions may present differently in male and female clients. One salient example is that of depression. Men's hidden depression was the subject of Real's 1997 book titled *I Don't Want to Talk About it*. In it, he argued against the widespread belief that depression is a woman's disease, writing instead that there is a cultural cover-up when it comes to admitting the degree to which depression plays a major role in the lives of contemporary men. Real (1997) stated that our society forces boys and girls, at very early ages, to metaphorically cut themselves in half with the result being that girls do not fully develop their public selves, assertiveness, and voice, while boys lose their expressiveness and connection to others.

Overt depression—the more classic type of depression exhibited through symptoms described in the Diagnostic and Statistical Manual of Mental Disorders (2017)—commonly known as the DSM-5—is what most individuals would identify as acute and dramatic. Allegedly, in the late 1990s, some 6–10 percent of the population suffered from this; however, Real (1997) felt that it was a much greater number, since men experience depression in ways that are not recognized and treated. The stigma of suffering from a mental illness or any medical condition, according to Real (1997), for that matter, was and is so much greater for men.

Real (1997) described in detail about covert or masked depression in males. Mental health professionals, he said, were far more likely to treat the symptoms of men's depression (substance abuse, marital tensions, and work problems) than they were to identify and treat the underlying causes. Left untreated, long-term, chronic covert depression can explode into overt depression. While many of Real's (1997) clients did report some of the more classic symptoms of depression, others spoke of the lack of capacity to feel—a sort of emotional numbness, similar to Sifneos's (1987) alexithymia.

Real (1997) called depression an auto-aggressive disease in which the self literally attacks the self. "In overt depression, that attack is borne; in covert depression, the man attempts to ward it off" (Real, 1997, p. 54). In covert depression men defend themselves against shame, fleeing into addiction, narcissistic disorder, or grandiosity (Real, 1997). Treating themselves, men feel better when the object of their addiction is continuous, but if disrupted, that very addiction plunges the man into deeper depression. This deeper depression triggers a greater need for the object of addiction, whether drugs, alcohol, women, or work (Real, 1997). In each case, an elevating intoxication attends the object of the man's addiction.

Many of these addictive choices are socially condemned, but others, like workaholism for men, actually are rewarded. The addiction defense moves men from the "less than" position—intolerable for traditional men—to a "better than" position; however, this happens without the man confronting his demons (Real, 1997). Without experiencing overt depression men can never be cured as "the only real cure for covert depression is overt depression" (Real, 1997, p. 68).

Without ever acknowledging it, traditional men depend on their partners to supplement deficiencies in their self-esteem; if those partners fail, the men become overcome with depression and shame, yet have only the familiar outlets of psychological and physical rage to medicate their depression (Real, 1997). Being socialized to externalize their distress, men escape overt depression, only to drive it underground.

Part of the route to cure involved what Real (1997) called "re-parenting" of the male self. This involves an awareness of the role that socialization has played in causing the man's initial distress as well as an acceptance of some of the responsibility for their behaviors, since men are socialized to see themselves as unfairly treated, rather than defective. This vision is compounded by the fact that they are under-socialized in the ability to express their emotions and needs.

Recovery includes identifying personal strengths and weaknesses in five areas to include self-esteem, protection, care, knowledge, and moderation (Real, 1997). These are key to developing relational maturity, first in the self, and then eventually in intimate relationships. Men must be educated to be skillful in these areas before they can hope to achieve authentic relationships that will help them to be emotionally mature (Real, 1997). In essence, men must be helped to "learn" intimacy. They also must learn to care for themselves, which is in direct contrast to the societal message that they must be the "sturdy oak" who defends and protects others (Pollack, 1998). Ultimately, if men are able to heal the disconnect, they will buffer themselves against the epidemic of debilitating depression.

An example of the difficulty in convincing men to seek treatment for depression, or other disorders, was depicted in the *Real Men. Real Depression* campaign (Rochlen, Whilde, & Hoyer, 2005). Recognizing that it would take a novel approach to get traditional men to address their symptoms, the *Real Men. Real Depression* campaign was created to raise public awareness about depression among men and to address the fact that "men are less likely than women to recognize, acknowledge, and seek treatment for their depression" (Rochlen et al., 2005, p. 2). Using the testimonies of traditional men with histories of depressive illness, a documentary filmmaker created a series of public service announcements for television. The campaign also utilized brochures, radio ads, and an interactive website. The slogan for the campaign was, "It takes courage to ask for help" (U.S. Department of Health & Human Services: National Institutes of Health, n.d., n.p.), and the public service announcements made use of real men in traditional occupations to be its spokespeople.

The entire campaign was based upon key strategies to counteract traditional men's resistance to mental health therapy. The first is "that men manifest depression through moods and behaviors and self-reports that are different from women, and that our diagnostic tools are too often blind to this gender disparity" (Pollack, 1998, p. 160). The campaign promoted the idea that men experienced depression very differently from women. By endorsing male-based depression, the campaign helped men to differentiate themselves from their stereotyped notion of women's illness.

Second, the campaign attempted to counter the stereotype that only the weak seek help by using hypermasculine participants as the "poster boys" and voices of the media presentations (U.S. Department of Health & Human Services: National Institutes of Health, n.d.). A traditionally masculine peer reference group was used to attract traditional men who are more likely to be persuaded by media figures who look athletic, professional, and heterosexual. The choice of "real men" as the title of the campaign was made deliberately to reach out to men who conform more rigidly to gender roles, since they are less likely to seek help (Rochlen et al., 2005, p. 5).

McGrath (2016) noted that the population at highest risk for depression and other serious mental health issues today is that of adolescent boys. Rates of depression and anxiety disorders are rapidly rising and for the first time in history, depression among males is almost the same as among females. The "disquietude" that has come in the wake of shifting gender roles and opportunities, positive as many of those have been, have left boys and young men in the dust in terms of clear expectations for their expression of masculinity. Along with family dysfunction and the lack of male role models and mentors for so many, the transition out of boyhood is rocky (McGrath, 2016).

The author equates boys' troubles with communicating their feelings and worries to having "a padlock on your tongue" (McGrath, 2016, n.p.). This puts boys at risk of seeking out alternative ways to deal with stressors, such as substance abuse, immersion in the world of cyber fantasy, or self-destructive risky behaviors. Depression, suicidal ideation, and even suicide are possible outcomes of unresolved struggles with masculinity, uncertain future plans, relationships with love interests and parents, sexuality, bullying, or other problems. The frequent male choice to disengage rather than seek out help leads to greater risk of emotional and mental health challenges (McGrath, 2016).

Given Brooks's (2017) observation that men arrive at the therapist's office only as a last resort, hoping to "fix" a pressing problem, it makes sense that the campaign acknowledged men's feelings about seeking help. The men who share their stories speak about the dire situations—impending job losses, broken relationships, and thoughts of suicide—which finally drove them to therapy. This disidentification with seeking therapy under less duress plays subtly into the male ego, while at the same time tacitly suggesting that it may be useful to seek help earlier than the speakers did. In being forced to carefully construct a campaign that "devises an alternative model of help seeking that is characterized by traditionally masculine qualities, including courage, strength, and purposeful action" (Rochlen et al., 2005, p. 6), the authors underscore the powerful societal taboo against traditional men desiring therapeutic intervention.

In direct contrast to popular assumption, men actually show greater physiological response when emotionally aroused than do women, and they take longer to return to their physiological baseline when aroused (Gottman & Gottman, 2015). This renders men more likely to avoid aversive or overwhelming stimuli by withdrawing from them. It is essential that an effective therapist shares this knowledge with both male and female partners in order to help them understand men's avoidance of emotionally difficult situations (Gottman & Gottman, 2015).

When men do submit to entering therapy, a key step is to demystify their emotional behavior (Wong & Rochlen, 2005). There is actual disagreement within the field of men's studies as to whether men actually are emotionally inexpressive due to gender role socialization, which equates being emotionally expressive with being female, or whether this is in fact a fallacy (Wong & Rochlen, 2005). If men are conditioned not to feel, or are unaware of their feelings, they may suffer from alexithymia; however, it may be that men simply are socialized to think that they shouldn't be expressive, rather than being limited in this capacity (Levant, 1995). Kennedy-Moore and Watson (1999) proposed a five-step model for understanding this concept.

1. First, a stimulus may activate a primary affective state and/or physiological arousal. The same stimulus may produce different emotional reactions in different individuals.

2. The second step involves conscious awareness of the basic affective state to which the individual is aroused. The authors argue that men often disrupt this awareness, repressing their reactions because that's not what or how men are supposed to feel.
3. The third step involves labeling and interpreting one's emotion; men's socialization to split off from undesirable emotions makes them have different identifications, descriptions, and expressions of such emotions.
4. The fourth stage involves personal evaluation of his response as acceptable. Unfortunately, there is a whole repertoire of emotions that are considered not manly.
5. This leads to the final step of perceiving whether or not he reads his social context as being accepting of such emotional expression. If the perception is that it is not safe, the emotional expression will be squashed.

Following this model, it may be realized that it is too unsafe for men to articulate emotions, rather than their being unable to feel or articulate emotions (Kennedy-Moore & Watson, 1999).

Rochlen, Land, and Wong (2004) found that men have a more favorable evaluation of online counseling rather than traditional counseling. They speculate that this may be because of a greater perception of anonymity, and thus safety, lowering fears of expression of emotions. The consequences of helping traditional men express their emotions more openly has both potentially positive and negative outcomes that must be considered.

Greater emotional disclosure can help men lower their distress if validated by a confidant or by male peers in a group setting; however, men may experience greater distress if they feel vulnerable as a result of expressing what they perceive to be as taboo emotions (Wong & Rochlen, 2005). It is the conflict between expressive style and that of his significant other or of societal norms that can be detrimental to men's health, so in considering the benefits of developing greater expressiveness in male clients, therapists also must help them to recognize and prepare for the consequences of this change. This very dilemma is one of the arguments for well-functioning men's therapeutic groups.

Wong and Rochlen (2005) stressed that rather than seeing males as inherently at greater psychological risk because of their emotional inexpressiveness, the degree of gender role conflict between the man and his interpersonal and social settings must be gauged. There are diverse possible causes for male inexpressiveness that do exist, and these must be recognized in order to be treated effectively. One possible cause is a disruption at the aforementioned stages two and three; therefore, clinical implications involve helping male clients learn to better identify and name their emotions.

At stage four, where a man may be evaluating his emotions negatively, cognitive therapy may be useful in challenging his negative beliefs about expressing his emotions. The therapist might need to take a psychoeducational approach to point out the value of expressing emotions and the research findings that suggest that there is very little difference in men's and women's emotions. This research finding (Wester, Vogel, Pressly, & Heesacker, 2002, p. 633) may liberate traditional men from the fear that they are like women if they are feeling or expressing emotions.

Some uses of inexpressiveness in males actually may be adaptive; it is the therapist's duty to observe important intra or inter-individual conflicts that need addressing and help clients resolve those (Webster et al., 2002). The therapist also may help his or her male clients to work on the situational aspects of expression versus non-expression in order to identify where it is safe and appropriate to share, with whom they should share, and how best to share (Chaplin, 2015).

Pollack (2005) proposed strategies to treat those he called "masked men" (p. 203). "It is the loss of men's emotional voice in boyhood," he wrote, "that puts them at risk for a hollow and stiff sense of self, covered over by a mask of false bravado" (Pollack, 2005, p. 203). It is the premature loss of psychic connection to self and others, and the development and reinforcement of the gender strait jacket that causes men to suffer psychic pain.

Boys experience a wrenching disruption of their early environment from their parents; therefore, they experience a sense of abandonment, and its accompanying shame, which forces them to repress what Pollack (1995) called "the voice of human vulnerability and tears, replacing it with the only acceptable proto-male affect: anger" (p. 204). With the loss of the love of his life (mother), psychic loss of the feeling half of his self, and the usual distance from the father—psychologically and/or geographically—the boy is set adrift from his nurturing self, and because this happens so early in life, he has no way to name his experience (Pollack, 1995).

This early disruption leads to a "disorder of the self: male type" (Pollack, 1995, p. 205). Starting in male adolescence and continuing through adulthood, this disorder manifests itself in a number of symptoms such as action blunting of empathic recognition, alexithymia, avoidance of interdependent object relations and the substitution of sexualized ones, harsh self-criticism or criticism of others, partial affective-intellectual split, anger/rage, walling off of the vulnerable core self, perfectionism, shame, the inability to grieve or mourn, and the vulnerability to substance abuse and male depression (Pollack, 2005). The therapist must employ specialized methods when treating such disorders.

One such method is not to put demands on men before they can handle them. Men must be allowed to think that any good ideas generated are their own, that they are in charge. Both therapy and the therapist must be seen as dispensable so that the client has a feeling of self-sufficiency. The therapist must allow the man to rely on him/her in a manner that "silently performs missing functions within the self without acknowledging this openly" (Pollack, 2005, p. 210). The stable transference constellation could not be broken until it can be interpreted from the male client's own perspective. In many ways the early phase of therapy is similar to an extended consultation without any attempt to interpret or confront the patient. The therapist might float "a trial balloon but if the man retreats, the therapist should back off. It is most helpful to assist the client in solving very concrete problems that are at hand and to avoid linking his present struggles to early experiences" (Pollack, 2005, 211).

The therapist must work slowly through stages of therapeutic intervention. It is important that s/he can recognize gender-specific syndromes; for example, how men experience and express depression (Pollack, 2005). It is crucial, too, to be sensitive to men's shame and avoidance of admitting their vulnerabilities. A neutral, non-confrontational, analytical approach works best in early therapy. Creating a safe holding environment in which men can develop trust but deny any need for the therapist or sessions allows clients to save face but begin to bond; this leads to finally building an alliance approach to therapy (Pollack, 2005).

Although most of the literature addressed so far deals with the therapy in terms of adult males, there is increasing attention to the plight of young and adolescent boys. As Levant (2005) has noted, traditional boys' emotional shaping has been influenced by seven predominant themes to include self-reliance, emotional inexpressiveness, aggression, seeking high social status, hypersexuality, the avoidance of anything "feminine," and the rejection of homosexuality (p. 162).

The male code begins its not-so-subtle influence in latency and reaches full-blown internalization in adolescence. This socialization results in adolescent boys who are dampened down emotionally and overcharged sexually and aggressively (Levant, 2005). Such states produce tremendous shame and sadness in contemporary boys and raise the likelihood of a constellation of problems that cry out for therapeutic intervention. There are several issues that therapists should be alert to when dealing with teenage male clients.

First are the issues of problematic sexuality. Levant (2005) reported on research that he and colleagues conducted with adolescent boys. Asking the boys what questions they would pose if they could have a confidential conversation with an expert on male adolescence, over 90 percent of the respondents posed questions concerning sex (Levant, 2005, p. 166). When analyzing why sex loomed so large for adolescent boys, Levant (2005) postulated that

> being lustful when you are needy is the only acceptable way a teenage boy trained under the code of masculinity can behave: powerful, dominant, aggressive, and self-sufficient and in no way vulnerable or needy. Teenage boys are rarely able to articulate this subterranean expression of caring emotions in their overt sexuality (2005, p. 166).

A second issue of concern is the impress of popular culture and its violent and misogynist stereotypes of masculinity. Adolescent boys are also likely candidates for abusing substances "because they can have the effect of temporarily deadening boys' sensitivity to their emotional turmoil—the struggle between their needs and emotions (if these are not yet fully suppressed) and their beliefs about how boys are supposed to behave" (Levant, 2005, p. 167).

A final concern is the lack of positive fathering and interaction with adult males to help boys navigate the passage into young adulthood. Since "fathers tend to be the transmitters and chief enforcers of the code of masculinity [they are often relegated to the role of] toughening up their boys by withholding affection and reinforcing traditional masculinity, with all of its emotional restriction" (Levant, 2005, p. 168). They also may be somewhat peripheral to the family by virtue of work and/or emotional distance, and therefore they cannot be held up as potential role models for more engaged fathering.

BOYS IN TROUBLE

Kraemer (2011) noted that boys are in trouble in terms of mental and physical health right from the get-go. Male fetuses have a higher risk of mortality than female ones and while more males than females are conceived, more girls are born. With the rare exception of spina bifida, almost any problem in utero is more likely to affect boys than girls (Kraemer, 2011). Boys born prematurely have a lesser rate of healthy survival than girls and pregnant women who suffer severe stress are more likely to lose male fetuses than females (Kraemer, 2011).

While the genetic blueprint for an individual's development is present at birth, they have to be activated, and the primary caregiver (most often female) is the main influence on socializing the infant to his or her view of the world. The primary tasks of regulation of an individual's emotion, forming safe and secure relationships with others, and forming a unique identity and personality undergird the human development process (Mascolo & Fischer, 2010;

Robertson & Shepard, 2008). In utero, and up into the second year of life, the right hemisphere of the brain is the dominant one (Berk, 2017). It is not until sometime in that second year that the left begins a growth spurt. Boys and girls begin their journey into life with a similar capacity for emotions, but this quickly changes (Berk, 2017; Robertson & Shepard, 2008).

As boys develop, their right hemisphere will still unconsciously store, regulate, and process emotional information; this emotional intelligence does not go away when the left begins its spurt. However, "boys often restrict vulnerable emotions, may speak a less emotional vocabulary than do girls, and tend to value aggression and competitiveness as hallmarks of masculinity" (Robertson & Shepard, 2008, p. 11). For most boys, their neurological instructions become overridden over time as powerful socialization forces reward some behaviors while punishing and extinguishing others. Culturally appropriate affect, behavior, and cognition are driven home through this process.

Kraemer (2011) summarized other telling facts about gender differences in childhood, such as: ADHD and conduct disorders are more likely in boys; and boys on the autistic spectrum outnumber girls four to one. Kraemer (2011) believed that the tendency of boys to be consumed by relatively impersonal interests is probably brain-related and noted the brain differences between the sexes. Children with autistic features, for example, are not less developed in terms of emotions; rather, they are aloof compared to typical children as they try to reduce anxiety and overstimulation. When placed in situations in which they need to articulate their emotional states (such as in a doctor or therapist's office), males are generally less expressive (Kraemer, 2011).

Male infants, according to Kraemer (2011), are on average, less physiologically mature, fussier, and more emotionally demanding than girls. While they have heavier brains and more bulked-up muscles as infants, they are not as mature. There is a misperception that boys are "little men" who are more independent and mature than girls, when in fact, infant boys are less mature and more emotional (Kraemer, 2011). This leads to the likelihood that young boys may receive less attentive care than girls and that boys and adolescent males are less likely to seek help when they are distressed.

Another male vulnerability that Kraemer (2011) mentions is that boys react earlier and more dramatically if they have a depressed mother (one tenth of all new mothers suffer postpartum depression and others may be clinically depressed prior to birth). Male children are more apt to become hyperactive and inattentive—signs of the inability to self-regulate—during and even after their mothers' mood improves (Kraemer, 2011). Along with biological and temperamental factors, ADHD, which is far more common in boys, is a disorder of self-regulation that can be the result of lack of good fit between the child's needs and parental caregiving. Kraemer (2011) also noted studies on conduct and hyperactive disorders, showing that a large percentage of boys who are diagnosed with one also have the other but that treatments are often given separately and without great attention to realigning parenting to children's needs.

While medication may be the choice for many doctors, Kraemer (2011) urged therapeutic intervention with all children and parents, even if medication is used. He also cautioned about the unwanted side effects, some carrying into the future, on growth, sleep, and motivation. The author also reported that about one in twelve boys (twice that of girls) will be diagnosed with a conduct disorder stemming from highly troubling behaviors such as aggressive bullying, repeated theft, running away, or setting fires. Kraemer (2011) acknowledged that there certainly are genetic and temperamental factors that contribute to this disorder but also that children are essentially wired for morality.

Hyperactivity and conduct disorder, taken as a pair, are connected to early childhood experiences while the brain is rapidly growing. Making sure that all parents have good prenatal care, nutrition, education about parenting and support as well as understanding gender differences and their implications for parenting and mental and emotional health, should be global imperatives, given the fiscal and societal costs of poor health and well-being among individuals (Young, Jean, & Mead, 2019).

Kraemer (2011) suggests to primary health providers that asking parents questions about birth and the early months of their children, as well as finding out what the parents' childhoods were like and how that impacts current parenting, is a helpful framework for assessing the family's wellness needs; yet he admits that fathers are rarely very engaged in their children's health visits, so constructing family health genograms needs to involve everyone. Helping fathers understand their son's vulnerabilities and health care needs developmentally can assist them in helping their sons to avoid some of the risks that plague so many males' emotional health (Yogman & Garfield, 2016).

BOYS ADRIFT

Sax (2016), a family physician and a psychologist, suggested that the health and emotional well-being of contemporary boys is affected by five factors. While acknowledging the serious mental and emotional health problems of girls (bullying, body image, eating disorders, sexual assault), he stressed that today's boys and young males are in deep trouble when it comes to their mental health. The first factor mentioned are the changes at school, where Sax (2016) sees the feminization of our educational systems as putting boys at a distinct early disadvantage.

Due to large brain differences between boys and girls, gray matter develops earlier and faster in girls; at adolescence, the majority of girls will be more than two years ahead of boys in maturation in areas that our schools prize. Higher testosterone levels at adolescence produce greater thickness in the visual cortex of boys and less in girls (Berk, 2017). While boys develop more quickly in perceptual and object recognition, girls advance in the language skills that affect reading, writing, and expression of ideas and emotions (Berk, 2017).

The bottom line, according to Sax (2016), is that formal education starts too early for boys and they are essentially doomed due to brain differences and maturation in all but the most boy-friendly schools. Wealthier parents who are aware of this disparity frequently hold their sons back a year, but the poor don't have this luxury; since the pace of formal education has accelerated so much in recent decades, the best solution would simply be to start at a slightly later age. Schools, in their shift from field trips to screens and the world of play to content mastery, have put boys under great stress at an early age.

A second factor cited by Sax (2016) are video games. Constructed as male-friendly experiences, boys are far more likely to become addicted to them. This is a form of addiction that is not discussed much in counseling theory as of yet; however, Sax (2016) argued that there are many mental health problems associated with gaming and the content and nature of many of the games themselves. This experience is addictive because it appeals both to boys' visual and spatial preferences and their will to power. Video games, Sax (2016) argued, are heroic in the sense that boys are socialized to power and mastery and most video games give a quick and easy shot of power and control over the life and death circumstances of their characters.

Sax (2016) also lamented the reinforcement of attention deficit among boys, writing that distraction is rewarded in video gaming. Since there are myriad variables for the gamer to pay attention to at once, he cannot concentrate on just one element in order to be successful. This rewards the already-distractible boy with greater value on diverted attention. Most games also reward male risk-taking. Since the gaming world is unreal, characters can take physical risks with impunity; in fact, risky behavior is a necessity in many games. Sax (2016) noted that

> researchers have found that adolescents who play these risk-glorifying games are more likely to engage in dangerous driving behaviors such as speeding, tailgating, and weaving in traffic; they are more likely to be in automobile accidents; and more willing to drink and drive. In another study, teens who were playing risky racing video games at age 17 or 18 were more than three times as likely, five years later, to have been involved in an actual car crash. (p. 81)

Boys who are frequent gamers are more obese even than those who binge on television viewing and they also risk greater dehumanization of others (Calvert, Staiano, & Bond, 2013). Sax (2016) cited frightening research studies that found that the more often young males played violent video games, the more they came to see themselves as less human. Those who regularly played these violent games over time were discovered to be more likely to abuse alcohol, smoke, and take part in risky sexual activities (Prescott, Sargent, & Hull, 2018). Those games that rewarded antisocial behavior increased the likelihood that the boy would actually take part in such behavior. When high school students were assigned to a group that played either violent or non-violent video games, those in the violent game group appeared to undergo moral detachment (Sax, 2016). Young men also preferred to continue to play despite being aware of long-term negative effects of addictive gaming on everything from relationships to employment (Sax, 2016).

Sax (2016) bemoans the mental health aspects of addictive gaming as "the most serious negative effects of video games are the effects on the gamer's personality, motivation, and connectedness to the real world. These boys may be highly motivated, but their motivation has become derailed" (p. 83). Boys' behaviors become less caring and more hostile, as well. Sax (2016) concludes this observation with the belief of psychology professor Craig Anderson who points out that the evidence linking playing video games to antisocial behavior is as powerful as that linking secondhand smoke to lung cancer. Ardent gamers destroy their relationships with their girlfriends, who get tired of their addiction and find other things to do (Sax, 2016). The bottom line for addicted gamers is that they replace real-world activities and relationships with those of incessant gaming.

Reasons three and four relate to over-prescription of medications for ADHD in boys and the general increase in endocrine disruptors in our environment, emanating from synthetic chemicals, pesticides, and plastics. Given the high percentage of boys diagnosed with ADHD, medications such as Adderall and Ritalin are frequently used; medications such as this improve the functioning of both normal children as well as those with actual ADHD, but at what cost? Sax (2016) wrote that the downside is a change in personality, loss of drive, motivation, and engagement.

Boys need to move, they translate motivation into action, and they engage through motor domains. Not only do these biological proclivities make boys more prone to diagnosis, but when medicated over time, they can lose access to the processes that most help them to learn. This is not to say that there are not instances in which medications may bring a world of good, but Sax (2016) argued that more boy-friendly learning environments might accomplish the same results without the inherent risks.

Sax (2016) cited findings about the effects of endocrine disruptors on male and female puberty. Given the alarming rise in synthetic chemicals in our environment, many researchers believe that they have found the cause for the speeding up of onset of puberty in girls (Özen & Darcan, 2011). Interestingly, though, the opposite effect occurs in boys—these same chemicals appear to delay or disrupt male puberty; thus, the gap between the genders has grown even wider in terms of sexual maturity. Evidence over the last fifteen years also seems to suggest that these hormone-mimicking chemicals may be linked to increased obesity, ADHD, and less dense bones in boys (Özen & Darcan, 2011).

The final of Sax's (2016) five factors is titled "the revenge of the forsaken gods" (p. 163). Noting that the transition from boyhood to manhood is about more than just biology and the passage of time, he laments the scarcity of rituals, safe passages, and guides to help in the psychological and emotional development of healthy males. Strong bonds across generations and the attention to the male spirit life are sadly missing in contemporary society, leaving boys and adolescent males adrift.

Sax (2016) recognized that some subcultures of larger American culture (such as Navajos and Orthodox Jews) continue to teach traditions and observe special rites of passage, few other subcultures do so in ways that are formal and explicit, leaving a large group of "lost boys" to figure manhood out for themselves. Ignoring rites and rituals that have eased boys into communal manhood has left too many to turn to less-than-positive peers and role models (many from mass media) to teach them what manhood is all about (Sax, 2016).

Sax (2016) points out that gender matters and ignoring the gendered needs of boys and adolescent males can have ramifications. He quotes a scientific panel convened at Dartmouth College that stated

> neglecting the gendered needs of adolescents can be dangerous. Boys and girls differ with respect to risk factors for social pathology. We recognize the perils of oversimplifying or exaggerating gender differences. But as the medical world has discovered, the risk of not attending to real differences that exist between males and females can have dangerous consequences . . . Young people have an inherent need to experience sexual maturing within an affirming system of meaning. (p. 219)

ADDRESSING ADOLESCENT MALE HEALTH ISSUES

Adolescence is the critical juncture at which mental health and emotional health issues with males must be addressed, albeit in new ways. Adolescence is the developmental stage at which gender differences in mortality rates begin (Rice, Purcell, & McGorry, 2018). Sadly, males will travel a path leading to shorter life spans, lower levels of immune system functioning, greater hazards on the job, and higher levels of risk-taking, especially at puberty. The authors note that a great degree of higher male mortality is related to mental ill health and that mortality risk factors can be lowered through more timely and effective interventions (Rice et al., 2018).

Every other year, the National Risk Behavior Survey (Centers for Disease Control and Prevention: Division of Adolescent and School Health, 2017; Robertson & Shepard, 2008) is conducted to gather data on the risk behaviors among adolescents that contribute to their disabilities, deaths, and social problems. From these surveys, one sees that the four leading causes of death among adolescents in America (ranked in order) are vehicle accidents, unintended injuries, homicide, and suicide (Robertson & Shepard, 2008). The authors cite the work of Mahalik and his colleagues (2003) in which they explicate the Conformity to Masculine Norms Inventory.

The inventory is comprised of eleven categories of traditional norms of masculinity that influence male decision-making and risk-taking; these include such things as dominance, winning, self-reliance, status, physical toughness, and dominance over women. The more a boy or adolescent male engages in behaviors that are consonant with the eleven categories, the higher his risk is of dying young from the four aforementioned causes (Robertson & Shepard, 2008).

Westwood and Pinzon (2008) remarked that while adolescent males have equal numbers of health issues and concerns to those of girls, they are far less likely to be seen in clinical or therapeutic settings. Both boys' attitudes and the construction and delivery of healthcare services account for this fact. It is more difficult to engage boys initially; however, if they can encounter health professionals who are comfortable initiating discussions about difficult topics such as substance abuse, sexuality and puberty, violence, or risk-taking behaviors during regular healthcare checkups, then boys may view these visits as a setting in which they can move beyond presenting symptoms into talking about what may lie beyond the symptoms themselves (Westwood & Pinzon, 2008).

Boys and adolescent males most often go to a clinic or doctor's office due to an injury (such as from sports), a chronic condition (such as asthma), or an acute illness. Westwood and Pinzon (2008) reported that while males age ten to fourteen have only a little higher mortality rate than females, by the time they are in the twenty to twenty-four range, that rate has increased almost three times. Most deaths are unintentional (accidents such as car crashes), suicide, or homicide, and all are associated with substance abuse or alcohol abuse. If there is a gun present in the home, young males are at a significantly higher risk of suicide (Westwood & Pinzon, 2008).

Boys and adolescent males often are woefully undereducated about how their bodies work and even less aware about mental and emotional health and well-being; therefore, physicians and other healthcare professionals can be vital in the frontline fight for better health and well-being. These practitioners may be aware of parental risk factors such as abuse in the home, bullying, or use of alcohol and marijuana (Griffin & Botvin, 2010). The latter is particularly important, as males are far more likely than their female counterparts to binge drink and to drive under the influence. Screening at a young age is critical, as the misuse of substances increases male involvement in multiple risk behaviors (Westwood & Pinzon, 2008).

Most boys and adolescent males have concerns about their reproductive health and sexual orientation. Around 50 percent of boys, according to Westwood and Pinzon (2008), have reportedly had intercourse prior to turning eighteen. Regardless of the campaigns for safe sex, fewer than 70 percent of males in the teen years say that they use condoms and if they take part in multiple-risk behaviors, they are even less likely to do so (Westwood & Pinzon, 2008). Many youth have had heterosexual sexual relations or experimentation, but clinicians know that this does not necessarily mean that they are heterosexual. Healthcare workers who establish a regular, positive relationship with their patients may create safe spaces for discussion of sexual orientation.

Among adolescents and emerging adult males, mood and anxiety disorders are on the list of common mental health conditions, yet many do not seek help or necessarily even recognize conditions such as depressive disorders (Westwood & Pinzon, 2008). Given that help-seeking behaviors are not seen as masculine or that they betray weakness or vulnerability, practitioners need to consider these conditions in the assessment of males who present with psychosocial changes; these may be somatic in nature or general malaise such as loss of interest or plummeting grades.

Skilled caregivers will bring up such information with their male patients, knowing that depression and suicide are skyrocketing among young men, but that overt signs such as aggression or agitation may be the only visible symptoms they display or discuss. The rate of completed suicides is higher for boys than girls, most likely due to greater familiarity with and access to weapons. Adolescence is also a time in which psychosis may present (Westwood & Pinzon, 2008).

Mental and emotional health needs do differ between majority, mainstream and marginalized, and minority or victimized populations of males. Boys from lower SES communities, the homeless, incarcerated youth, gay or transgender youth, those with disabilities, minority males and new immigrants, and victims of abuse and neglect all are at higher risk for emotional problems and threats to their well-being, physically and mentally (Westwood & Pinzon,

2008). One reason for this is lack of quality healthcare that is affordable and easily accessible; yet other reasons may relate more to perceptions of what it is to be male. Boys are unlikely to see connections between psychological and emotional stress and physical discomfort (Westwood & Pinzon, 2008).

The authors also mention that primary caregivers and other healthcare professionals who offer more routine services may be the best buffers against escalating mental health problems. Since it is most likely overwhelming to explore highly personal topics in one visit, contact over time may permit disclosure on boys' parts and affords clinicians the opportunity to slowly move from more neutral to more personal topics (Westwood & Pinzon, 2008). Providers should take a problem-solving approach rather than trying to delve deep into emotional territory and to stress that confidentiality is always part of their work, with certain limitations (Westwood & Pinzon, 2008).

Westwood and Pinzon (2008) offered some natural opportunities for providing important information about psycho-emotional well-being, such as during wellness checkups or routine physicals for sports teams or camps. Parents should receive information about the importance of regular health care; the developmental issues and typical health concerns for adolescence, specifically of boys; and the critical nature of building protective factors and lessening stressors (National Academies of Sciences, Engineering, and Medicine, 2016). Because men are generally not prone to taking as good care and seeking help when needed as women are, programs that help fathers become better healthcare role models are essential.

Patton, Darmstadt, Petroni, and Sawyer (2018) applauded global gains in agendas addressing the health of women and girls, particularly in areas such as contraception, reproductive health, maternal health, and nutrition; however, they expressed grave concern about health gains of boys and adolescent males around the world. This concern came in light of the fact that boys are more prone to specific health problems such as substance abuse, violence, homicide and accidental injury, completed suicides, and poor nutrition (Patton et al., 2018). Globally, boys are far more likely to be homeless, forced to become child soldiers, or in trouble with juvenile justice; not only do these threaten childhood health, but the ramifications follow them well into adulthood (Patton et al., 2018).

Socialization in most cultures puts boys and young males in the unhealthy positions of having to adopt traditional hegemonic definitions of masculinity (Patton et al., 2018). Such definitions, at their worst, require that they seek dominance over others, particularly women, minorities, those of different sexual orientations, and males who are perceived as weaker. Such norms intensify the risk-taking behaviors of males, and their need to assume independence and autonomy make it less likely that they will seek out help. Girls and young women are forced into greater health-seeking behaviors because they are at greater risk for pregnancy, while in most countries and cultures, birth control and pregnancy concerns are thought to be women's responsibilities; such attitudes relieve adolescent boys and young males of engaging in medical conversations that explore sexual responsibilities and protections, for the most part (Patton et al., 2018). It is critical that we bring a global gender lens to health care services and education, in both physical and mental health arenas since the two are inextricably linked (Patton et al., 2018).

Rice et al. (2018) described adolescent boys and young adult men as an "underserved population relative to their mental health needs" (p. 509). Citing the large discrepancy between young men and young women in terms of health profiles in this age demographic, Rice et al. (2018) argued that to ignore the effects of suicide, substance abuse, conduct disorder, and physical violence during some of the most productive years of a man's life, is to court disaster due to the social and economic consequences of mental health problems throughout the life span.

There are myriad factors that interfere with boys and adolescent males receiving the mental health care that they need such as

> mental health literacy, self-stigma and shame, masculinity, nosology and diagnosis, and service acceptability. A call is made for focused development of policy, theory, and evaluation of targeted interventions for this population, including gender-synchronized service model reform and training of staff, including the e-health domain. (p. 509)

Rice et al. (2018) emphasized the greater mental health risks for certain young males (sexually diverse, those from culturally diverse backgrounds, and those involved in the juvenile justice system) as well as those from low-income brackets; one-third of all deaths among adolescent males who grow up in low or middle-income countries in the Americas is the result of interpersonal violence. Psychotic disorders tend to emerge earlier in boys, males with psychosis are more apt to have comorbid substance abuse disorders, and males are more likely to be homeless; yet they are less likely to interact with evidence-based mental health counseling (Rice et al., 2018).

Despite young men in most modern societies having greater opportunity, privilege, and power than young women, their mental health and emotional well-being is poorer (Rice et al. 2018). The root of these issues is socially determined very early on; yet changes in the way mental health for males is conceptualized and delivered can rewrite this history. Any successful initiative to improve male mental health must begin with improving mental health literacy, since "in school-age adolescents, men are less likely than women to correctly label depression-based vignettes, are less likely to endorse concern over a depressed peer, and have less confidence in their ability to identify individual symptoms of depression" (Rice et al., 2018, p. 511).

Some of this restricted diagnostic ability most likely lies in decreased ability to identify and describe emotional states, in self and in others. Rice et al. (2018) have seen benefits of programs that build literacy in the context of male peers and that help frame discussions of mental health topics in language that is boy-friendly; therefore, having good relationships with healthcare providers, mentors, coaches, and fathers or other significant males can furnish safe grounds for education, as well.

Analyses of studies of self-disclosure, males report self-stigma more highly than do females when it comes to disclosing experiences that may lead to diminished mental health (Rice et al., 2018). This is particularly true in sensitive areas such as sexuality or sexual abuse; participants in studies reviewed by Rice et. al (2018) described shame as a primary motivator for remaining silent and not seeking help; the more they felt their masculinity was threatened, the more shame they experienced and the less likely disclosure of mental or emotional problems or questions.

Western cultural views of masculinity are the biggest threat to positive health and prosocial behavior among boys and adolescent males. Masculinity is seen as a finite capital—hard fought to win, easy to lose and in short supply if a boy shows vulnerability or weakness, such as seeking help or admitting to mental health problems (Drew, 2019; Powell, n.d.). Boys and adolescents may also deviate from female patterns of symptoms accompanying different mental disorders. Males tend toward risk-taking and inhibition; thus, externalizing psychopathology, while girls are more apt to internalize their symptoms through emotions such as sadness, hopelessness, or worthlessness (Ogundele, 2018; Robertson & Shepard, 2008). Life span studies have found that after disruptive or stressful life events, males are much more likely than females to engage in externalizing behavior such as gambling, substance abuse, or activities involving physical risk-taking (Rice et al., 2018).

Robertson and Shepard (2008) found that one of the biggest psychological challenges to male adolescents' health is the need to play parts determined by particular scripts. These scripts represent the socialized expectations of males and as males become older, they are pressured to adopt one as their dominant sense of identity (Robertson & Shepard, 2008). Among the most common types are (1) strong and silent, (2) playboy, (3) independent, (4) tough guy, (5) winner, (6) give 'em hell, and (7) homophobe (Robertson & Shepard, 2008). Contemporary adolescent males may be choosing among jock, gansta, nerd, preppy, stoner, good ol' boy, or other images. A small percentage may be able to juggle several roles and often boys adopt a protective image (such as playing a sport to obtain "jock insurance") that allows them also to participate in activities that may be their true passion but are not considered masculine enough such as art, drama, fashion design, and others (Robertson & Shepard, 2008).

Adolescent males use shame to reinforce masculine codes of behavior; for example, they may not necessarily think that a particular boy is homosexual, but they may call him out for being "gay" if they feel his behavior doesn't conform to the Boy Code. Shame was once used to prepare boys for almost-certain combat; in modern times, with fewer and fewer involved in wars, it becomes a tool for gendered social conformity (Robertson & Shepard, 2008). The psychological pitfalls of this are that boys feel pressured either to take part in things at which they will fail or opt out and suffer shame for not measuring up.

New modes of service delivery for counseling boys and young men need to be considered in order to entice more males into preventative health and therapy when needed. Data cited by Rice et al. (2018) indicated that strengths or assets-based counseling and that which is based on male relational styles, courage, humor, and positive aspects of the "warrior culture" have the greatest successes. Environments that are free of judgment and in which males feel competent, peer-oriented programs, genuine clinicians, and active rather than talk-based therapy are most beneficial, and there is also some suggestion that the internet could play a much larger role in providing education, answering embarrassing questions, or providing direct counseling.

GENDER ROLE CONFLICT, GENDER ROLE STRAIN, AND GENDER ROLE STRESS

Long contending that cultural standards for masculinity that are inherent in gender role socialization have potentially negative effects on mens' well-being, Pleck (1995) looked at three particular themes that have run throughout his work and that of other men's studies scholars. The first is what has been called "gender role discrepancy or gender role incongruity" (Pleck, 1995, p. 12). Pleck (1995) noted that "there is only one complete unblushing male in America: a young, married, white, urban, northern, heterosexual Protestant father of college education, fully employed, of good complexion, weight, and height, and a recent record in sports" (p. 13). Obviously, the vast majority of American men cannot come close to meeting these ideal criteria; therefore, the discrepancy between the "real" and the "ideal" may lead to low self-esteem, competition, and possible negative mental and physical effects on their health.

A second construct is "gender role trauma" (Pleck, 1995). If a man were able to meet the ideal criteria, the socialization process leading him to fulfillment is traumatic, culminating in negative side effects even when the man is apparently successful (Pleck, 1995). Such socialization is fraught with repression of many of a boy's natural proclivities toward expression and connection, leaving him at risk for less than developmental wellness. Finally, a man may suffer from "gender role dysfunction" (Pleck, 1995). Successful attainment of ideal masculinity cannot help but have negative side effects for the man and his significant others; for example, while a man may invest heavily in work-role behaviors that will lead to high performance in the provider role, his low-level family participation puts him in jeopardy with regard to dysfunction in the roles of partner and father. Whether or not particular gender roles are important to the man or not is key to understanding research on gender role strain. If men subscribe to the dominant masculine ideology, they share "common dimensions, including achievement, emotional control, antifeminism, and homophobia" (Pleck, 1995, p. 20). A man's degree of endorsement of traditional masculine ideology is an expression of the gender expectations to which he holds himself; however, traditional male role expectations have dysfunctional correlates, and Pleck (1995) found that these cut across different racial-ethnic groups, although to different degrees; however, there are "generally similar concomitants" (Pleck, 1995, p. 21).

Why do men pursue ideal masculinity despite its often obvious negative side effects? Pleck (1995) concurs with those who hold that men are socialized to believe that their masculinity is something that must continuously be proved. Eisler (1995) further probed the notion of gender roles in his work on masculine gender role stress. Bem (1981) also investigated this concept, "sex-typed attitudes and behaviors are learned when one is willing to process information primarily according to society's mandates of what is appropriate for one's own sex and to ignore information associated with the opposite sex" (p. 356). Bem (1981) proposed that both genders learn at an early age to evaluate their adequacy as people on the consonance between their behaviors and those socially sanctioned for their particular gender. Clearly, some men and women become more committed to rigid gender identity than others.

Eisler (1995) articulated five propositions about the "masculine gender role stress paradigm [that have helped him understand] stress arousal and the subsequent health problems in men" (p. 212). The first is that there are powerful social reinforcers (such as parents, teachers, and coaches) who reward traditional masculine attitudes and punish, often harshly, behaviors that they consider feminine; thus, even young boys develop and internalize masculine schema, and these schema are then used to evaluate potential threats and challenges to their very masculinity.

Different men have different degrees of commitment to these schema, however, so there is a continuum of commitment ranging from hypermasculinity to androgyny (Eisler, 1995). Excessive commitment to rigid masculine schema can limit the array of coping strategies that a man has, while gender role stress can rear its ugly head when men perceive themselves as being or exhibiting behaviors that are less manly or feminine (Eisler, 1995).

Using the Masculine Gender Role Stress Scale, Eisler (1995) explored men's stress using a forty-item tool that has five interpretive factors. The first measures men's fears of physical inadequacy and another, their level of comfort with emotional expression, both their own and that of others. A third factor rates fear of subordination to women in the sense of being less successful than women in traditionally male arenas. Finally, fears of intellectual inferiority and "performance failure," in the worlds of work and sexual activity, were measured (Eisler, 1995).

Men with high scores on socially desirable masculine traits are not necessarily at higher risk for health problems; however, men's commitment to some of the traditional dimensions does seem to render them at a higher risk for psychological and physical distress (Eisler, 1995). The perception that a man was weak or sexually "below par" was a severe threat to a man's self-esteem. This was also true for women whom the men perceived as equal or superior to them in "traditional masculine domains" (Eisler, 1995, p. 218).

There was a pervasive need for men to see themselves as highly decisive and self-assured, drawing on rational skills rather than being emotional similar to women (Eisler, 1995). Traditional men needed to see themselves as high achievers occupationally and sexually, and they were uncomfortable with vulnerable emotions expressed either by themselves or others. High-scoring men showed greater cardiovascular response (blood pressure rise) when appraising situations as potential threats to their masculinity, and the greatest stress arousal occurred when dealing with feminine-type emotions or when feeling challenged (Eisler, 1995).

Although most literature on the gender role conflict has been confined to grown men, with a few articles on college-aged students, it appears from the work of Watts and Borders (2005) that such a conflict begins to be experienced in adolescence. Their qualitative study of boys' perceptions of what it means to be male turned up evidence that the hallmarks of gender role concern are present earlier than might have been expected. Using O'Neil, Helms, Gable, David, and Wrightsman's (1986) description of gender role conflict, and its accompanying four gender role conflict patterns, Watts and Borders (2005) set out to discover if these applied to the experiences of high school boys ranging in age from fourteen to eighteen.

The first research question—do adolescent boys experience restricted affection between men—demonstrated that fear of being criticized for sharing feelings of affection for other boys is present even in adolescence (Watts & Borders, 2005). Moreover, the social sanction against such expression or demonstration of affection is powerful and homophobic. As one participant said, "I think there is a fear, just because there's that fear of criticism and that fear that someone will jump on you and be like 'What!? What's going on?' And you don't want to get that started. You could be the next gay dude at your school" (Watts & Borders, 2005, p. 4). The theme of homophobia ran through many of the respondents' answers. Some boys claimed never to have feelings of affection for male friends. Friendship was tolerated, but a "real boy" would not experience a feeling of love for another. Those boys who did express feelings of affection admitted that they did so knowing that they would be criticized or ridiculed (Watts & Borders, 2005).

The boys in the study also appeared to suffer from what O'Neil et al. (1986) referred to as "restricted emotionality" (p. 2) as to share emotions seemed "unmanly." As one said, "that's like a stereotype thing. Like that I'm supposed to be all hard and tough" (Watts & Borders, 2005, p. 4). The participants, however, did feel that the emotions of anger and rage were perfectly acceptable to display and often these emotions were the only ones that transpired openly in a relationship between male friends. As one boy said about anger, "that's the only emotion I really have" (Watts & Borders, 2005, p. 4).

It appeared that the more sensitive the emotion, the less likely a boy would be in having the capacity and/or the comfort to express it. Sadness and grief, for example, were bottled up inside, or denied, because they were not seen as acceptable emotions to vent (Watts & Borders, 2005). In one boy's equation, crying is tantamount to drama, "It's not that I'm really afraid to cry. I'm not that dramatic. I don't have a very dramatic life" (Watts & Borders, 2005, p. 4).

Fathers, boys admitted, were the role models from whom they had learned emotional inexpressiveness, with several mentioning that they had never seen their fathers cry, and that fathers appeared to avoid emotional display (Watts & Borders, 2005). Adolescents, most likely due to their age, were less likely to report conflicts between "work" (school), family, and other relationships; yet the closer the boys were to graduation, the more they reported stress between the demands of schoolwork and relationships with friends and family (Watts & Borders, 2005). Their achievement needs reflected a struggle to define what success really meant; however, they agreed that boys need to be in control or in charge, "There will be a bunch of guys, and they will be like each trying to take, like, you know, control. Three people will try to be the leader" (Watts & Borders, 2005, p. 6).

In the final aspect of the project, the researchers read a simplified version of gender role conflict theory to the boys and asked if the definition resonated with their own experiences. On the whole, boys responded in the affirmative and while they felt that some of it "was worded too strongly [they seemed to believe that] the theory that you just read is actually like the theory that everyone envisions as a male" (Watts & Borders, 2005, p. 6).

Concluding that gender role conflict appears to begin its developmental trajectory in adolescence, the Watts and Borders (2005) noted that there were very clear messages sent to boys about what was and was not acceptable male behavior. That homophobia, restricted affection, restricted emotional expression (with the exception of the sanctioned emotion of anger), and alexithymia impinged upon boys' relationships was confirmation of what many other researchers had discovered in studying the traditional male experience (Watts & Borders, 2005).

O'Neil (2015) adapted his earlier Gender Role Conflict scale to become the Gender Role Conflict Scale for Adolescents-GRCS-A as a means to conduct more longitudinal research on boys and young men, since there is a dearth of information readily available. Eight recent studies that involved adolescent boys using this scale demonstrate that boys' reports that they were undergoing family stress, anger, problems with their conduct, and difficulty expressing emotions were significantly correlated with gender role conflict (O'Neil, 2015). This seemed to occur at the onset of adolescence and played out in their emotions, their family experiences, and athletic endeavors.

O'Neil (2015) wrote that the boys with problems in the aforementioned areas scored high on "restrictive emotionality," "conflict between work and family relations," and "restrictive affectionate behavior between men." Restrictive emotionality was correlated with lower help-seeking and higher levels of depression; higher scores on RABBM led to lower levels of depression (O'Neil, 2015). Underclassmen in high school had higher levels of GRC than upperclassmen (O'Neil, 2015). Much more research needs to be conducted with these models and populations of boys and adolescent males.

Zakrzewski (2014) attempted to debunk the myth that boys are unable to feel or connect with others as effectively as girls can; rather, it is the early socialization of boys that prevents their developing natural tendencies toward emotional connection and attunement. Chu (2014) firmly believed that it is cultural conditioning, rather than nature, that tamps down boys' inherent abilities in the emotional and social domains. It seems, however, most likely that the answer is both nature and nurture when considering boys' lag in language processing and difficulty in finding labels for their emotions.

SUICIDE AMONG THE SCHOOL-AGE POPULATION

Korte (2017) cited a frightening statistic: a doubling in the number of patients aged five to seventeen who have been hospitalized for suicidal thoughts or actions in the period from 2007 to 2015. It appears medical staff believe that as school systems are becoming more challenging, and bullying and weapons more common, many students are driven to consider suicide as a solution to their problems (Korte, 2017). There also seems to be a "seasonality" to suicide, as Korte (2017) noted that while more adults commit suicide in the summer, it is during the fall and spring that school-aged students attempt the act.

While society is primed to believe that suicide is not an act performed by children, recent statistics prove otherwise. A new report shows that, for the first time, suicide rates for U.S. middle school students have surpassed the rate of death by car crashes (Rock, 2017). The suicide rate among youngsters aged ten to fourteen has been steadily rising, and doubled in the U.S. from 2007 to 2014, according to the Centers for Disease Control and Prevention (Rock, 2017). In 2014, 425 young people ten to fourteen years of age died by suicide, and for all other age groups, suicide rose by a margin of 30 to 63 percent as well (Rock, 2017). The American Academy of Pediatrics rates suicide as the third most prevalent cause of death among those fifteen to nineteen years old (Rock, 2017).

Korte (2017) painted a picture of not only the increase in suicides among school children but also the use of more dramatic ways of self-harm. Hanging and suffocation have become more common, as have suicidal thoughts that may not be acted upon, or may be thwarted (Korte, 2017). While girls are more likely to unsuccessfully attempt suicide, boys and young males are far more likely to complete their attempts. Kraemer (2011) wrote that masculine isolation is at the root of male suicide and that signs of hopelessness, hostility, social isolation, and self-loathing are common among males who make an attempt. Interestingly, social and economic conditions affect male suicide rates; they go down during war time and rise during economic depressions (Dos Santos, Tavares, & Barros, 2016).

It is a relatively recent phenomenon to consider adolescent depression as common, chronic, and serious enough to merit greater attention. One advancement is in understanding how the genders experience depressive incidents differently. Prior to adolescence, boys have a slightly higher rate of depressive symptoms, but this rate changes when puberty starts. Fleming and Englar-Carlson (2008) question the rates as they feel that "many cases of depression among teenage boys may go undiagnosed because they might be masked by substance abuse and acting-out behavior" (p. 127) and that actual numbers are closer to 20 to 35 percent.

Physical or sexual abuse, late puberty, and long-term poverty are risk factors for depression in young males. While girls generally experience depression as the result of disruptions in their relationships, boys report that school-related problems and non-interpersonal factors lie behind their depression (Fleming &

Englar-Carlson, 2008). A high-risk factor is that a boy reported having fewer than two friends, raising doubt about whether relational factors don't play a role in their distress as well (Fleming & Englar-Carlson, 2008). Having poor adaptive functions within school and family settings and weak or nonexistent support systems influences mental health and well-being.

Risk Factors in Male Suicide

The American Academy of Pediatrics (Shain, 2017) noted that certain groups were at greater risk for suicide; for example, Native American boys and adolescents have the highest suicide rates in the nation. Almost a third of bisexual and gay males in grades 7 through 12 revealed that they had attempted suicide (Shain, 2017). While some may have had mental health problems that put them at greater risk for this act, almost to a boy, respondents in several major studies mentioned harassment, bullying, marginalization, religious bigotry, and family rejection as root causes of their consideration of ending their lives (Shain, 2017).

When traditional ties and supports are weakened, boys are at greater risk, this is clearly seen as one of the causes for the high suicide rate of Native American Indian males (Fleming & Englar-Carlson, 2008). While substance abuse and the availability of firearms are contributing factors, the forced loosening of tribal ties and the replacement of social integration as a tribal member in the face of having to fit in to the majority culture given the historic dislocation and relocation of many tribes, are primary factors in depression among this population (Fleming & Englar-Carlson, 2008). Latino males also are believed to have an elevated risk.

African Americans historically have experienced lower rates of suicide than other ethnic groups but in the last several decades young African-Americans between the ages of fifteen and nineteen have become a very high-risk group (Balis & Postolache, 2008). Now, young African American males are as likely to commit suicide as their white peers and the reasons for that skyrocketing figure, the authors believe, lie in a postmodern society that is characterized by the falling away of many traditional institutions, lack of community, an increase in people's feelings that things are beyond their power to change, and an increasing exposure to toxic risk factors (Balis & Postolache, 2008). With fewer connections among individuals and between individuals and the society in which they live, there is an increased chance of depression, related pathologies such as drug or alcohol abuse, and suicide (Recovery Worldwide, 2019).

African Americans tend to be more vulnerable because they are more likely to be relegated to living in resource-poor, low income areas, and institutions that provided social support (family, religious, community) and protected individuals from societal risk factors have gradually been dissolving in postmodern societies (Nutt, 2018; Williams, 2018). Young African American males face greater exposure to stressors that increase psychological distress; they are thus more prone to depression and pathologies such as suicide (Williams, 2018). Fleming and Englar-Carlson (2008) noted that African American males who move into the middle and upper classes face unprecedented pressures to succeed and may also struggle to forge an identity in the face of class expectations and the necessity of leaving peers behind.

Media Influences on Suicide Rates

Korte (2017) raised concern about the fact that the internet and other media are both increasing rates of cyberbullying (which itself can be a cause of depression or suicide) and suicide, since teens and young adults have ready access to reams of information about how they can do bodily harm. Both those who have harmed themselves and those who have acted violently against others have utilized the internet to learn about ways to carry out their actions (Korte, 2017). Posting on the internet may be a means for broadcasting their plans or alerting others of impending trouble; although when males were alerted to distress among their peers, they were less likely to report or respond to it in preventative ways (Korte, 2017).

Social media continues to be a growing problem. Kutner (2016) wrote of another concern about social media prevalence, that is its ability to memorialize victims of suicide in ways that make death seem heroic, glamorous, or an efficacious way to solve pressing problems once and for all. Unstable or impressionable children and adolescents can be influenced by these social media postings or other memorials even if they have no connection with the deceased. Those who actually have a real-life connection to a suicide victim are twice as likely to develop their own suicidal thoughts as someone who never knew the victim (Kutner, 2016).

Social media also may be at the root of the "cluster suicides" that have become rampant in schools. Kutner (2016) called these cluster suicides "contagious," and wrote of the violent ways in which they were carried out in the neighboring counties of El Paso County, Colorado, and Douglas where teen suicides were accomplished by gunshot, hangings, choking, and drug overdoses. While historically, theorists believed that social bonds prevented suicide or other forms of violence, it was established in the 1990s that suicide can actually be transmitted between and among individuals, with those aged fifteen to nineteen up to four times more susceptible to suicide contagion than any other age group (Logan & Mercy, 2018).

The widely reported Silicon Valley (Palo Alto) suicides raised awareness that it is not just students on the fringes or in the throes of social inequities who can be suicidal; these were the best and brightest—students who were high achievers, socially respected, and college-bound. Research examined the psychiatric risk factors of students with behavioral issues, trying to ascertain if these issues correlated more positively with the stage of adolescence or with poverty (Rosin, 2015). Needing a school to compare with an inner-city site, where 86 percent of the population was on free and reduced lunch, an extremely affluent site was also examined. Results showed that not only did students at the affluent school use drugs and alcohol at significantly higher rates, but that they also suffered from greater incidences of serious anxiety and depression (Rosin, 2015).

The most affluent youth had not previously been even considered as being an at-risk group for mental health problems due to their high grades, seemingly limitless future possibilities, and material wealth; however, results proved that many of these students were under huge stress that peaked in adolescence (Rosin, 2015). This was certainly true in Palo Alto, where students felt the pressure to excel in everything they attempted—pressure often created by their parents' lofty expectations, while at the same time they felt isolated from their parents (Rosin, 2015). This research should remind practitioners and parents to be on the alert for signs of excessive stress and pressure as well as withdrawal within the family unit.

RISK FACTORS

The Colorado Child Fatality Prevention System investigated and discovered common risk factors among the victims (Kutner, 2016). These included family arguments, physical or emotional abuse, breaking up with a boyfriend or girlfriend, and the number of students who were children of parents serving in the military, who are at higher risk for suicide than the general public (Kutner, 2016). For young males, confrontations to or failures of their masculinity lay at the heart of violence against self or others. In general, if boys and adolescent males do not possess the coping skills to get through stressful times, even much smaller events, such as not making a team or being spurned by a love interest when coupled with larger ones, it may prompt a chain reaction that moves from depression to suicidal ideation to an actual suicide attempt (Kutner, 2016).

There also are common suicide warning signs that too frequently are either not noticed or not reported and may include talking to others or sharing on social media emotions such as wanting to die, experiencing feelings of hopelessness or seeing no way out, or believing that they are a burden to others who will be better off without them (American Foundation for Suicide Prevention, 2019). Stockpiling firearms, medication, online resources, or possessing specific items that could lead to implementation are also telltale signs of intent (American Foundation for Suicide Prevention, 2019). Those considering suicide often part with their possessions or call or visit others to say their goodbyes. Having made a final decision, their moods can suddenly change depression or agitation to calm and cheerfulness (Korte, 2017).

When considering young males and suicide, one of the most informative questions is whether there are guns in the home, as firearms used in suicide attempts make rescue nearly impossible. According to the Violence Policy Center (2018), there were just shy of 23,000 firearm-related suicides in 2016. Given the gun culture in which so many young men grow up, the choice of firearms is understandable. Even in homes in which guns were stored safely or locked up, the risk of adolescent suicide was higher (Violence Policy Center, 2018). The use of alcohol combined with weapons is almost always fatal.

In those who suffer depressive and suicidal moods, there are compounding cognitive problems that promote faulty thinking; among these are cognitive constriction, distortion, and rigidity (Cartreine, 2016). In each of these cases, the thinker sees few options for his behavior, generalizes an incident to all situations, and can't think his way through to better alternatives for action. If he suffers a series of negative events, it is likely that each subsequent event will lower his threshold for actual suicide because his thinking becomes patterned by an ever-narrowing list of options (Cartreine, 2016; Fleming & Englar-Carlson, 2008).

WHEN MASCULINITY TURNS DEADLY

Violence against self can also be nested within acts of violence against others. There is probably no better modern-day example than that of Columbine shooters Eric Harris and Dylan Klebold. Their diaries reflect a long history of depression and a wish to end their own lives, which was accomplished at the end of the shooting spree (Young, Michael, & Smolinski, 2019).

Given that almost all the school shooters throughout American history were males, Langman (2009; 2015) offers inner glimpses of the male mind gone awry. Langman (2009; 2015), formulated psychological profiles of school shooters in the contemporary times. He depicted three types of shooters—psychopathic; traumatized; and psychotic (Langman, 2015).

Psychopathic killers are arrogant, narcissistic, and entitled (Langman, 2015). They are compelled to meet personal needs before those of others and rarely demonstrate any sort of empathy toward peers or their victims (Langman, 2009; 2015). Common traits of psychopathic killers include a strong impulse for excitement; the lack of guilt, remorse, or the ability to relate to others' emotions; grandiosity and a sense that they are entitled to respect; and the ability to deceive others through the ability to read them and know how to manipulate them (Langman, 2009; 2015). Eric Harris, architect of the Columbine shootings, is the perfect embodiment of a psychopathic killer (Langman, 2015).

Because of their exaggerated sense of their own importance, a psychopath doesn't care if he hurts others, either emotionally or physically; sadly, doing so may provide them with a sense of euphoria or self-grandeur (Hirstein, 2013). Having highly polished social skills permits them to lie with impunity and they thrive on their ability to manage others' impressions of them so that their true goals are hidden, and they appear in positive light (Hirstein, 2013). Most psychopaths are extremely charismatic if they choose to be; thus making them charming but deceitful.

Langman (2009, 2015) also wrote of psychopaths as possessing little to no regard for social norms, values, ethics, or the law; they most often believe that they are the embodiment of the law themselves. Their attitude gives them a particular disdain for authority figures such as teachers or law enforcement. Lacking the emotion of fear, they remain calm and high-functioning in situations that cause typical people to experience stress or malfunction (Hirstein, 2013). They do not take responsibility for their actions, instead blaming their victims for what happened. They believe that any punishment that befalls them is unjust, a personal wronging, which permits them to act out as they think is justified.

Psychopaths are highly sensitive to any slights, rejections, or put-downs; since these are part of regular male bantering and posturing for leadership positions in groups, a psychopathic boy is prone to acting out because he cannot control the situation (Hirstein, 2013). They feel under attack or disrespected even in typical "guy" situations and they tend to target a girlfriend, teacher, parent, or others who have rejected or frustrated them with acts of fury or violence (Langman 2009; 2015). The author differentiates between "explosive" psychopaths, who erupt in fury when they perceive they have been disrespected or rejected and "tyrannical" psychopaths, who derive a high degree of pleasure in exerting power over their victims. Eric Harris, for example, possessed both types of psychopathology (Langman, 2015).

School shooters, Langman (2015) discovered, suffered from psychotic symptoms such as major depression and bipolar disorder; these symptoms ran the gamut from being chronic to episodic and some were considered narrowly problematic while others were completely debilitating. The school shooters in Langman's studies (2015) seem to have suffered from schizophrenia or schizotypal personality disorder. Schizophrenia, which is more severe, led the boys to have hallucinations or delusions; they also experienced social struggles, described being extremely lonely, and were frequently depressed (Langman, 2015). These young males were seen by others to be outcasts, odd in their behaviors, speech, or dress, and held atypical beliefs. Those living with schizophrenia often speak of not trusting their own brains, of being exhausted from trying to separate what is real from what is delusional (American Psychiatric Association, n.d.). Their very personalities are disturbed in that they may not even know whether they are human or not. West Paducah, Kentucky, school shooter Michael Carneal questioned whether he was a human or an alien (Young, Michael, & Smolinski, 2019).

Langman (2009, 2015) refuted the notion that most school shooters must have had horrific childhoods but did recognize that there was a percentage among them who went through childhood trauma or abuse, and they are labeled the traumatized shooters. They may have grown up in poverty, been neglected or abused as children, or suffered traumatic losses or disruptions such as the death of a parent, homelessness, or institutionalization. Chaos, violence, or psychological absence due to substance abuse or mental illness characterized their upbringing, and, for boys in particular, this engendered shame and rage that later became focused on self or others (Langman, 2015).

Langman (2009) wrote that regardless of circumstances surrounding the shooters, they were similar in some ways and a lack of empathy, above all else, typified their behavior, allowing them to commit terrible acts, often at close range, without feeling for the victims. Because of their feelings of justified anger, shooters were able to detach from their actions relatively easily. While Michael Caneal questioned whether he indeed was of alien stock, other shooters describe their victims in terms of being less than human (zombies) or enemies or "different." Rage bound them together, but the sources of that rage could emanate from feeling that others were controlling them, having a limited sense of personal freedom, thinking of themselves as a superior race forced to suffer with inferior beings, being slighted, being abandoned, feeling victimized or outcast, and being unfavorably compared to others of their gender (Langman, 2009; Young, Michael, & Smolinski, 2019).

With many journals, videos, and other artifacts left for him to pore over, Langman (2009) found that shooters experienced existential angst that often led them to have suicidal thoughts and ideation. Many had suffered for years and had developed intricate suicide plans; these were seen as the only way to end the suffering, but it was not enough to go out alone; rather, their tormentors must go with them as well.

Langman (2009) saw extremely reactive natures among the shooters, meaning that these individuals could fly into rages if they thought they were being disrespected in any way. Unable to engage in normal give and take, they flew off the handle into accelerated rages at the slightest provocation. Langman (2009) believed that their fragile identities and their sense of failed masculinity put them at almost constant risk for escalated emotions that could quickly become translated into plans for revenge. It is easy to understand how these psychopathic males, with their knowledge of and access to weapons, could pose a threat to themselves and others.

FINAL THOUGHTS

Boys and adolescent males are socialized in many ways that do not lead to optimal mental health and well-being. Social norms around masculinity can lead them to negative consequences such as restricted emotionality, repressed expressions of affection, early separation from parents, gender role conflicts, and dysfunctionality in their relationships. They are also less well-educated than women about mental health and well-being and tend to seek help when in distress less frequently; sadly, they are less able to even recognize or articulate their emotional distress. Having to be "a man" means fearing being viewed as weak or vulnerable if mental health help is sought.

Boys and adolescent males are diagnosed far more frequently than are girls and adolescent females in just about every category of behavioral and emotional issue during these developmental periods. They are at greater risk for becoming a special education statistic, being medicated for ADHD, be diagnosed with a conduct disorder, or be considered on the autism spectrum. But while girls are more likely to internalize their mental and emotional health problems, leading to higher incidences of depression and suicide attempts, they are less likely to complete those attempts and more likely to seek or receive help.

Boys more often turn their problems into outward behaviors such as risk-taking, substance abuse, or violence against others; they also are more likely to complete a suicide attempt. Ninety-four percent of all school shooters are male and another growing health hazard for young men is addiction to violent video games. There is a prevalent belief that our nation's schools are becoming less boy-friendly, and the institution of more formal curriculum into lower and lower grade levels puts slower-developing males at greater risk for failure and punishment.

Fathers and other prominent role models most likely were not raised in a culture of taking care of their own mental and emotional health and thus cannot serve as guides, nor are they often able to be observant of signs of mental health distress in their sons. This means that there is less of a safety net around boys if they encounter stressful or unhealthy situations. This puts a greater onus on primary health providers and others, such as physicians who provide sports physicals, to be on the frontline of protection and diagnosis of potential health risks. From a therapeutic standpoint, it is essential that practitioners develop male-friendly strategies to reach out to and engage traditional men and boys in examining gender roles and the negative effects that they may have on their health.

POINTS TO REMEMBER

- Males begin their lives at greater risk than females, being less likely to survive to birth and more emotionally needy and in distress than girls as infants.
- Parents are more likely to give attention to girls' emotional distress, more likely to keep girls closely connected to them for longer periods of time, and less likely to see them as ready for greater independence and separation from their mothers than their male counterparts.
- Certain subpopulations of boys and adolescent males—such as Native American, African American, members of marginalized groups, gay and transgender males, those living in poverty, and those with disabilities—are at higher risk for poor or compromised emotional and mental health.
- Contemporary boys and adolescent males are raised in a culture in which men have not been socialized toward identifying, articulating, and seeking help to address emotional and mental health problems.
- Boys and adolescent males can suffer from gender role conflict, just as men do, which can lead to depression, restrictive ability to express affection with other males, and problems with conduct, family relations, and anger.
- While females tend to internalize mental health issues, boys tend to externalize, which can lead to violence toward self and others, particularly if weapons are available.
- Researchers see changes in early childhood education, environmental factors, lack of positive male role models and guides, over-diagnosis and medication of certain disorders, and the rise in violent video gaming and addiction as contributing factors to poor male mental and emotional well-being.

Chapter Three

Manhood in the Making

Social and Cultural Influences on Masculinity in America

The influences on manhood are many and confusing, perhaps none more so than what happens socially and culturally to young men trying to break the code. In 2017, there were 53,716,518 school aged (5–17) children in the United States (United States Census Bureau, 2018b). Half of those children were white, 25 percent Hispanic/Latino, 14 percent African American/black and 5 percent of Asian descent with all other ethnicities comprising the remaining percentage (Kids Count Data Center, 2017). Just over half of all students were male (51 percent), for a total of 27,395,424 boys in American classrooms in 2017 (United States Census Bureau, 2018b).

MASCULINITY

For thousands of years, there were three touchstones for a male to be considered a man in practically every culture—the 3 Ps: procreate, provide, and protect (Daloz, 2011). These touchstones are no longer relevant in most of the world today. Daloz (2011) noted that "in an increasingly urban world, it no longer makes sense for a man to sire as many children as he can; in a society where a single income has lost its potency and women share the workplace, few men can be the sole provider; and in a world of terrorism and roadside bombs, protection is rarely about just being tougher" (p. 78).

Becoming a man in today's world is not so clear cut. The definitions of masculinity, manhood, and maleness are less certain. Each man has an untold number of ways to demonstrate his masculinity. Similarly, each culture, society or social context has many forms of manhood, of which hegemonic masculinity is the dominant, highest ranking form (Carberry, 2017; Griffith,

Brinkley-Rubinstein, Bruce, Thorpe, & Metzl, 2015). Hegemonic masculinity is the "standard by which males' status and esteem are judged, even though few boys and men ever achieve this ideal" (Yavorsky, Buchman, & Miles, 2015, p. 7).

While hegemonic masculinity varies across cultures and time, several core traits are demonstrated in almost all cultures, societies, and organizations. Besides maleness, the prime characteristics of hegemonic masculinity are heterosexuality, domination and subordination of women as well as other non-macho males (Schrock & Schwalbe, 2009). Additional common characteristics include mental and physical strength, competitiveness, risk taking, rationality, and stoicism, demonstrated as minimal and guarded emotional expression (Schrock & Schwalbe, 2009). In current Western society the definition of hegemonic masculinity also includes white and moneyed (Schrock & Schwalbe, 2009).

Hegemonic masculinity is not a natural phenomenon; rather, it is a social construct. It is not the same in all cultures and social environments; for example, in a school setting, school-wide policies, administrative priorities, curriculum, direction and type of teacher attention, pedagogical practices, and peer cultures all play roles in determining which masculinities are reinforced and valued over others (Tischler & McCaughtry, 2011). Even within a school setting the characteristics that determine the dominant masculinity may not be the same in all situations. The fitness, strength, and athleticism that may dominate in the physical education arena may not dominate in literary or theater environments, or even the science lab (Tischler & McCaughtry, 2011).

Masculinity vs. Femininity and Others

Hegemonic masculinity, the summit of masculinity, is situated "as oppositional and as superior to femininity and other lesser forms of masculinity—often those that incorporate femininities (e.g., gay masculinities)" (Yavorsky et al., 2015, p. 8). Actions, behaviors, and traits that could be interpreted as feminine are avoided at all costs by any male seeking to establish himself as a man. These feminine behaviors include studiousness, expressions of feelings, dependence, weakness, warmth, and empathy (Gosse, 2012). A male exhibiting any of these traits as well as a host of others deemed feminine that do not fit with hegemonic masculinity, is subjected to domination and subordination by those males who do portray hegemonic masculinity (Carberry, 2017). Bullying, both physical and verbal, of the subordinated male is common and seen as "an abusive ritual of condescension" (Carberry, 2017, p. 84).

Toddlers, Childhood, and Adolescence

A child's first relationship, in most cases, is with its mother. Mothers are female. At some point a toddler begins to understand he is different from his mother and this "comes as a profound shock to a tender three-year-old just discovering he is a boy" (Daloz, 2011, p. 79). The effect of the discovery by a toddler that he or she is not his or her mother is substantially different for boys than it is for girls. Girls, while discovering they are not their mother, also learn they are not dissimilar from her. This similarity of mother and daughter both being girls allows the daughter to identify and connect with her mother. The same is not true for boys. Boys must separate from their mother. It is in this need for separation from their mother that boys begin to feel the necessity to separate from the feminine. According to Daloz (2011), "This need to separate from Mother in order to be a real man is rooted in the male soul from the earliest years, as boys learn they will not grow up to be like Mama" (p. 79).

As children learn the world is divided into boy/male/man and girl/female/woman, they must also learn how to show they understand this organization and where they fit in. Research by Bussey (as cited in Jordan, 1995) into early childhood gender beliefs reveals that most children have adopted a gender identity by age two; however, they are not clear what behaviors are appropriate for their gender. Even by age four children may still not grasp or be prepared to accept the stereotypes presented by adults and other sources of influence (Berk, 2017; Jordan, 1995). Children enter school knowing their gender; however, they do not have a fixed image or idea of what it means to be a boy or a girl and what behaviors are acceptable and look to adults and peers for answers and to make sense of the mystery of how to be a boy or a girl (Berk, 2017; Jordan, 1995).

During toddlerhood and childhood, boys worked on separating themselves from their mother and, then by extension, anything feminine. According to Cahill (as cited in Schrock & Schwalbe, 2009) young males "reject and devalue . . . symbols of female identity" in order to "confirm their identities as boys" (p. 281). This work continues and intensifies in adolescence; thus, studiousness, classified as "feminine" by hegemonic masculinity, may be considered "white" or "gay" (Gosse, 2012). Similarly, reading is gendered as female and, as such, is an activity that a boy seeking to establish his masculinity will shun, despite the likely negative impact on his academic achievement (Berk, 2017; Froschl & Sprung, 2004).

Adolescence is a proving ground for boys. Their childhood was spent learning how to be a boy, how to present as a male in society, and learning to avoid anything that might be feminine (Berk, 2017). Adolescence brings a mandate to leave behind childlike behaviors and possibly childhood friends

(Oransky & Marecek, 2009). Boys feel the demand to begin to lessen their reliance on family for guidance and support. It is at this time, early adolescence (ages 10–14 years), that "is a critical period for shaping gender attitudes, particularly because the onset of puberty brings new and intensified expectations related to gender" (Amin et al., 2018, p. 1). Not only is manhood difficult to attain for a boy, it can feel like a contest that must be won, and then constantly re-earned.

One of the ways a boy can present his masculinity is through bodily performance. For adolescent boys, this bodily performance is critical in demonstrating that they are performing being a boy correctly, as if they are actors perfecting their personal character (Tishcler & McCaughtry, 2011). These bodily performance activities and characteristics, often sports related, denote hegemonic masculinity and include strength, speed, power, muscularity, fitness, athleticism, injury, and risk acceptance (Tischcler & McCaughtry, 2011).

In addition to sports-related bodily performance, boys use their bodies to communicate in considerable and complex ways that form a potent body language. These macho posturing actions, gestures, and behaviors are powerful, bolster a boy's masculinity and, therefore, are very desirable to adolescent boys (Dalley-Trim, 2007). It is common for boys to practice "shouting and being loud, call out and interruptive behaviours, laughing, joking, misbehaving, acting tough, acting cool, play fighting and refusing to affirm the teacher's authority" (Dalley-Trim, 2007, p. 203). Boys quickly figure out that they can impress their peers if they break rules, are defiant, talk back to teachers, and disdain academics. These behaviors and other actual or symbolic acts of intimidation and defiance serve to elevate a boy to manhood status (Schrock & Schwalbe, 2009).

Adolescent boys in current Western society practice emotional restriction and withdrawal from close relationships (Tischler & McCaughtry, 2011). They begin to distance themselves from their families and close friends. Teasing is a major tactic boys use to egg on other boys to be tough, to refrain from expressing emotion or feelings, to be stoic (Tischler & McCaughtry, 2011). Ostracism is used to police boys who fail to eliminate or restrict their emotional displays. The parents of a boy who exhibits emotionality may be particularly disposed to encourage stoicism in order to keep his masculinity from being threatened and from becoming a social outcast (Schrock & Schwalbe, 2009).

THE BOY CODE

From early childhood on, a boy is constantly building his masculine identity, presenting his manhood and trying to live up to the "Boy Code"—a code of conduct, a set of rules or expectations on how to be a real boy (Neu &

Weinfeld, 2007). This code is present, learned, and reinforced in almost every environment in which a boy might find himself—sandboxes, playgrounds, classrooms, camps, places of worship, after-school activities, athletic venues, and more. They learn the code from their family, peers, teachers, coaches, media, and most anyone else with whom they come in contact (Cleveland, 2011).

The Boy Code, originally developed by educator William Pollack (as cited in Neu & Weinfield, 2007), is a list of do's and don'ts for boys.

- Do not cry (no sissy stuff)
- Do not cower, tremble, or shrink from danger
- Do not ask for help when you are unsure of yourself (observe code of silence)
- Do not reach for comfort or reassurance
- Do not sing or cry for joy
- Do not hug your dearest friends
- Do not use words to show tenderness and love (p. 24)

This code clearly articulates the restrictions placed on boys' emotional development. Boys are expected to be "strong, silent, and self-reliant and that they should inhibit any feelings or desires that might be construed as feminine" (Neu & Weinfield, 2007, p. 24). Young males come to believe that they must repress most emotions and attain autonomy at all costs. The cost of violating the Boy Code can be harsh. Boys who fail to follow the code may be seen as girly or gay and "are labeled in ways that leave them feeling isolated, shamed and vulnerable to teasing and bullying" (Froschl & Sprung, 2004).

Implications for Academic Achievement

The consequences of not adhering to the Boy Code in school for boys are twofold—emotional and academic and encompass many factors. The stress of an academic environment, and not being able to deal with it emotionally, causes many boys to feel estranged and unconnected to the school environment. The stereotypical and narrow conceptions of hegemonic masculinity which reject all things feminine and categorizes academic achievement as feminine may cause some boys to underperform in school. Several behaviors that are conducive to achievement in school, such as cooperation, attentiveness, and being studious, are deemed feminine and tend not to be displayed or practiced by boys striving to demonstrate their masculinity; thus, adhering to the Boy Code and working to present as masculine may curtail academic accomplishments in boys (Yavorsky et al., 2015).

Males value school success accomplished through a process of "effortless achievement" (Yavorsky et al., 2015). This contradictory process requires boys to present their school successes as the "result of innate capabilities, not effort—especially since studying has become associated with femininity" (Yavorsky et al., 2015, p. 9). Being studious and achieving academic success requires hard work, discipline, effort, and commitment. Males who practice "effortless achievement" will find real academic achievement difficult.

The fear of failure, which is paramount among the fears fostered by the code, renders "boys less likely to reattempt something at which they have previously been unsuccessful, and they are also less willing to try something new because of the possibility that they might fail" (Cleveland, 2011, p. 43). This avoidance of trying is acceptable because, to the boy striving to present as masculine, it is better than trying and failing; however, such avoidance stops learning in its tracks. Should a boy attempt something new, he may reduce his chances of success by utilizing defensive pessimism (setting unrealistically low expectations) and self-sabotage such as setting obstacles in the path to success (Cleveland, 2011).

The code compels independence; therefore, "boys are unlikely to seek the help they may need or even to indicate, in a direct way, that they need help" (Neu & Weinfield, 2007, p. 24). Two other facets that may also be factors in boys' reluctance to ask for help are emotional restriction and social teasing; they do not want to appear weak or be teased. Accordingly, boys who endorse hegemonic masculinity are less likely to seek help and, in particular, to seek help in language arts which is seen as a feminine subject (Leaper, Farkas, & Starr, 2018).

A boy's ability to function in school can be, and often is, seriously hindered by a deep-seated fear of not belonging, mixed with anxiety of being different or labeled girly or gay. Cleveland (2011) stated "belonging, in fact, is so important that some boys will do almost anything, endure almost anything, and inflict on one another almost anything in order to be *part of the group*" (p. 42). Boys may cover up or hide their inability to be part of the group by acting out, being disruptive, or becoming the class clown (Cleveland, 2011).

Literacy skills such as reading, writing, and speaking are considered something girls do and, therefore, are feminine skills. Such feminized activities are to be avoided at all costs by boys seeking to adhere to the Boy Code (Neu & Weinfield, 2007). Boys who shun these literacy skills impede their ability to master the skills needed for success in school and out. Equally as harmful, boys who inhibit their feelings, rein in their emotions, as directed by the Boy Code, will have little practice in identifying and talking about those emotions, or those of others and without this ability will be at a loss to connect with characters in a story or discuss what a character may have been feeling in a book (Neu & Weinfield, 2007). Using any of these feminine skills will leave a boy vulnerable to being labeled as girl-like and gay (Neu & Weinfield, 2007).

The stereotypical and narrow conception of hegemonic masculinity rejects all things feminine and categorizes academic achievement as feminine.

Cleveland (2011), described how the Boy Code affects learning as it plays

> into a boy's natural need to build and protect his burgeoning masculine identity. It negatively affects his attitudes and willingness to engage in learning on many levels: by labeling literacy or being smart as feminine and, thus, something to be avoided at all costs; by emphasizing being tough and uncommunicative; and by convincing boys to adopt a host of counterproductive hypermasculine behaviors and defensive maneuvering, including the willingness to fail in order to secure a sense of belonging. Its influence is as pervasive as it is pernicious. (p. 44)

According to Eliot (2009), professor of neuroscience at the Chicago Medical School of Rosalind Franklin University of Medicine & Science, a child's brain is exceptionally malleable, continually responding to all experiences from prenatal life to adolescence. If gender differences are constantly being reinforced and exaggerated, even if not consciously, the danger is that the harmful and limiting stereotypes about what it means to be a boy—the Boy Code—congeal and become cemented as truths, not only in the minds of children, but also in the minds of parents and educators (Martino, 2011).

BECOMING A MAN

Manhood—or masculinity—is not something a boy either has or does not have; it is something he must earn (Tishcler & McCaughtry, 2011). In the past, manhood could be achieved by successfully completing a culture's coming of age ritual—often brutal physical tests or risky exhibitions of toughness—or demonstrating mastery of procreate, provide, and protect (Tishcler & McCaughtry, 2011). Achieving manhood marked a change in status from juvenile to adult. Today the shift from boyhood to manhood is not guaranteed; rather, it is a social status that must be earned (Bosson & Vandello, 2011). Manhood is both elusive and tenuous, it "is not delineated by adulthood and there is no enduring standard by which masculinity can be proved once and for all. Instead, masculinity is inherently 'precarious' and must be proved repeatedly" (Smiler, 2016, p. 1). The uncertainty of manhood is in "such a shaky state that it is unattainable for any significant period and must be constantly re-earned" (Gosse, 2012).

To prove or preserve his masculinity a boy must put on a convincing manhood act. Unfortunately, this act is often demonstrated by conforming to stereotypical hegemonic masculine ideals of strength and violence (e.g., fighting); risk taking (e.g., excessive alcohol consumption, high-speed reckless driving); and promiscuous sexuality (Smiler, 2016). The traits that signify masculine can vary, not only historically, but also culturally. They can also vary depending on race, ethnicity, and class (Schrock & Schwalbe, 2009). A boy must learn how to present a masculine self to various audiences and situations and this "process of learning how to signify a masculine self in situationally appropriate ways continues throughout life" (Schrock & Schwalbe, 2009, p. 283).

Race and Ethnicities

The definition and traits of what it means to be a man varies by race, ethnicities, nationalities, age, generation, and life stage; for example, younger generations of men may be more emotionally expressive and less homophobic than older generations of men such as the baby boomers and those who preceded them (Smiler, 2016). In addition to demonstrating traditional hegemonic masculine traits, African American males often include responsibility and accountability, autonomy, respect, and spirituality as important components of masculinity, whereas Latino males include the concepts of familismo (the importance of family relationships), personalismo (establishing a personal connection with everyone regardless of their social or professional status), simpatia (establishing agreement and harmony in relationships) and respeto (respect) (Smiler, 2016).

The most important characteristics of masculinity identified by Asian American males included having a good job, being honorable, being in control of one's own life, being a family man, and having lots of money (Smiler, 2016). With non-white races and ethnicities comprising half of school-aged children, the ways that boys perform manhood can vary widely (Kids Count Data Center, 2017).

Social and Cultural Reinforcements

Children, adolescents, and adults, from their birth forward, all piece together their understanding of gender from multiple sources in their social world which provide both clear cues and unspoken, hidden clues (Arbeit, Hershberg, Johnston, Lerner, & Lerner, 2017). Family members, peers, teachers, media, toys, and many other sources of influence teach boys of the need to identify as boys and how to indicate their maleness through societal pressures such as which clothing to wear, emotional guardedness, and sport selection (Davies, 2018; Schrock & Schwalbe, 2009).

Boys are told, initially by their parents and then others, from their earliest days "don't cry," "shake it off," "take it like a man," "man up," and other euphemisms exhorting him to ignore and reject his physical and emotional feelings (Davies, 2018). Everywhere a child turns there are hints, signs, and reinforcements for "proper" gender performance, often including examples of consequences of not performing gender as prescribed.

A boy's first role model is his father and he will strive to be like this larger than life role model. It is vital that the older males, those in positions of modeling give "messages about being a man. Boys want to grow up to be like their male role models. And boys who grow up in homes with absent fathers search the hardest to figure out what it means to be male" (Canada, as cited in PBS Parents. n.d., n.p.) The lack of a male role model in a boy's life is a major factor in his underachievement in school and beyond. More than ever before, there is a lack of male role models; thus, the only exposure for young men is what they see on paper media, film, television, the internet, and video games (Cleveland, 2011). This becomes an issue as this generation ages as "they will gravitate towards those negative male mentors, peers and behaviors who are best able to duplicate the unrealistic images they may associate with a strong male identity" (Cleveland, 2011, p. 48).

Peer group expectations exert a powerful influence on boys and their quest to become men. Adolescent boys will align their manhood act, their friendships and many of their emotion presentations with "peer group expectations and assumptions about masculinity and what they identified as its antitheses, girlishness and homosexuality" (Oransky & Marecek, 2009, p. 234). Young men's gendered behavior is policed by peers in both blatant and subtle ways. Blatant control includes outright mockery and public humiliation of boys who showed emotions in public or displayed emotional vulnerability. Subtler ways of regulating boys' emotional practices include making light of friends' problems, joking about their fears, urging an upset friend to be stoical, and avoiding friends when they were upset. These practices effectively eliminate much meaningful emotional content from boy–boy friendships and, as a result, they may be unable to recognize feelings in themselves and others, becoming emotionally illiterate (Oransky & Marecek, 2009).

Conceivably, sports, whether a boy is a participant or spectator, is one of the most powerful sources of the meaning of masculinity—what it means to be a man. This source of influence comes from multiple arenas: from the highly visible "pageantry" of television sports broadcasts to local organized high school and recreation sports to casual pickup games at local athletic fields and courts, including park and backyard games (Connell & Messerschmidt, 2005).

Simply watching or participating in sports is an effective way for boys to demonstrate their manhood (Schrock & Schwalbe, 2009).

Sports reinforces the Boy Code (Neu & Weinfield, 2007). Boys who cry in sports, from disappointment or pain, are teased, demeaned, and ostracized. The message is clear that boys must not show fear or pain (Schrock & Schwalbe, 2009).

Violence and aggression is reinforced and celebrated in sports and therefore is an effective way for a boy to establish his masculinity (Schrock & Schwalbe, 2009). The message that acting macho is manly leads boys to engage in risky, even violent, behaviors like their sports heroes, and often results in injury to themselves or others (Gosse, 2012). Additionally, the valorization of violence and aggression may be credited for the "pervasiveness of bullying" (Schrock & Schwalbe, 2009, p. 282). Successful resistance to bullying is an effective way to defend a manhood. "Men don't share pain, physical or mental. Men are 'bulletproof,' even the nastiest words should not affect a man's psyche. And, perhaps the most dangerous message, men don't walk away from confrontation or from bullies" (Roberts, 2013, n.p.).

Intimidation, control, and dominance are also encouraged in sports, providing another clear example of how a real man acts. Katz (as cited in Jhally, Ericsson, Talreja, Katz, Earp, & the Media Education Foundation, 1999) explains this through a basketball example when a "player does an 'in your face' dunk over his opponent, and then rubs it in. The lesson about manhood is clear. You gain respect by disrespecting another person" (p. 20).

Sports clearly provide multiple and powerful messages about masculinity. Fortunately, not all messages are negative. Positive lessons include sportsmanship, hard work, confidence, teamwork, dedication and commitment, among others (Connell, 2008). Unfortunately, not all boys are regularly exposed to encouraging and affirming role models, whether in person or through media and these positive qualities may be overlooked (Chen & Curtner-Smith, 2013).

FINAL THOUGHTS

Over half the students in American classrooms are boys. From early childhood until adulthood and indeed beyond, boys struggle to become a man, to be seen as masculine. There is no clear cut definition of a "real man" to which a boy can refer. The dominant masculinity—hegemonic masculinity—varies in different cultures and environments and is the standard against which a male and his behavior is measured. Not only is it difficult for a boy to achieve this manhood, it must constantly be performed and proven again and again—throughout a boy's entire life.

Hegemonic masculinity, as the summit of masculinity, is positioned opposite and superior to anything feminine; therefore, any behaviors or actions that might be seen as feminine will be avoided at all costs by any boy or man working to prove himself a real man. Anything classified as feminine is considered girly, gay, or sissy, and is, therefore, considered unacceptable for a real boy or man. This avoidance includes actions and behaviors that are gendered as feminine and that could improve a boy's academic achievement if they were practiced.

Body performance and body language are important ways a boy can express his masculinity. Often sports related, a boy may perform his manhood through his strength, speed, power, and his willingness to accept risks. Boys use their bodies to communicate in multiple and complex ways. They quickly realize that they can impress their peers; thus, gaining status by breaking rules, talking back, showing disdain for academics, and demonstrating other actual or symbolic acts of intimidation or defiance. These behaviors serve to elevate a boy to manhood status.

From early childhood on, a boy is continuously crafting and reaffirming his masculinity and trying to live up to the Boy Code—a code of conduct—on how to be a "real boy." The cost of violating this Boy Code can be ruthless. Academic achievement can be severely hindered by a boy's quest to adhere to the Boy Code and secure his masculinity. Studiousness is considered feminine; thus, boys will avoid studying, paying attention, and cooperating. Anything literacy related, such as reading and writing, will be shunned. Young men who practice emotional inhibition, as dictated by the Boy Code, may be at a loss to identify with characters and their emotions in a story. The Boy Code also inhibits the boys from seeking help, particularly in language arts, a subject viewed as feminine.

Fear is a major factor in boy's behavior. The fear of not belonging, mixed with anxiety of being different or labeled girly, may be covered up by acting out, being disruptive or by becoming the class clown. Fear of failure, which is the paramount fear for boys, may render a boy unwilling to retry something at which they were previously unsuccessful or to try something new because they might fail.

Everywhere a boy turns there are clear cues, hints, and reinforcements for "proper" gender performance—how to appropriately perform hegemonic masculinity. Frequently, these signs also come with examples of consequences for not properly performing this act. Boys receive these messages from their parents, other adults, and peers. Strong, dominant, powerful, and intimidating men are glorified and any man not meeting these attributes is demeaned, belittled, and feminized. For a man, the importance of masculinity, of being a man, cannot be understated. The ramifications go far beyond his home, his friends, his school, or his community. Indeed, the consequences may well be global.

POINTS TO REMEMBER

- The primary characteristics of hegemonic masculinity include heterosexuality, domination and subordination of women or other men who display feminine traits.
- Failing to follow the Boy Code can result in a boy being labeled as girly or gay, leaving them isolated and shamed, as well as very vulnerable to teasing and bullying.
- Whether a boy is a participant or a spectator, sports can be a powerful influence on a boy seeking the meaning of masculinity.
- Boys learn early on that they must separate from their mother, who is female, and thus begins their quest to separate from anything feminine.

Chapter Four

Education for Self-Efficacy

Breaking the Cycle of Male Underachievement in Postsecondary Education

As young men enter their high school years, a greater emphasis is placed on college and career opportunities. These students, who may have struggled throughout their schooling experience, may find they are not ready for college, but they are unsure what to do next. Some go to college because they are told it is the next step, not necessarily because they are ready or have a clear vision of what their life could be. This is a tough enough task for most students; yet those who have been historically underrepresented at the college level may struggle even more.

Data documenting four-year college attendees in 1970 showed that 58 percent were men and 42 percent were females, while in 2017 the percentages were 56 percent female and 44 percent male, almost completely reversed (Marcus, 2017). An example of this change was easily seen in the Boston Public Schools graduating class of 2007 when it was noted that blacks and Hispanics were going to college at a rate of 186 females to every 100 males, and 153 white females to every 100 males (Sommers, 2013). This, despite a trend that shows that "parents who have only boys are doing more to support their children's college education than parents of all girls" (Ashford, 2017, n.d.).

Further data describes the disparity between race, gender, and college completion (Wang & Parker, 2011). In 2010, only 37 percent of black college graduates were men versus 47 percent in 1988 (Wang & Parker, 2011). In addition to the black male, during 2010 approximately 45 percent of each race, Hispanic, white, and Asian, were male college graduates versus the 1988 census that showed these same races at approximately 53 percent for graduating males (Wang & Parker, 2011). This shift in postsecondary degree completion began several decades ago and continues to grow (Semuels, 2017; Statista, 2019).

While the term "big man on campus" (BMOC) has denoted college males who ruled the collegiate scene, the Urban Dictionary (2013) describes a BMOC this way:

> A guy in college with connections. The Big Man on Campus (or BMOC) knows people. He's privy to the locations of the best parties, the coolest hangout spots, and the loosest women. The term isn't used as much anymore due to the advent of internet social networking, allowing everyone to "know people"; but still, being a BMOC takes skill in real-world networking. (n.p.)

The definition also notes that the BMOC "may have a slightly more inflated ego than most" (Urban Dictionary, 2013, n.p.).

Historically, the college campus has been the province of males, albeit males of privilege. College was, as Bowman and Filar (2018) termed it, a "masculine endeavor" (p. 28). Those of high economic standing sent their sons off to college "to learn more about the world and their place in it" (Bowman & Filar, 2018, p. 28). The wars of the twentieth century culminated in the G.I. Bill and a rededication to the sciences, engineering, and other disciplines that were seen as vital in the global race. Men overwhelmingly were the recipients of the postwar, postsecondary benefits available (Young, Michael, & Jean, 2018).

The movements promoting women's, civil, and disabilities rights of the second half of the last century leveled the playing field to a certain extent; yet as Bowman and Filar (2018) point out, as campuses scrambled to make their classrooms and social environments more accessible and inclusive, they moved away from some of the male-oriented practices of the past. Classrooms became less competitive and more cooperative, more open to self-exploration and expression; there was greater emphasis on career as a tool for promoting social good. Behaviors once excused as "boys being boys" now fell under greater scrutiny.

The end result of these changes is that young males currently are transitioning to college campuses less frequently than young women, having less success and more problems, and leaving before earning a degree at unprecedented rates (Marcus, 2017; Somers, 2013). Rather than big men on campus, some writers have labeled them "lost boys" who have not adequately grown up, found a purpose for their academic pursuits, or developed the kinds of social and personal skills needed to succeed on the contemporary campus (Dreher, 2018).

SECONDARY SCHOOL AND PARENTAL RESPONSIBILITIES TO PREPARE STUDENTS FOR A COLLEGE EDUCATION

The male student needs support prior to leaving high school in order to be prepared for a career or college. A recent report described a $20,000 yearly income difference between those with a high school diploma and a bachelor's degree or higher (DeSilver, 2016). Those students who were enrolled in and graduated from a career and technical education (CTE) program had better yearly incomes than their peers who did not go to college (Kreisman & Strange, 2017).

Another report analyzed responses from high school graduates on their preparedness for college or career opportunities and found that half of the respondents felt there were gaps in their high school education (Hart Research Associates, 2014). This pervasive feeling was up from ten years prior by 8 percent of college students and 2 percent of non-college students (Hart Research Associates, 2014). Gaps were noticed in categories such as oral communication skills, work habits, research and application of learning, computer and technology skills, as well as academic content areas (Hart Research Associate, 2014). As many of these skills are feminized in primary and secondary school, it is conceivable that young men struggle with these skills at higher percentages than female students (DiPrete & Buchmann, 2013; Reichert & Hawley, 2010). Additional findings from the Hart Research Associates (2014) report included

- For students who went on to college, the report found that those who felt there had been gaps in preparedness also struggled more once in college;
- At least half the respondents felt that the high school they attended held only moderate expectations for their students and that was a contributing issue to their college success or struggles; and
- Regardless of whether respondents were in college or a career, they felt more prepared for their future if had they taken advanced high school courses.

The report offers solutions for high schools as a means to increase student preparedness for college or career to include setting rigorous standards for all students, more emphasis on academic graduation requirements, encouraging all students to take more advanced courses, communication expectations, connecting classroom learning to the real world, and supporting student learning with tutors and labs as needed (Hart Research Associates, 2014).

Familial Responsibilities

Families, too, must do their part to ensure college or career success; however, this is very much planned years in advance as they show their child the value in education, hard work, and commitment to completion. According to McConville (2018), there are three very specific tasks that encourage college and career readiness to include (1) ensuring the student can manage personal, behavioral, and medical needs such as setting an alarm each day and taking care of medical needs, (2) taking ownership of academics, study skills, and knowing when and how to find help, and (3) completing forms, maintaining a calendar, and meeting deadlines, the administrative tasks necessary to stay on course. These tasks can be taught at a young age and as the children grow, they are given more responsibility for each task. Parents who model these tasks provide a non-verbal visual of high expectations and independence (McConville, 2018).

Gap Year as an Option to College Success

For those boys who are just not ready to go to college or are unsure of their next step toward adulthood, Wichard-Edds (2015) suggests having them take a structured gap year "between high school and college—to travel, work, learn a new language or pursue independent study" (p. 1). Not meant as a procrastination technique, a gap year gives boys time to mature and become a "more focused student with a better sense of purpose and engagement in the world" (Gap Year Association, 2019). Students who avail themselves of the gap year are perceived to be more independent, self-reliant, and mature than non-gap year students (Birch & Miller, 2007). Detractors, meanwhile, cite the gap year as a potential waste of time financed by unsuspecting parents (Pendoley, 2017).

Students who opted for a structured gap year reported that the top three most significant outcomes were that it (1) helped them develop as a person, (2) allowed time for personal reflection, and (3) increased personal maturity (Gap Year Association, 2019). Respondents on a career path noted the ability to acquire much needed skills, clarity of career choice, and success in securing a job (Gap Year Association, 2019). Interestingly, out of twenty-three possible impacts, the top six reported outcomes were related to personal growth, while the bottom five were related to attending college with responses such as increased interest in attending and completing college (Gap Year Association, 2019). Overall, students who successfully completed a structured gap year were more likely to graduate college with a higher grade point average than their more traditional college-bound peers (Crawford & Cribb, 2012).

Helping Transition to College

For the most part, college campuses are not racial and gender equal in terms of admissions. The latest data shows that women and whites are the majority members of each college class (Marcus, 2018; 2017). At the high school level, Purnell-Mack (2017) suggested that there were four assumptions that could turn the tide of the underrepresented male on the college campus to include:

- Race and gender intersect to impact postsecondary success;
- Postsecondary achievement is a social imperative;
- Data is necessary to inform and shape accountability and commitment; and
- Activating advocates to engage in this work systemically and programmatically is a critical lever. (p. 5)

This translates into specific and focused outcomes for students such as awareness of college and its importance, a readiness to attend college, enrolling in a college that is a good fit, and completing college despite frustrations and potential setbacks (Purnell-Mack, 2017). Using a model called the College Bound Brotherhood (Purnell-Mack, 2017) at the secondary level, student feedback from the program showed that the one year retention rates were better than peers not included in the model, support systems were able to guide students to be more successful in their first year of college, and mentorship was an integral part of making decisions that led to postsecondary success.

LOST ON CAMPUS

While the enrollment and graduation rate gaps have already been referenced, the academic discrepancy between males and females starts almost as soon as matriculation. Males are apt to enroll for fewer credits and earn lower grades than females beginning in their first semester, and male rates of academic probation and disciplinary problems are higher (University of Oregon, 2010). One likely explanation for these disparities may be that young males are more likely to matriculate in college with fewer or less well-developed skills in non-cognitive areas such as organization, dependability, and self-regulation. Their mind-set may also differ from that of females, as Kleinfeld's (2009) research seems to indicate. That research found patterns of avoiding asking for necessary help, choosing social events over studying, general laziness, poor planning, and not working to required levels for success, patterns not found among female students (Kleinfeld, 2009).

Using semi-structured interviews, the researcher spoke with high school seniors about their mind-sets regarding post-secondary education. Interviewees had "folk theories" about the causes for the gender gap in school success and college attendance, such as young men are (1) lazy, (2) do not plan ahead, (3) easily distracted, and (4) prone to peer pressure (Kleinfeld, 2009). One of the more interesting findings among these themes is that what was labeled as laziness by both genders masked other emotions when Kleinfield (2009) spoke with the young males, such as (1) insecurity, (2) difficulty in understanding the application process, (3) trouble with writing essays, (4) lack of goals, and (5) unwillingness to reach out for help.

When coupling the variables of being male and being a first-generation student, risks for attrition increased. Research by Chen (2005) shows that first-generation students generally matriculate with less academic preparation than that of peers whose parents attended college. Mehta et al. (2011) found that they had less support than their non-first-generation peers and also tended to have more financial stress and responsibilities outside of school. These first-generation students were less able to partake in co-curricular activities while enrolled and were more likely to drop out of college.

Minority students also are at higher risk, as race is negatively related to persistence in college and minority males persisted at significantly lower rates than other student populations (Houshmand, Spanierman, & Tafarodi, 2014). Minority status presents many challenges and stressors on most campuses. Among these are three main barriers to minority success: poor secondary academic preparation, financial stressors, and negative racial climates on campus. The first two barriers are generally the result of low SES, poorer schools, and disproportionate placement in lower academic tracks while in secondary schools (Banerjee, 2016).

Houshmand et al. (2014) write of the toll that racial microaggressions can take on minority males' mental health and academic achievement, while Kugelmass and Ready (2011) found that the academic achievement gap between minority and majority students actually widens during college. While male student enrollment has decreased, first-generation and minority student enrollments have been increasing in recent years; however, even though there are still large numbers of male students who enroll in college, the numbers of risk factors that may complicate their successful persistence to graduation still remains a serious concern (Snyder, De Brey, & Dillow, 2019).

In addition to academic and financial challenges, ethnic minority students may suffer from internal pressures such as extra performance anxiety, imposter syndrome, or stereotype threat as well as feel intimidated by large classes or perceive their faculty members or advisors to be disinterested in them as individuals (Snyder et al., 2019). Bowman and Filar (2018) noted the decline in attendance rates for males in college and the significance this has for later-life success. For males who do attend college, they are less likely to be engaged, more likely to take part in destructive behaviors (toward both self and others), and more apt to encounter difficulties (Bowman & Filar, 2018). According to Bowman and Filar (2018), too many young males are socialized away from college attendance due to gender role conformity in which it is not "cool" to aspire to be an academic achiever.

O'Neil's (2015) work on gender role conflict illuminates six major conflicts that have implications for college attendance and success to include (1) emotional constriction, (2) health care issues, (3) restrictive expressions of affectionate behavior, (4) homophobia, (5) socialized control, power, and competition issues, and (6) achievement and success orientation leading to perceptions about which curricula and campus experiences will directly translate to future goal attainment. The more that young college males subscribe to traditional masculine ideals, the more at risk they are for failure on campus.

In general, Bowman and Filar (2018) believe that young males present challenges to colleges on multiple fronts; they urge college personnel to examine these challenges and propose more male-friendly practices where needed. Enrollment is the first challenge encountered due again to socialization factors mentioned previously. This is tied to the issue of educational engagement, which Bowman and Filar (2018) feel most boys and adolescent males have scant experience with.

The authors were not surprised to see a lack of success and exceptionally high rates of diagnosis with ADHD given that most contemporary schooling is not geared toward boys' socialization to be "active, and outspoken, and adventure-seeking" (Bowman & Filar, 2018, p. 16). Without prior experiences of being actively engaged with their education, it makes sense that many young men would eschew college for vocational education, the military, or a trade—all of which are far cheaper and appear to offer a more immediate payout.

Men's behavior in terms of well-being, health, and help-seeking also are challenges. On campus, substance abuse and sexual conquest appear to be equated with being a "real man" (Randolph, Torres, Gore-Felton, Lloyd, & McGarvey, 2009). College males are hospitalized for alcohol abuse twice as often as females, peer groups and media can influence behavior by normalizing these behaviors, and they are four times more likely to complete a suicide (Bowman & Filar, 2018; Randolph et al., 2009). College-aged males want close relationships with others; yet they are less likely to sign up for activities such as community service, study abroad, or mentoring programs that can provide these things and are more likely to take part in activities such as athletics or fraternity life that, at its worst, can push them to their limits physically and emotionally in the pursuit of being part of "the team" (Bowman & Filar, 2018).

These behaviors are even more challenging among members of racial minorities and other marginalized groups (Bowman & Filar, 2018). These students are underrepresented, often academically underprepared, may have suffered discrimination or have different cultural norms regarding masculinity (Bowman & Filar, 2018). They may have been forced to grow up in a more self-reliant fashion; as one interviewee put it, he was raised by the "pull yourself up to success" philosophy (Bowman & Filar, 2018; p. 15).

Marginalized students are less likely to have been adequately prepared academically to enter college and critical issues such as time management, study skills, and willingness to accept forms of academic assistance when needed are often lacking; while their own beliefs about their ability to succeed, or the presence of imposter syndrome, can derail their progress (Bowman & Filar, 2018). Academic probation remains one of the strongest predictors of males' dropout rates from college (University of Oregon, 2010).

Young males, particularly from marginalized groups, also are confronted with institutions that value the modern liberal arts education, while economic and cultural pressures to provide put their emphasis on career preparation; thus, academic experiences that do not appear to be relevant to career preparation are often dismissed or are the cause of frustration over time wasted (Bowman & Filar, 2018). Gender socialization in previous educational experiences relegates education purely for the "life of the mind" (Bowman & Filar, 2018, p. 17) to lesser status.

Bowman and Filar (2018) commented on the gendered bifurcation in social and classroom roles on campus as assertiveness, risk-taking, and activity, which are hallmarks of male learning styles; yet they are not necessarily the styles of preference in teaching in the contemporary college classroom. Simply getting young men to enroll is not enough. College personnel must specifically program to address some of the barriers to male persistence to graduation. Addressing personal failures by proactively seeking, rather than posturing or disengaging, is one example of how to help academically underprepared males who may encounter initial struggles and disappointments at the college level (Bowman & Filar, 2018).

Creating college classrooms that bridge the styles of both genders with collaboration and competition, risk and reflection, can invite male students into a more comfortable academic tradition (Young, Michael, & Smolinski, 2018). Building resiliency and promoting scholarship as an integral part of masculinity are key to long-term academic success.

For those from the aforementioned groups, poor academic preparation, lack of guidance, and families who cannot provide college capital through sharing their own experiences on campus conspire to put young men at academic risk. There is greater pressure for males not to enter what they perceive to be female professions and academic disciplines than there is for females to break gendered barriers (Bowman & Filar, 2018). There are implications for gender socialization that extend beyond the classroom as well.

Bowman and Filar (2018) bemoan the erasing of spaces that permit strong male friendships and homosocializing, pushing these activities into undesirable settings. While athletics and intramurals provide such a space for some, the vast majority of campus men are not necessarily seeking bonding through sports. The authors also postulate that while young males desire social connections with other men, they lack "friendship 'approach' skills" (Bowman & Filar, 2018, p. 17) that are necessary to form these connections in the first place.

Marcus (2017) cited the need for more direct appeals to men as he quoted one college administrator as admitting that in the past, colleges did not need to provide "role models and mentors for males" (n.d.). The biggest gender issue on campus, that administrator says, is how to attract and retain more men (Marcus, 2017). At that particular institution, more sports and specific academic programs, such as business, are being added in the hopes of boosting male attendance.

Another college administrator sees the origins of males' disengagement from college as beginning as early as elementary school, with economic forces driving men to see college as a waste of time and money (Marcus, 2017). Beginning college recruitment with boys as young as fifth grade in order to instill the value of a college education can be seen as a valuable endeavor, according to one interviewee, although another suggested beginning as low as kindergarten, as the anti-boy bias is displayed in so many elementary schools as another cause for educational disengagement (Marcus, 2017).

Many boys, Marcus (2017) believes, have never seen male role models who have succeeded at college; this is particularly true for those in rural and low-income urban districts. With professionals few and far between in these settings, boys don't see men who have made profitable and respected careers out of their college majors. Even further, they often see classmates who have gone to college drop out with huge debts or graduate only to find low-paying jobs that could have been accessed without their degree. Boys, Marcus (2017) notes, may feel that they have a larger number of alternative paths than girls do. They make up a larger percentage in trade schools and vocational programs than do females and often earn as much as those who graduate college; yet those with a bachelor's degree will make 56 percent more over a lifetime (Kroeger, Cooke, & Gould, 2016).

If colleges are to pitch higher education to men, campuses must be framed to seem more of a masculine endeavor (Bowman & Filar, 2018). This can come through programming, mentoring, or rehabilitating fraternities and other spaces to accentuate authentic masculinity. Marcus (2017) quoted one source who has run one of the few male-centered support centers as saying that while he set out believing that these would be a key solution, "at most college campuses the attitude is that men are the problem . . . I've had male students tell me that their first week in college they were made to feel like potential rapists" (n.d.). Colleges grapple with empowering women, who were long shut out of the academy, and acknowledging some of the real crises contemporary male students face.

Marcus (2017) sheds light on the fact that males of all groups, including white males, are struggling on campus; their pressures are very real, he says, and revolve around many of the same issues. This is particularly true for white males from underserved areas and backgrounds. Yet, as is noted, "we're uncomfortable as a nation having a discussion that includes white males as a part of a group that is having limited success" (2017, n.p.).

GENDER GAP AMONG LOW-INCOME STUDENTS

Semuels (2017) depicts the rising gender gap among low income students as females who are "leaving their brothers behind" (n.d.) in terms of accessing and completing higher education. While 17.6 percent of females from low-income and minority families have become college graduates in the last few decades, only 12.4 percent of young ethnic men who were high school sophomores in 2002 had completed their bachelor's degree (Semuels, 2017). In 2016, 22 percent of Hispanic women in the twenty-five through twenty-nine age range had earned a bachelor's degree while only 16 percent of Hispanic men in that same age range had completed their degree (Semuels, 2017).

The author cited the early struggles of boys from low SES families, noting that they struggle right out of the gate to compete with girls. Despite data indicating that they are just as healthy and cognitively primed to learn, they fall behind as soon as kindergarten. Semuels (2017) noted that evidence indicated that boys are more greatly impacted by stress and poverty and less resilient than their female peers and they appear more sensitive to negative environmental factors than are girls.

These problems start young and relate to socialization and early preparation (Semuels, 2017). Girls arrive at school more primed to please their parents and teachers and more prepared for the kind of schooling that early elementary schools in the United States provide. Girls are more likely to think that earning good grades is important and they possess more of the behavioral and social skills that early elementary teachers demand.

Boys are too frequently under social pressure to act in what is perceived to be more masculine ways that are often at odds with schools' expectations. Semuels (2017) remarked that they often avoid acting too interested in academic achievement because that is seen as the province of girls and gays; however, boys who avoid such stereotypes and actually participate in activities such as art, music, dance, or theater perform better academically than other middle school boys and are more likely to complete college than those who do not perform well in middle school. The author cites statistics showing that males who earn "As" in middle school have a 70 percent likelihood of completing a college degree by age twenty-five while those earning "Cs" have only a 10 percent chance (Semuels, 2017).

How parents raise their boys has a great deal to do with college aspirations and success. Those boys who feel pressure to adhere to traditional masculine norms are less academically successful (Semuels, 2017). This often occurs in working-class or lower-income families in which boys are socialized to see school success as the domain of girls and women and the world of physical, blue-collar labor as the province of males. They may not have any immediate role models who have accessed higher education or risen to professional jobs that require college degrees (Semuels, 2017). There may also be a greater emphasis on immediately being able to provide for extended family.

In an economy in which blue-collar jobs are rapidly disappearing, it is imperative to parent boys and adolescent males into the belief that masculinity may also include higher education and may embrace fields that are traditionally not associated with men. Parents who have achieved higher educational levels themselves are more likely to raise boys who value academic achievement (Semuels, 2017). They may also have access to more male role models and mentors who can stress the importance of career and academic readiness through postsecondary education (Semuels, 2017).

DiPrete and Buchmann (2013) contributed an additional perspective—boys may also be more fixated on short-term, immediate gratification than their female counterparts are; therefore, the journey that college competition requires, with its continuous need to achieve, may not seem palatable, particularly if there are available jobs that pay an immediate dividend without the college degree. While in the short term, the wages from such jobs are motivating, over the long run, boys can expect far less income and less job security than those with degrees.

Johnston (2012) reiterated many of these perspectives in his research for the Oregon Gear Up Program and the Ford Foundation. He found that the desire for short-term material and economic gains, the perception of higher education as being not "masculine," fewer discussions by high school guidance counselors with boys about attending college, and negative school experiences lead young males to avoid college enrollment.

HISTORICALLY UNDERREPRESENTED MALE POPULATIONS

Young Men of Color

While access to college has improved for historically underserved populations, retention and graduation rates have not. Some institutions have implemented programs to specifically address the retention and academic success of male students of color. Brooms, Clark, and Smith (2018) investigated the lasting effects of a summer bridge program for men of color (B4US) to determine which components participants identified as most critical to their positive outcomes.

The summer program aimed to develop a group of mentors for each of the young men, while building community from cultural wealth. Brooms et al. (2018) spoke to three kinds of capital that were developed and employed in this effort to include aspirational, family, and navigational. Aspirational capital lay in bolstering the young men's abilities to maintain their dreams and goals, even in the face of real or perceived barriers (Brooms et al., 2018). Family capital provided motivation, as they carried their community and family history to college with them and drew upon it for resiliency and resistance efforts (Brooms et al., 2018). In some cases, family members served as social role models for college success while in others, students found the drive, as in being the first in their family to graduate.

Navigational capital was essential to success in transitioning to college culture and expectations. The summer program introduced participants to faculty, staff, and other personnel who gave them the skills to navigate the campus and its resources successfully, even among institutions that did not provide adequately for their marginalized students.

The researchers found that brotherhood, identity formation, and personal development lay at the heart of the commitment to college. In forming a true community of males, the program leaders brought in others who could share both heart and stories about how they overcame challenges to graduation, as well as how opening their hearts and minds helped them to become better men (Brooms et al., 2018). The students were urged to move with a purpose, serving both the B4US family and themselves. In addition to providing the tools for academic efficacy, the participants were presented with opportunities to exert leadership, learning to be a role model to others. This could take the shape of helping their peers or paving the way for younger males of color through mentorship (Brooms et al., 2018).

Participants spoke of the need to "be the change" and to keep their academic focus so that they could model for others (Brooms et al., 2018). They learned through leadership, in terms of deeper understanding of self, their validity as scholars, and their power in being transformational models for others. In many cases, the participants were invited into leadership roles that they might not have sought themselves and they also benefitted from networking and exposure to professional guides and mentors through service projects and conference attendance (Brooms et al. 2018).

Brooms et al. (2018) noted that the bridge program promoted caring that was culturally caring in nature and offered critical mentoring and was viewed by participants as "family work" in which they serve as brothers to each other and brothers or often father figures to the young males of color whom they mentor. Recognizing that exerting leadership and mentorship is very much needed in their communities, they prided themselves on helping young males discover their own voices (Brooms et al., 2018).

An ancillary benefit of the bridge programming was the opportunity to reimagine manhood and masculinity (Brooms et al., 2018). Through workshops, retreats, guest speakers, and mentorship, participants were pushed to examine their inherited definitions and beliefs and came to the understanding that there should be equality for everyone. This recognition led the young men to push back on hegemonic concepts of masculinity in which women were not treated respectfully or as equals (Brooms et al., 2018). Understanding where such behavior came from, including the fear of the feminine and its relationship to homophobia, marked a huge step forward in these males' development.

Expressing emotionality and feeling that it was permissible to open up allowed the participants to resist societal restrictions on their self-expression. They were urged to "step out of the things you've been conditioned to do" (Brooms et al., 2018, p. 95) and develop a strong sense of self that included a broad, inclusive definition of manhood, including embracing both the masculine and the feminine.

These college men, through this innovative program, were able to form a tight, connected group to take the place of the families and communities they had left behind. They were able to build a supportive network of both other men and of women and felt compelled to give back to the college and to young men of color around them (Brooms et al., 2018). Their experiences, as captured in the research by Broom et al. (2018), illustrated some of the keys to academic success, personal growth, service to others, and college connection. Chief among these keys were investing in the personal lives of students of color, encouraging distributive leadership, and providing opportunities for mentoring, networking, and professional engagement (Brooms et al., 2018).

Males Transitioning from Military Culture

Many young men on contemporary college campuses are transitioning from military service or still are actively engaged. While many of their transitional issues are consonant with those of other male college students, they have unique challenges that many have likened to those shared by underserved students (Young, Michael, & Jean, 2018). Branker (2009) proposed that while low-income students, those of color, and first-generation students comprise what has been historically considered to be underserved populations, student veterans are underserved as well. Equally important, many may have suffered disabilities that are visible or invisible, making their acclimation process even more challenging (Young, Michael, & Jean, 2019).

Entering college, for so many student veterans student military (SVSM) students, is like traveling to a foreign land without a solid grasp of the culture and norms (Young, Michael, & Jean, 2019). There may be little college knowledge or capital, especially if the soldier is first-generation and there are many transitional losses that such students lament when they first matriculate. How well they adjust to this transition and what kinds of supports they receive tell the tale of whether they will persist and be successful ultimately.

Arminio, Grabosky, and Lang (2015) noted that these students must become bicultural in the sense of transitioning from military to college culture. Qualitative research found that military culture was normed on collectivism, masculinity, and a strict hierarchy—traits that competed with those prized at most colleges (Arminio et al., 2015). The soldier-students experienced what was both culture shock and cultural dissonance, leading many to feel uneasy on campus.

The loss of structure and of well-defined, commonly held values that is prevalent in the military clashed with the encouragement of independent thinking and creativity encouraged by faculty in college classrooms and beyond. The loss of collectivism and a ready-made "family of men" made many feel isolated from the majority campus (Arminio et al., 2015). In some cases, students only felt comfortable with others who had transitioned from military branches. Given that one of the assumed benefits of college is the opportunity to interact with diverse individuals, sticking with "one's own" complicated individual growth, critical thinking, and social integration on campus.

Loss of masculinity was expressed by the interviewees as a confrontation with college campus and classroom norms that did not necessarily embrace or even understand the kind of joking, shaming, and interactions that characterized life in the military (Arminio et al., 2015). They spoke of the hypersensitivity that they perceived in the classroom environment, and there were sometimes palpable tensions between civilians and military students and between female and male authority figures in the classroom (Arminio et al., 2015).

Many military students arrived on campus bearing the literal and unspoken scars of their service. The mental health issues that plagued non-military males, and the corresponding avoidance of help-seeking, put male military students at higher risk for mental health issues such as PTSD, depression, and anxiety. There also are identity formation issues that are pressing for these students. While some students may envision a clear path for their transition from service to their next career step, others will struggle with what DiRamio and Jarvis (2011) called "finding the fulfilled civilian self" (p. 62). Juggling his military identity, new identity as college student, and future envisioned self-in-civilian-world may be stressful for many young males, necessitating skillful counseling and psychoeducational interventions, individually or in targeted groups.

Fraternity Brothers

Robbins's (2019) fascinating look into fraternity life on campus illuminates the search for identity and belonging that so many young males undergo during emerging adulthood. Robbins (2019) followed a year in the life of two young males while also making sense of information gleaned from hundreds of current and past fraternity members. The book makes it clear that while there are certainly chapters whose members and activities confirm the worst popular stereotypes of *Animal House* behaviors, there are deeply rooted personal needs that the best fraternity chapters help to fill for so many young men searching for a sense of self and recognition in our campus communities.

Like many other researchers, Robbins (2019) noted the difficulty of being a young male in contemporary American society

> during what's been called "a collapse in the American construction of masculinity." Unsure about what's expected of them, they're growing up in a world where women can be doctors, but men still face stigma for becoming nurses; where the majority of high school dropouts are male; and where experts point to "toxic masculinity" as a driving force behind everything from mass shootings to international terrorism. (p. 12)

Robbins (2019) quoted statistics showing that more than 50 percent of college men have felt very lonely in the last twelve months and a fifth within the last two weeks. Males are not as adept at socializing and making connections as are women at this age, and 75 percent of suicides among fifteen to nineteen-year-olds are male (Robbins, 2019).

The author described the social hierarchy of fraternities, both within the houses themselves (lowly pledges to officers) and within the college (low-status fraternities to high-status ones). Beyond this is the social netherworld that is made up of those not cool enough to even get a bid. While on the one hand, "Jake" has positive motives in pledging (finding connection, guides to help navigate college life, taking part in philanthropy, and seeking leadership roles), he is also acutely aware of the negative side of fraternity life such as hazing, drinking, disrespect of women, and discrimination that can be found in many fraternity chapters (Robbins, 2019).

Being accepted into a fraternity provides a sense of relief because young males, Robbins (2019) found, felt that they then would not have to navigate their college years alone. This was particularly true of freshman year, where pledges were mortified that they could not even find their way around campus or "know where the food is" (Robbins, 2019, p. 275).

Two of the most prized aspects of Greek life were noted to be (1) looking out for one another and (2) having a second family to rely on (Robbins, 2019). These aspects fulfill the basic needs of belonging and help ease the transition from family and community of origin to the unknowns of the college campus. The fact that the members live, eat, study, and recreate together in the best of circumstances can create an intimacy that leads to personal growth and transformation. As one brother wrote:

> Because I went to college 3,000 miles away from my family, these brothers became my support. In three to four years, it's almost guaranteed that someone is going to have a tough time in their life. For family issues, deaths, financial crises, and mental health issues, brothers have always flocked to help. This goes above and beyond what you expect from ordinary friends. (Robbins, 2019, p. 151)

Houses that place a high value on philanthropy also help to develop community connections through service, charity, and volunteering. The best fraternities also help brothers "branch out and explore different types of campus organizations. My brothers have pushed me out of my comfort zone and made me a more well-rounded man" (Robbins, 2019, p. 250). The chapters that were made up of first-generation students, those that were Latino or black centered, or openly encouraged members of the LGBTQ+ communities, placed particular emphasis on academics, personal development, service, and leadership (Robbins, 2019). "Hermandad," otherwise known as the brotherhood, is noted as the most powerful support system during males' college experience, providing motivation, academic intervention, accountability, and deep discussion about issues that related to personal growth and meaning making (Robbins, 2019).

The same held true in gay/bi/trans/progressive fraternities. Finding communities within the larger college campus that aided young males in developing and expressing their sexual identities was critical to their sense of well-being, particularly in conservative areas such as the South or rural campuses (Robbins, 2019). This was vital to members who might be struggling to piece together identities from multiple perspectives, such as being black and gay. In fraternities in which straight members of majority cultures openly advocated for minority members and supported their expressions of self, positive personal development was allowed to flourish (Robbins, 2019).

Interestingly, interviewees frequently used the word "intimacy" to describe their fraternity brotherhoods. They spoke of the importance of learning through initiation into their chapter's values and ways of expressing interpersonal bonds through mandated activities such as community service, mandatory study halls, and rites and rituals. Rituals that required fraternity brothers to get to know each other through discussion and emotional connections not only promoted self-awareness and self-acceptance but also often served as a lifeline to better mental health (Robbins, 2019). One young man praised his fraternity for learning

> how to accept my shortcomings. The fraternity gave me a space to learn about myself after a tumultuous time where I was so unhappy with the person in the mirror that I would rather have killed myself than be that person. I'm forever in debt and grateful to those people. The fraternity saved my life. (Robbins, 2019, p. 158)

Other Forms of Family

Athletics, service clubs, and other organizations on campus also can provide family experiences and the bonding and intimacy found in fraternities. While so much national attention is paid to men's varsity sports, Weaver, Forte, and McFadden (2017) explored the role of club sports for male students, both in terms of recruitment and retention. While club sports, other than rugby, had little effect on recruitment efforts, they contributed to the overall retention of male students for a variety of reasons (Weaver et al., 2017).

One male who took part in the research study explained the relationship between club sports and a sense of belonging at the institution by saying, "I think for men, it does help them connect to the institution, and often, they connect through sports. Once that connection is built, students want to stay here." While another said, "I think absolutely there is a lot of potential to continue to retain males. I think there is a great opportunity . . . to keep men engaged in that kind of team atmosphere" (Weaver et al., 2017, p. 47).

An interesting observation was made by one study participant who related that on campus "Men can have tougher times finding their identity . . . club sports is an excellent way for that identity piece" (Weaver et al., 2017, p. 47). Another saw the connection to something bigger than the self—a natural "social relationship" as he termed it. It could also be that club sports help retain males because since they are part of a team, they have ready-made relationships with college personnel who keep an eye on their progress toward graduation.

> In terms of retention we go into every first-year experience classroom . . . and talk about the process of starting clubs. [Personnel commented] As counselors, we do not forget about them once they get on campus and move to the next class. Part of our job is to see that through and get them involved and encourage things. (Weaver et al., 2017, p. 49)

Club sports were also a way to encourage student leadership, since they are often organized and led by students themselves. This provides a venue for leadership development that might not take place on a larger, more formal scale. Obviously, there are far fewer male students who will attain varsity status than who could take part in club sports, so the chance of impacting student success is more likely (Weaver et al., 2017). In all institutions studied, participants reported that when students are involved in activities outside of the classroom, they "become more successful in and out of the classroom, [retention rates increase, and participation in clubs can help] with an overall better college experience" (Weaver et al., 2017, p. 47).

MEN'S MENTAL HEALTH ON CAMPUS

In addition to academic struggles on campus, many males also wrestle with mental health issues. Overall, college students, regardless of gender, are affected by problems hindering mental health and well-being; among these were depression, addiction and substance abuse disorders, anxiety, eating disorders, depression/suicide, self-injury, ADHD, and schizophrenia (McWhirter, 2019). A recent study by the American Psychological Association (as cited in McWhirter, 2019) found that roughly 86 percent of students who had a psychiatric disability left college without a degree. A third of college students reported being so depressed during their previous year on campus that they were barely able to function (McWhirter, 2019). Nearly 60 percent of polled faculty said that they did not feel confident that they could work effectively with students with hidden disabilities, and between 80–90 percent of college students who died by suicide had not gotten help from the counseling services available on campus (McWhirter, 2019).

There appear to be well-documented gendered differences when considering campus-based mental health issues. Women are more likely to experience depression, anxiety or eating disorders; men have higher rates of substance abuse and suicide (Whitley, 2018). Suicidal ideation appears to occur at much higher rates among males than females. According to Whitley (2018), male college students are far less likely to access available mental health services on campus. The result of this fact is that young males may be suffering from the aforementioned conditions alone or may turn to self-medication with drugs and alcohol.

Many contemporary researchers and writers feel that men's mental health problems on campus are ignored or silenced (Hess, 2018; Whitley, 2018). Whitley (2018) sees campus-based discrimination against men's groups, citing that they have been met with protests and lack of funding or sanctioning by their institutions. Men's issues groups are characterized as misogynistic and are misunderstood by those who see them as continuations of male power and control in society; however, socialization to masculinity may be at fault (Whitley, 2018). Males tend to be their own worst enemies in terms of help-seeking behaviors that could address mental and emotional health challenges; yet these groups can be instrumental in promoting discussion and psychoeducation on topics related to male health and well-being.

According to Hess (2018), a recent massive survey found that one-third of college freshmen struggled with mental health issues, most notably massive depressive disorder and general anxiety disorder, at rates of 21 percent and 19 percent respectively. Colleges and universities are ill-equipped to handle these increasing levels of mental health problems, so in addition to ramping up the resources of campus-based counseling centers, college students must become better advocates for their own health and well-being. This comes especially hard to those males who have been raised to "tough it out" or "go it alone," or who believe that help-seeking is the stuff of "sissies."

Hess (2018) depicts several steps that college students can employ to prevent or lessen campus mental health problems or threats to their well-being. The first is to avoid stereotypes about what life is really like on campus; these stereotypes are so pernicious because they can easily lead students to substance abuse and self-medication that masks true symptoms of trouble. Heavy alcohol and drug abuse and acts of casual sex are presumed to be the norm; however, students actually are quite surprised to discover that excessive drinking is not the norm, the average number of sexual partners per year is one, and 20 percent of students never drink at all (Hess, 2018). Each misconception about campus life behaviors can be potentially damaging, as it is not uncommon for students to self-medicate for anxiety or depression. Resorting to this approach over time may cause physical damage as well as psychological and physical addiction.

Transitions can put students at risk of ignoring health routines or at least relegating them to a secondary spot in the day (Hess, 2018). Diet, exercise, sleep, and relaxation all are critical to college success; while building mental health capabilities helps to bounce back from stressors or disappointments while in college (Hess, 2018). Students can proactively prepare to face the inevitable failures through resilience training.

Strayhorn (2016) discussed college student development in terms of grit and hardiness and urged all students to become familiar with the tenets of positive psychology. Increasingly, colleges are including the deliberate teaching of coping skills in their orientation and freshman seminar classes. Knowing that transitions are inherently stressful, colleges are upping their efforts to provide for positive, prosocial mental health and well-being. These attempts include classes, yoga, meditation, peer counseling, stress management techniques, and new approaches toward training faculty to be early spotters of students who may be in trouble.

Hess (2018) reminds students that it is far better to seek early help than to wait until mental health concerns are at a crisis point; however, students may not always be aware that issues with such things as interference with memory or concentration can be indicators of problems. Students need to know the signs of stress, anxiety, or depression so that they can help themselves and their peers. Finally, students need to know when it is time to reach out to a professional counselor. While peers, residence assistants, faculty, coaches, mentors, or other valued relations can be extremely helpful during more minor or typical crises, there are times when only trained mental health professionals can provide the proper diagnoses and treatment plans or can prescribe medications. With so many models of counseling, such as individual, group, or psychoeducational, most students should be able to find a model that meets their needs.

According to Riseman (2016), only one-third of those seen in college campus counseling centers are males. The pressures of masculinity, combined with academic stress and transition, may require even the most independent of young men to recognize that they could use additional support. College personnel are now looking to do greater outreach in places like dorms, gyms, athletic teams, and fraternities to reach potential male clients; yet young males are almost twice as likely as young females to live at home with their parents during emerging adulthood, with nearly 60 percent of the male population aged eighteen to twenty-four doing so (Riseman, 2016).

Reksodiputro (2018) argued for campuses building cultures in which mental health services are perceived to be more gender-inclusive. Young males are moving out of families and communities of origin, but they most often are subjected to less-than-ideal eating, sleeping, and living conditions during freshman year (Reksodiputro, 2018). Given that it is easier to become physically or emotionally taxed under these situations, it is no wonder that so many freshmen suffer mental health problems or challenges to their overall well-being. Men are disproportionately affected by stigmas about help-seeking, necessitating new approaches to enticing them to utilize services when they are called for.

Males are less likely to perceive mental illness to be as common a problem as it is and they are less skilled than their female counterparts in estimating depression or sadness among their peers (Reksodiputro, 2018). One of the most effective approaches to building a culture that removes stigmas around male help-seeking is to enlist those males who have taken advantage of services and succeeded in college to share their stories with other young men. This practice works well within different affinity groups or groups with identities held in common; using high-profile males who are known on campus, as well as mentors, coaches, and popular faculty, can build a communal sense that mental health issues cut across all human variables and are the concern of all on campus (Reksodiputro, 2018).

June has been designated as Men's Health Month (Men's Health Month, 2019). This is a good time for college personnel to ponder new approaches to getting men to improve their health, reduce their risks, and cut the number of college deaths, 75 percent of which are male (Men's Health Month, 2019). Some campuses have emphasized men's health clinics, a course on men's health, and a men's health committee; yet many campus initiatives, while highlighting physical health and well-being, are relatively silent on the topic of mental health concerns.

Lynch, Long, and Moorhead (2018) identified seven key barriers to young males seeking professional health care for mental health issues. The first is a perceived lack of acceptance by peers if they seek help. Being seen as a "weak member of the group" is a definite deterrent. In worst cases, young men feared ridicule or rejection by their peers.

Personal challenges is the second theme; these cluster around the communications issues with identifying and expressing emotions and the fear of finding out that you are not normal. Help-seeking behaviors are simply not integrated into males' coping frameworks and are seen as a last resort. As one interviewee told the researchers, "It takes a point where I'm actually about to have a meltdown . . . to actually go see someone" (Lynch et al., p. 143).

A third theme was that self-medicating with alcohol (and sometimes also drugs) was viewed as a more acceptable way of dealing with problems than was help-seeking. For some, being under the influence made it more tolerable to express their emotions, although often this was done in exaggerated ways. Fears and lack of knowledge about the medical and counseling fields also exacerbated men's problems. They often expressed fears that they would be medicated or held negative opinions of counselors due to previous encounters.

Cultural and environmental influences also served as barriers and include religious factors, generational divides, and rural life. Seeking strength through prayer, as opposed to counseling, fear that medical information would spread in small towns, and being told, in essence, to buck up when expressing mental health concerns all acted as deterrents to help-seeking.

Lynch et al. (2018) uncovered fear of homophobic responses among gay interviewees; this arose as help-seekers were forced to reveal their sexual orientation in order to receive meaningful help, but often they had encountered bias in the past. For some males, this fear was so great that they preferred to suffer in silence rather than risking homophobic backlash. The most common barrier to seeking counseling lay within socialization to traditional male ideas in which, as one put it, "if you go and ask for professional help, you are not really a man" (Lynch et al., 2018, p. 143).

Luckily, Lynch et al.'s (2018) informants had suggestions for improving mens' mental health behaviors. The first was through tailored mental health advertising that was positive, male-centric, and inviting. It needed, in their opinion, to seem masculine, cool, and tough. Media and social media should be employed and should target young males through sports, gaming websites, and other places that appealed to men who would typically avoid help.

Many participants believed that the best route involved integrating mental health into formal education, beginning as early as possible and continuing through college was most effective (Lynch et al., 2018). This included integrating more counselors into all levels of schooling and normalizing help-seeking from professionals. Low mental-health literacy could be combated through early and consistent education involving increasing levels of sophistication (Lynch et al., 2018).

Education also could be effective if provided through semiformal support systems. Professional youth workers in communities and community mental health settings were valuable and paved the way for young males being more comfortable with accessing campus-based services. It should also be recognized that some male college students may be more comfortable with off-campus sites rather than those offered on campus.

Lynch at al. (2018) cited making new meaning as a critical component of changing men's behaviors. Too many participants found mental health discussions laden with jargon, stigmatizing language, and discrimination, and instead wished for discussions that furthered normalized mental health issues and set them in the context of positive masculinity (Lynch et al., 2018). Accessible conditions that provided the key information in a language that felt comfortable to young males were the opening that many needed to take steps toward greater health.

Thomas (2018) put a spotlight on new initiatives that fell into the tailored advertising approach; among these were Heads Together, led by Prince William and Prince Harry, and recent mental health wellness programs sponsored by the NBA in which star players openly discuss their battles. With more dedicated sites online, males can access information, read stories, and communicate with others, lessening the stigma and isolation. Particular counseling approaches such as those that are strength-building, group-oriented, problem-focused, and informal are more successful with college men and fit male preferences; rather than counseling settings that provide equal power relationships, choice, and control (Thomas, 2018).

Some campuses have had successes with new definitions of what masculine strength and prowess entail. Complementing traditional strength and fitness regimens with yoga, tai chi, meditation, mindfulness, and other forms of strength training can expand ideas of wellness and conditioning (Thomas, 2018). As even prominent athletic teams begin to regularly incorporate these into their training, the paths to fuller wellness, including stress management, increased focus, and emotional regulation, become easier.

PRESSURES OF MASCULINITY

The college years are most often where young males are expected to break from their family and communities of origin and somehow magically transition from boys to men. Freshman year, in particular, places great emphasis on this transition, yet it is the time in which most young males express the greatest sense of confusion, loneliness, and the need to conform to what they think other males define as masculine behavior.

Mahalik et al.'s (2003) work on traditional expectations of masculinity enlightens readers as to what young males believe to be the dominant, acceptable expressions of manhood on our campuses and in society in general. These include winning at all costs, having multiple sexual partners, being heterosexual, having power over women, demonstrating emotional control, desiring social status, being physically aggressive and dominating, prioritizing career and work, taking part in risky behaviors, and being independent (Mahalik et al., 2003).

The more that young men adhere to these expectations, the more that they are likely to engage in risky behaviors. Robbins (2019) points out that while many do not necessarily want to behave according to these dictates, their perceptions are that they need to in order to fit in. They believe that other males support these toxic and dangerous dictates more than others actually do, thus perpetuating the myths about what is masculine behavior and what isn't. This becomes a vicious cycle in which most college males do not endorse traditional masculine norms but believe that others do, including the misperceptions that others drink more, engage in sexual acts more, and are more independent and emotionally stoic than they actually are.

THE CAMPUS EXODUS OF YOUNG MEN

Riseman (2016) called the exodus of young male college students from their campuses "the silent epidemic" (n.p.). Within the past decade, approximately one third of young men who had matriculated dropped out during or at the end of their freshman year; those who did persist graduated with a bachelor's degree within four years only 38 percent of the time, and it took six years for 58 percent of them (Riseman, 2016). While the challenges of college completion, especially during the freshman year, have not changed much for young men over the years, it appears that their level of resiliency or ability to cope with challenges has weakened (Riseman, 2016).

Riseman (2016) blames human development to a certain extent for this change in resiliency, citing research that shows that boys don't develop as quickly as girls do and that this fact accounts for boys' behavioral choices that only compound their poor approach to challenges. Interpersonal skills, such as friendship building and creating buffering social networks, may result in greater isolation and that isolation, in turn, can exacerbate other social, academic, and mental health problems (Riseman, 2016). Male students appear to be less adaptable and turn to familiar behaviors, even if those have not been particularly effective in the past. There are also biological and educational contributors to the greater incidences of disabilities such as ADHD, dyslexia, and other learning differences and disorders; yet we know that students with identified learning differences often see college as the time to break free of the labels and supports they have received in high school.

The 2014 study, the State of Learning Disabilities (Cortiella & Horowitz, 2014), demonstrated how profound this break is for students as they move from high school to college. The report stated that in less than two years after they leave secondary school, 52 percent of all identified Learning Disability (LD) students do not self-identify with having a disability; while eight years out from high school graduation, that number had risen to 68 percent (Cortiella & Horowitz, 2014). Whether this was done out of ignorance about the need to self-identify or the deliberate choice to break free of the label, students failed to make postsecondary officials aware of their disability (Horowitz, Rawe, & Whittaker, 2017).

While a scant 24 percent of high school graduates told their postsecondary institutions of their disabilities, 44 percent of them who did not access services in college later reported that they wished they had because they now believed that these supports would have helped them achieve success (Cortiella & Horowitz, 2014; Horowitz, Rawe, & Whittaker, 2017). The study did not break down statistics by gender; yet it is fair to assume that with gendered differences in help-seeking, male college students with disabilities would be more likely to eschew services than females.

Hadley's (2007) research on learning disabled students' transition to the college campus highlighted three of Chickering's (1969) vectors of competence that need to be developed in early adulthood. Of these, "managing emotions" was the most challenging for students with disabilities (Chickering, 1969). PK–12 schooling provided students with so much individualized attention and support services that they were unaccustomed to the greater autonomy that college required. Managing emotions, one might hypothesize, would be challenging for male students without disabilities too, as their socialization results in greater denial, posturing, or avoidance of failures in order to save face. When confronted with campus setbacks, they are likely less emotionally and psychologically equipped either to seek help or to bounce back. Escape appears to be the best route.

According to Riseman (2016), social media also has ratcheted up the anxiety around college performance. Posts on social media can make it seem that everyone else has more friends, better grades, and far more fun; these posts rarely lay bare the truth of failure. Social media may even lower self-esteem among some college students. Absent is the ability to pierce these idealizations; therefore, young males can feel that they are not measuring up (Riseman, 2016). If the standard is to "drink, smoke, and hook up" and one is not doing so or does not even desire to do so, college can be a lonely place that can make young males very vulnerable.

Riseman (2016) pegged depression as the number one reason for college dropouts and sees that the task of identity solidification is primary to positive self-regard. For those males who are not making the grade, either academically or socially, it is a blow to the ego that may result in shame, isolation, or denial. Another source of their sense of failure, Riseman (2016) felt, is the incredibly unrealistic expectations that they hold, such as becoming the next Steve Jobs, Jeff Bezos, or Steph Curry. With images of male success stories so large in the public eye, it is hard for many young males to find purpose or to be satisfied with being just good enough.

The Hostile Campus

In much the same way that critics have blamed the feminization of PK–12 education for many of boys' and adolescent males' learning problems and disengagement from school, there are those who believe that the male flight from college can be blamed, at least in part, to hostility toward males on contemporary campuses. Some have crudely called this the "rape culture" (Jordan, 1995). The requirement of statistics related to campus assaults and the subsequent mandating of workshops on topics such as consent, date rape, and sexual respect can lead to the perception that college campuses are hostile to men.

As an example, Bremmer (2017) quoted James Shelley, the director of the Men's Resource Center at Lakeland Community College in Kirtland, Ohio, who told the *Denver Post* that he believed that date-rape-prevention programs are frightening men away from college campuses because the programs are tantamount to telling young males that "they are potential rapists" (n.p.).

A 2011 Department of Education national letter to institutions of higher education requiring them to come to their own decisions about the guilt or innocence of those accused of sexual assault on their campuses brought an onslaught of lawsuits by young male college students seeking to overturn what they believed were false rape charges (Bremmer, 2017).

Greer (2017) titled his book *No Campus for White Men*, raising the claim that not only are colleges hostile to males, but that statistics on women and sexual assault on college campuses are vastly overamplified. Further, Greer (2017) decried that programs that raise awareness about diversity issues, victimization, and identity politics promote white male flight from higher education. Affirmative action and movements for greater equality for marginalized groups have pushed white male college students into a marginalized group of their own.

The Finances of College

Dwyer, Hodson, and McCloud (2013) examined finances as one reason so many more men than women drop out of college these days. Men, it appears, are not as willing to take on a large debt to pay for their college education; however, the authors say that this is not due to greater fiscal caution; rather, it can be tied directly and historically to the gender gap in wages. Men, essentially, can drop out more frequently because they will not see financial penalties for doing so in their entry-level salaries, while the same cannot be said for women; however, the sad fact is that while the initial decision doesn't impose a penalty on young men, it will have powerful negative impacts later on and over the life span (Dwyer et al., 2013). According to Dwyer et al. (2013), by midlife alone there will be a $20,000 per year differential in salaries between males who completed and did not complete college. Young males, it appears, can be lured away from long-term investments in themselves due to perceived advantages in the short term (Schwyzer, 2013).

SUPPORTIVE SOLUTIONS FOR COLLEGE-BOUND YOUNG MEN

The first challenge in college success for young males is actually to get them onto campus; thus, recruitment efforts need to be tailored to male images and interests. To make the commitment to postsecondary education appealing to young males, Bowman and Filar (2018) suggested that colleges need to reframe traditional requirements such as the liberal arts or common core in a manner that is more career-focused to meet males' orientation toward seeing this as a worthwhile investment of time and money only if it directly fits into the career trajectory. Outreach from employers, successful male alumni, and current students who are finding success in internships and other job settings can lessen some men's skepticism about whether college is worth the effort and time (Bowman & Filar, 2018). The pursuit of a college degree needs to be recast as an act that exemplifies contemporary masculinity.

Bowman and Filar (2018) described many proven practices that may help engage and retain male students on today's campuses. Classroom, co-curricular, and extracurricular strategies have been shown to benefit young men academically and socially through higher levels of achievement and engagement and may include first-year seminars, common learning experiences, living/learning communities, and writing-intensive early courses as beneficial practices (Bowman & Filar, 2018).

Mentorship as a Means to Success

Since connection to at least one other significant individual on campus has been linked to successful college retention, mentoring programs and those that intentionally build community are likely to help young males persist and succeed (My Brother's Keeper Alliance and MENTOR: The National Mentoring Partnership, 2016; Tinto, 2007). Brooms et al. (2018) wrote of one such program, the Black Male Initiative Program (BMIP) at the University of Cincinnati, after conducting qualitative research to understand the participants' experiences. The thrust of the interview process involved uncovering how participants made meaning of their membership and what efforts they utilized to persist and Brooms et al. (2018) discovered four major themes that emerged from the data that help shed light on how to help young black men succeed.

The first theme was a "sense of belonging" that echoed Maslow's (1987) belief that one must feel he fits in and has community in order to maximize potential. According to participants, the project felt like a home in that it provided ready-made connection in those perilous early weeks of college. The group also allowed for "the benefits of accessing resources and capital beyond their own individual efforts" (Brooms et al., 2018, p. 146). One BMIP member noted that he was helped to "build sociocultural capital; BMI was both a space that helped him see his connections and responsibilities to the community (social capital) and aided him in his personal development (cultural capital)" (Brooms et al., 2018, p. 146).

A second theme was that the program helped to keep the student on track (Brooms et al., 2018). In connecting students to peers, faculty, staff, and other key personnel, the participants learned what resources were available to them in a more personal way. Many admitted that without this connection to human capital, they might have been ignorant of or avoided supports that ended up being vitally important to their success (Brooms et al., 2018). Personnel knew the students individually; therefore, they were able to tailor their services and encourage even further networking to participants. In many ways, this approach addressed males' lack of help-seeking early and head-on so that there was less stigma attached to reaching out to the various offices involved.

A third component that students believed led to their success was how the program led to increased academic motivation and efficacy (Brooms et al., 2018). BMIP itself had an academic focus; yet there were numerous formal and informal activities that lent themselves to building skills, confidence, and commitment—among these were academic coaching sessions (both individually and in groups), study tables organized by students, didactic experiences to boost study skills, and faculty lectures to increase interaction between participants and faculty (Brooms et al., 2018). Financial literacy, goal setting, and professional development were stressed in workshops as well (Brooms et al., 2018).

Finally, participants lauded the program because it lifted them up. One participant noted

> It's about committing to brotherhood. It's about holding each other accountable. It's about participating when you don't want to participate. It's about reaching out to every African American brother that you see on campus. It's about finishing—in life, on campus and off campus. It's about talking about your problems. It's about reaching out to your mentors if need be. (Brooms et al., 2018, p. 150)

Participants also saw that the program helped them to cultivate a positive masculinity, through deep discussions and self-reflection. Manhood, to them, became intertwined with acts of responsibility, collective concern, accountability, and caring. They were allowed to be vulnerable to each other in this safe space, ask for help when needed, and share emotional material. As Brooms et al. (2018) saw it,

> this vulnerability as a masculine construct pushes back against hegemonic masculinity, which informs and encourages males to be tough and emotionless . . . provided space for the students to explore alternative masculinities and even engage in cooperative masculinity, which is centered on working together to achieve shared goals and supporting each other for the greater collective gain. (p. 151)

It is not difficult to see how a model such as BMIP could be adapted to work for other groups of young college males. The component pieces could work equally well with veterans, members of other ethnic groups, first-generation students, or those with other shared backgrounds. The model is particularly powerful in that it both bolsters academic performance and retention while building positive group identity and fostering healthy masculinity. Some campuses have found similar successes in building living/learning communities that incorporate the same features, while it could be argued that the best of fraternity living may do the same.

Traditionally, mentors have been older, powerful male figures such as faculty. Today's mentors can range from peers to student affairs personnel to faculty, but they share a developmental role in helping the young man form his identity, understand healthy masculinity, and find ways to express it in prosocial manners. Successful mentoring programs also use a male-centric pedagogy that are single-sex, experiential, and developed for men by other men (Bowman & Filar, 2018).

A contemporary definition of mentoring is receiver-based, meaning that one can act as a mentor only if the mentee perceives him to be one (Bowman & Filar, 2018; Brooms et al., 2018). There are both formal and informal avenues for mentoring, and those college males who have mentorship earn better grades, have a higher level of interest in their studies, and are more competitive in the sense of being more highly motivated to achieve. Beyond the classic mentorship on campus, community-based mentorship may be perceived to be extremely valuable because it relates to advancing the young man's future through networking and building his résumé. Bowman & Filar (2018) pointed out that those young males who perceive mentorship to be valuable are more likely to see opportunities and be aware of resources available to them; sharing research on the value of mentorship and having peers speak about its role in their success can help to motivate more reluctant students to take advantage of formal and informal mentorship in a variety of settings.

Engaging the Male Student in Academic Pursuits

Bowman and Filar (2018) remarked that young men on campus are looking for a sense of belonging and are not sure where to turn; therefore, they often look for community in the wrong places or activities, engaging in risky relationships or behaviors. This powerful desire also has the "potential for serving as motivators towards increased campus participation" (Bowman & Filar, 2018, p. 86). The trick is to reach young males early in their college enrollment and to reframe such participation in male-friendly language and recognition.

Strategies that include active learning, peer-led instruction, case-based learning, and the integration of social media into both the formal and informal learning environments will be more readily accepted by young men (Young, Michael, & Smolinski, 2019). Connections outside of the classroom and college-community partnerships round out a sound college education and these active ways of building on classroom experiences may be particularly enticing to young males' ways of learning (Bowman & Filar, 2018; Young, Michael, & Smolinski, 2019).

Bowman and Filar (2018) recognized that young males may need to be coaxed into particular practices such as service to others or roles, such as a secretary of a club that they have been socialized to believe fall more into the province of females. Reframing these to be more inviting may assist males who have been socialized to be more outcome-driven, assessing a potential involvement in terms of how it looks on a résumé or relates to future occupational success (Bowman & Filar, 2018). Young men weigh the value of engaging in an activity in terms of its power, visibility, or career advancement potential; therefore, a community service day might need to be recast as a challenge with a community champion crowned at the end. Leadership or service activities might need to be commoditized with a certificate or something that can be recognized more formally.

Virtual academia

The college of today is very different from that of even a decade ago. Students participate in learning a variety of ways to include face-to-face, online, and hybrid (Young, Jean, & Quayson, 2017). While face-to-face might appeal to some students, online and hybrid can be geared to the working student, or the man who has other responsibilities. With each passing year the number of online learners, those who have enrolled in at least one online class, has increased from 27 percent in 2014 to 30 percent in 2016 (Lederman, 2018). Each teaching method must take into account student learning style and offer a balance of lecture, hands-on, and independent research that will appeal to all students (Celli & Young, 2014; Young, Celli, & Mumby, 2019). Even at the postsecondary level, male students gravitate toward competitive, hands-on, and independent learning tasks.

Learning styles and differentiation

Universal Design for Learning (CAST, 2019) and Gardner's Multiple Intelligences (Gardner, 2006) can guide the professor toward teaching and assessment that engages the male student and propels academic instruction to higher and more rigorous levels. UDL promotes independent learning that is hands-on, and student centered (CAST, 2019). Here, professors are responsible for offering a variety of learning opportunities that address the how, why, and what for the topic and the student (CAST, 2019). It does not matter if the instructor is teaching elementary, secondary, or postsecondary students, the tenets of UDL remain the same.

Gardner's Multiple Intelligences, although originally embraced by preschool through twelfth grade (P–12) teachers, offers a road map of sorts for professors who aim to teach to individual student strengths (Armstrong, 2018). Based on brain research, eight intelligences were identified to include linguistic, logical-mathematical, spatial, bodily-kinesthetic, musical, interpersonal, intrapersonal, and naturalist (Gardner, 2006). These intelligences can be seen as a framework that exemplifies best teaching practices for professors (Chen, Moran, & Gardner, 2009).

First year seminars

Starting off early with targeted experiences may be even more important for historically underserved male students in order to decrease the gender gap in academic achievement between males and females. Swanson, Vaughn, and Wilkinson (2015) discovered that participating in a first-year seminar boosted GPA and first-year retention of male students and gains for minority males were even higher than for male majority students. These academically oriented seminars appeared extremely useful in promoting male persistence and academic success, especially during that critical first year of enrollment.

Swanson et al. (2015) wrote of the value of these seminars as being a semester-long, credit-bearing experience that prepared young men for the rigors of college work. Since the instructors are able to get to know their students, they can individualize approaches to the required work, building upon student strengths and individual interests. As students rise to the challenges under this individualized tutelage, they gain confidence about their academic self-efficacy. This factor is highly positively correlated with persistence and success (Swanson et al., 2015). It also erases feelings of impostership among students who may not feel that they fully belong on campus.

Savvy instructors in first-year seminars with male students must emphasize the real-life application of the skills they are imparting (Swanson et al., 2015). They help their students understand the rationale for and utility of what is being learned—key elements to male students. If they buy in to the importance of the work, even if it is challenging, males are much more likely to maximize their engagement with classroom activities and the life of the mind overall.

The results of these seminars can be attributed to different factors beyond just the academic skills imparted. Instructors of such seminars receive special training that tunes them in to reaching out to and keeping tabs on students in a more proactive way than usual (Swanson et al., 2015). Intervening early and not necessarily when asked (often considered an intrusive practice) has demonstrated results in terms of increasing retention and academic success. Because males are less likely to seek help or reach out when they are challenged, this kind of intervention breaks down masculine norms and stigmas since all students in the seminars received such attention (Swanson et al., 2015).

Academic advising

Young, Michael, and Smolinski (2019) wrote about the values of faculty and academic advisors taking more active approaches in reaching out to students, especially those from fragile groups. Institutions are urged to adopt advising models that are developmental in nature and that define the advisor's role in ways that far outstrip traditional models of academic advising alone (Young, Michael, & Smolinski, 2019). In working with student populations who may not take advantage of advisors' office hours or services, the authors suggest using intrusive or proactive models to require early connection on a personal level. Advising models that draw heavily from counseling techniques are encouraged, such as motivational interviewing and appreciative advising, as these can build personal relationships, help students set goals, support desired personal development, and keep tabs on potential mental, emotional, and social health issues (Young, Michael, & Smolinski, 2019).

Co-Curricular Engagement for Men

Participating in co-curricular activities is an integral part of college life (Kuh, 2001). Male students who engage in programs, activities, and learning experiences are more likely to experience "self-efficacy, satisfaction, feelings of support and institutional challenge, retention, academic achievement and intellectual engagement, enhanced understanding of others, a deepened sense of spirituality, and practical skill acquisition such as interview skills and networking abilities" (Stirling & Kerr, 2015). These skills transfer to all aspects of student life and can promote the success of students who may otherwise fail.

According to Stirling and Kerr (2015), there are myriad positive outcomes to include personal wellness, identity formation, leadership, professionalism, and career awareness. For men who struggle with the academic aspects of college, co-curricular activities offer an outlet as well as a time to meet others who may be able to help. Sterling and Kerr (2015) outline several ways in which co-curricular activities can occur to include:

- Curricular Learning/Professional Practice: Applying learning experiences gleaned from co-curricular activities to academic experiences.
- Co-Curricular Pre-Training: Workshops that teach leadership skills, diversity training, team-building exercises, and other skills that will be applied to the co-curricular activity chosen.
- Purposive Co-Curricular Participation: Linking learning outcomes in the classroom to the co-curricular activity to balance "all four learning modes of experience, reflection, conceptualization, and experimentation" (Sterling & Kerr, 2015, p. 3).
- Professional Development Workshops: With a strong focus on integrating theory and practice, the workshops would begin after the activities are underway and "enhance students' theoretical knowledge on specific learning outcomes" (Sterling & Kerr, 2015, p. 4).

- Co-Curricular Portfolio: A capstone project that brings together the co-curricular learning and professional practice in a way that exemplifies the overall experience.

Other important co-curricular initiatives that build males' interest in fully investing in academic experiences include community-based learning, field trips, undergraduate research opportunities, internships, capstone experiences, and travel abroad. These experiences are engaging because they rely more upon male-friendly methods of instruction that focus on a male's need for visual and spatial ways of learning, movement, activity, interactions with others, mentor-based learning, and courses that deliberately bolster reading and writing skills in exciting ways as, even in college, young men lag behind young women in these critical skills for college success (Bowman & Filar, 2018; Wong, 2018).

THE STRUGGLING MALE STUDENT AND CAMPUS STRUCTURES

Not every student can walk onto a college campus and be successful; as a matter of fact, many struggle. For male students who have a disability, it is vital that they work with the disability center to ensure they receive the accommodations and modifications that can help them meet the expectations of success. Postsecondary institutions that accept public funding are obligated to "provide appropriate academic adjustments [that do] not discriminate on the basis of disability" (U.S. Department of Education, 2011, p. 2). Students who struggle must have coping mechanisms that will propel them forward such as self-reflection and self-monitoring, planning and strategizing, and metacognition (Young & Jean, 2018). These are often missing in students with disabilities; therefore, it is incumbent upon the professors and disability center to "understand and assist" (Young & Jean, 2018, p. 136) in order to ensure success.

Benchmarks for Inclusive Teaching

The University of Massachusetts–Boston is the site of Think College, a national organization dedicated to ensuring the success of students with intellectual disabilities (Institute for Community Inclusion, 2017). Any student with a disability, and therefore any male student with a disability, would benefit from the standards they seek to ensure. The standards include ensuring academic access, career development, campus membership, self-determination, alignment with college systems and practices, coordination and collaboration with faculty and services, sustainability of programming, and ongoing evaluation of all aspects of programming (Institute for Community Inclusion, 2017; Young & Jean, 2018).

Professional Development for the Professor

Colleges should offer professional development for professors to ensure proficiency in teaching students with disabilities (University of Washington, 2017). Professional development is necessary to ensure that postsecondary staff can support students with a variety of needs. This may mean that professors need to modify work assignments or accommodate longer delivery times. Some of this will come naturally as a result of teaching to individual learning styles or multiple intelligences (MI), while some of it must be very specifically tailored for students.

The University of Washington (2012) has developed a professional development training model with six different options for learning in which each module is "designed to improve the knowledge and skills of postsecondary faculty and administrators" (University of Washington, 2012, p. 1). From ADA compliance to instructional videos on teaching best practices, the trainings are web-based and self-paced (University of Washington, 2012). There are many other programs and options for professional development; however, the end goal must always be the same—to develop professors and staff to interact and teach students with disabilities in the most equitable way possible.

FINAL THOUGHTS

Barriers to college exist for young men in greater proportion than to young women. Having struggled throughout elementary and secondary school, young men are often turned off by the prospect of four more years of schooling. In recent years, more females went on to college and graduated than males, and the statistics for minority men are even more dismal. There are a number of strategies, however, that help the young male succeed when they might have succumbed to a different outcome.

Beginning in high school, teachers, counselors, and families have an obligation to prepare students for college success by increasing oral communication skills, encouraging good work habits, and ensuring knowledge in content areas. Technology and computer skills are also vital to success. At least one study showed that not being prepared for college was a major factor in the higher drop-out rate. Families should model appropriate skills such as managing personal behavioral and medical needs, taking ownership of academics and administrative tasks. These visual models remind students of the high level of independence needed to be successful at college.

Whereas once in this country college attendance was the province of males only (and essentially white, upper-class males), women have now surpassed men as college attendees and graduates and our campuses are far more diverse in their populations, reflecting the greater diversity of America as a whole. Young males are struggling to find a path to manhood without traditional rites and guides, just as they are wrestling with whether college is worth their investment. For many, finding a sense of belonging and community once on campus is a daunting task.

Men are far more likely to engage in risky behaviors while on campus, including abusing alcohol, attempting and completing suicide, or taking part in physically dangerous activities. Their mental health issues are growing, but many campuses have not yet implemented male-friendly mental health education and services. Young males are far less likely to seek help or even to recognize the seriousness of states such as depression, isolation, or disengagement while experiencing them. At some colleges and universities, personnel are offering male-centric programs, counseling, and psychoeducational experiences in order to get men to feel more comfortable in identifying and speaking about their mental health concerns.

Bereft of their families and communities of origin, young males on campus seek alternate families. Fraternities can fill this need and the best of them not only provide support, companionship and mentorship but service to others and professional connections as well. But too many such institutions are built around a culture of toxic masculinity that can further harm young males' development and derail academic achievement. LGBTQ+, progressive fraternities, and those for students of a specific racial or ethnic group tend to be more proactive in agendas that develop healthy, alternative masculinities.

Other campus activities, such as affinity groups, club sports, living and learning centers or summer bridge programs can help build connections that can boost persistence to graduation. But these also provide rich opportunities for building "brotherhoods," providing mentorship and professional networking, creating alternative masculinities, and encouraging egalitarian relationships with women and those outside one's own group. In offering safer spaces in which to infuse curriculum and leadership with opportunities to reflect upon definitions and expressions of positive masculinity, colleges cannot only serve their own retention efforts but raise up the next generation of young men capable of full partnership, brotherhood, and fatherhood.

POINTS TO REMEMBER

- Males are falling behind females in rates of college attendance and graduation.
- Many young males do not see the value of investing in a college education, although statistics show that they suffer fiscally from this decision later in life.
- Males arrive at college campuses looking for connection and belonging, just as females do; they can find these in positive environments, or lacking such connections, seek a false sense of belonging through risky behaviors and relationships.
- Historically, male college students have found connection in athletics, fraternity membership, clubs, or leadership roles.
- Many researchers and college personnel have validated the importance of mentors—whether peer, faculty or student affairs personnel—in the persistence of male students; effective models of mentoring take a developmental approach, focusing on masculine identity and development, and using male-centered pedagogy.
- Many young males feel that there is hostility on campus toward males because of histories of acts of toxic masculinity that have pervaded many campuses.
- Males suffer a number of challenges to prosocial behavior and positive mental health and well-being, but their socialized help-seeking behaviors too frequently prevent them from understanding or accessing help for their problems.
- There are proven practices that benefit male students in terms of self-efficacy, engagement, and investment in their studies. Among these are active learning activities, field experiences, problem-based studies, internships, undergraduate research opportunities, first-year seminars, living and learning communities, and mentorship.
- Specific programming and organizations for different male populations (racial, ethnic, international, gay/bi/trans, military veterans and active duty) can have salutatory effects on male identity formation, bonding, and service to others.
- Ensuring success for all students is vital. Those who have a disability must seek out the disability service center to ensure they get the help they need. Colleges have a responsibility to meet the needs of students who might struggle.
- Inclusive teaching and professional development for staff are two ways to ensure student success through strategies and new learning that bring equitable practice to the classroom.

Chapter Five

Making Their Way into the World
Finding that Just Right Career Fit

Graduating from high school is a major turning point in a young man's life. No longer is he considered a child; yet he may not be ready for the complexities of adulthood. While some high school graduates choose to attend college, others are confused about next steps or are convinced that more schooling is not for them. These young men find themselves at an uncomfortable crossroads as research shows that those with only a high school diploma have lower earnings and higher unemployment rates than their college graduated peers (Ford, 2018; Kroeger et al., 2016; Ross & Bateman, 2018). This, however, is in contrast to the fact that only 27 percent of jobs in the current economy require an associate's degree or higher (Constable, 2017; Hogan & Roberts, 2015).

On average, the unemployment rate of those under twenty-five during the Great Recession, which technically ended in 2009, was 2.2 times higher than that of the overall unemployment rate (Kroeger et al., 2016). This number has persisted due to a slow market recovery and millions of young people looking for work (Kroeger et al., 2016). In 2016, the unemployment rate for all high school graduates was 17.9 percent (up by 2 percent from 2007), while the underemployment rate was 33.7 percent (up by 7 percent from 2007) (Kroeger et al., 2016). Unemployment refers to those who are jobless but actively seeking work, while underemployment refers to those who work part-time, yet are actually looking for full-time jobs as well as those who have given up looking for work (Kroeger et al., 2016).

In 2019, more than 9.6 million young men aged sixteen to twenty-four were employed either part- or full-time, while just over 1 million young men were unemployed but looking for either part- or full-time work (U.S. Department of Labor, 2019). For those men who seek work, however, a plethora of options are available. Many young men will find work in a variety of places; start a business; travel abroad; serve in the military; intern, apprentice, or trade school; or take a gap year in which they volunteer or provide a service to others (Anderberg, 2019).

TAKE AN ENTRY-LEVEL JOB

For those young men who aren't sure what their next step should be, considering an entry level position in a company might give them a chance to see the variety of jobs available. Examples of entry level jobs include a store clerk, a factory worker, or other hands-on task-oriented jobs (Heathfield, 2018). In these positions, employees gain valuable experience and learn about the business, which can lead to better jobs later in life. Those who take on an entry-level position are usually trained to complete a task; later on, they may be trained to take on more complex tasks. In this way, the employer has a constant supply of individuals who have the specific skills necessary to keep the company going (Heathfield, 2018).

According to Farrington (2014), jobs in the service industry or retail offer basic positions usually at an hourly minimum wage; and with a good work ethic, employees can move into supervisory and management positions, often earning salaried positions and better benefits. Between 2014 and 2024, the retail industry and related occupations is expected to grow by 5 percent, which will add approximately 778,000 new jobs, making a job in retail a viable consideration for young men (Hogan & Roberts, 2015).

Entry-level jobs require both generalized and specific skills. Specific skills are those that the job itself requires, while generalized skills are those that all people should have regardless of the job. These are defined as soft skills and hard skills (Santi, Hawkins, Antonelli, & Phipps, 2018). Soft skills include leadership, interpersonal communication, problem solving, motivation, collaboration, positivity, and efficiency; while hard skills are knowing computer programs such as Microsoft Office, Photoshop, HTML, analytics, and social media (Moore, 2018; Santi et al., 2018).

Doyle (2018) also describes the ten traits employers will be seeking in the workforce of tomorrow and they include being self-aware; an ability to prioritize; organizational awareness; possess technical acumen; work well in teams; effective problem solving; ability to influence others; being proactive; being an effective decision maker; and the ability to learn with agility. Entering the workforce gives the employee life experiences and independence and allows them to decide if this is the path they want to take. Young men who have these traits may find their niche by taking on an entry-level position.

BE YOUR OWN BOSS: START A BUSINESS

While starting a business fresh out of high school may seem counterintuitive, Anderberg (2019) reported that there were "over 22 million individuals who are self-employed in the U.S." (p. 2). While many of these individuals did not attempt this at age eighteen, some did and were successful. Even of those who failed the first time, they continued to try until success happened and they credit their failures with their future success (Seth, 2019).

A study completed by Kerr, Kerr, and Xu (2019) stated that the Big-5 model influences "career choice and work performance" (p. 10). The Big-5 includes agreeableness, conscientiousness, extraversion, neuroticism, and openness to experience, and individuals with these qualities as well as a healthy risk attitude are more likely to be successful entrepreneurs (Kerr et al., 2019). According to billionaire Michael Bloomberg (as cited in Seth, 2019), to be an entrepreneur young men need certain qualities to include risk taking, embracing failure, persistence, ensuring there is a target market for the product, never stop learning, and giving back. Young men also benefit from a mentor, a business plan, and assistance with financing (Anderberg, 2019).

According to Toren (2011) and *Gentleman's Journal* (n.d.), a few examples of successful entrepreneurs who never went to college, dropped out of high school, or never went to school at all include

- Sir Richard Branson: Dropping out of school at age sixteen to build a string of successful businesses, he bought a Caribbean island at age twenty-four.
- Simon Cowell: At age sixteen he dropped out of school to open his own record label.
- Charles Culpeper: A high school dropout, he was the owner and CEO of Coca Cola.
- Walt Disney: Dropped out of school and founded his namesake company.
- Henry Ford: Born into extreme poverty, he never attended school; yet built Ford Motors and was "one of the richest men in history" (*Gentleman's Journal*, n.d., n.p.).
- Ray Kroc: Having never gone to school, he bought the McDonald's chain and "turned it into a multi-billion dollar company." (*Gentleman's Journal*, n.d., n.p.)

Other individuals attempted college and found it was not for them. Dropping out proved to be the catalyst to their success. According to Toren (2011) and Rampton (2016) a sampling of these individuals includes:

- Michael Dell: Although he briefly attended the University of Texas, he created his company, Dell Computer Corp., at age nineteen.

- Jack Dorsey: After leaving New York University without a degree, his start-ups include Twitter and Square.
- Larry Ellison: Founded Software Development Laboratories, which would become Oracle after dropping out of two colleges—the University of Urbana and the University of Chicago.
- Bill Gates: left Harvard to found Microsoft.
- Steve Jobs: After one semester, he left Reed College, worked at Atari, and then founded Apple and Pixar.
- Russell Simmons: Left City College of New York to promote musicians, launched Def Jam Recordings and Phat Farm clothing line as well as several other ventures.
- Mark Zuckerberg: Built Facebook in his dorm room, then dropped out of Harvard.

While it can be said that these men might have had savant-like qualities, the average young male who is willing to work hard and not give up in the face of failure can also succeed in opening his own business.

LEARN A TRADE

There is more than one pathway to learning a skilled trade. Students can enter a trade school or pursue an apprenticeship. Both paths provide a student with a desired skillset for employment in a trade. Trade schools provide a program of classroom instruction and hands-on training. Students generally pay for these programs and may incur some student debt; yet upon completion, they are free to seek skilled labor employment anywhere (Pearson, n.d.).

An apprenticeship is paid employment with hands-on training and some classroom instruction. Upon completion of the training, the student is guaranteed employment for a specific period of time with the company that trained them and is debt-free (Pearson, n.d.). Apprenticeship programs help employers recruit and retain a highly-skilled workforce (U.S. Department of Labor, n.d.a).

Trade Schools

Trade schools, also known as technical or vocational schools, teach skills related to specific trades and jobs, often with apprenticeships to hone those skills (Career Now Brands, 2019). This approach to education focuses on developing the skillset and knowledge base for a particular career, rather than receiving a general education as provided by a four-year college (Hamm, 2019). Trade schools have been underrated for quite a while, and the careers generally associated with them are often considered "blue collar" jobs (Hamm, 2019). This reputation, or stigma, is swiftly changing as more students and their families begin to search for a different and less expensive path to a career—particularly in light of the high cost of postsecondary education, which results in some students leaving college with enormous debt (Ross & Bateman, 2018).

Mike Rowe, former *Dirty Jobs* host and the founder and CEO of Mike Rowe Works Foundation, believes the pressure for high school students to pursue a college education in America is contributing to a large skills gap, leaving numerous manufacturing jobs unfilled (Wisner, 2017). Rowe, long a vocal advocate for skills training, maintains that our culture of stressing the importance of a college education not only results in many college graduates entering the work force saddled with high debt, but also without skills that could have been obtained more affordably at a trade or vocational school (Wisner, 2017).

Average starting salaries for trade and vocational school graduates range from $35,720 to $42,000 versus starting salaries for a four-year college graduate from $45,000 to $46,900 (Anderberg, 2014; Hamm, 2019). While this is not a vast difference, the trade school graduate enters the workforce and starts earning a salary and potential raises two years earlier than a four-year college graduate (Hamm, 2019). Examples of median annual salaries for trade school graduates include dental hygienists at $72,910, electricians at $52,000 and HVAC technicians at $45,910 (Career Now Brands, 2019).

Vocational school graduates also carry a lower educational debt load than a four-year college graduate—an average of $10,000 for the trade school graduate versus $37,000 for the college graduate (Career Now Brands, 2019). The college class of 2016 had the largest student debt of any graduating class in U.S. history with over 70 percent of the graduates carrying a student debt of over $37,000 (Career Now Brands, 2019).

Traditional college can take four, five, and even six years to complete, depending on a student's course load, whether they attend full time or part time or take time off to pursue other interests or work (Career Now Brands, 2019). Trade school programs are generally completed in six weeks to two years, again depending on whether a student attends full or part time (Career Now Brands, 2019). Some of the most common trade school programs and their average length include HVAC technician/2 years; dental hygienist/2 years; welder/4 years including apprenticeship; electrician/2–4 years including apprenticeship; mechanic/2–5 years including apprenticeship; and commercial trucking/6 weeks (Career Now Brands, 2019). It should be noted that trades listed with higher years include an apprenticeship in which the student is working in the trade, practicing his or her desired trade, and earning a salary.

One benefit of trade school is smaller class sizes (Hamm, 2019). Compared to colleges and universities with classes that can reach over 100 students, a trade school class can average thirty—or fewer—students. A smaller class size provides students the opportunity for more one-on-one interaction with the instructor (Career Now Brands, 2019). Another benefit is most of the training is hands-on with practical, real life applications (Career Now Brands, 2019; Hamm, 2019). With smaller classes, hands-on training, and shorter completion times, trade school is an ideal educational environment for many types of learners (Hamm, 2019).

Yet another advantage of trade school is that a student is almost guaranteed a job after completing school. Stories abound of large projects that had to be canceled due to a labor shortage and companies that simply cannot find people with the skills to complete the work needed (Anderberg, 2014). Skilled trades such as plumbing, electric, welding, healthcare, technology, and trucking are experiencing shortages of qualified people, creating vacancies with no one to fill them; and one out of three businesses are struggling to be fully staffed (Career Now Brands, 2019).

There is an additional benefit of the skilled labor that trade schools provide—job security. Skilled labor is not as exportable as those jobs performed in a cubicle or office every day (Andenberg, 2014). With more jobs being outsourced regularly to places where labor is cheaper—even work previously performed by lawyers and doctors—employment in some sectors is becoming difficult to find. Skilled labor jobs, such as carpentry, electrical, or plumbing, require a physical presence and cannot be outsourced (Anderberg, 2014; Hamm, 2019). Additional job security, according to Hamm (2019), is imparted by an aging work force where "skilled trade workers are a disproportionately older population, and will only continue to get older, creating increased opportunities for young workers to fill their shoes" (n.p.).

Attending a four-year college may be the right choice for someone who has chosen a career path that requires a bachelor's degree, wishes to pursue a master's or professional degree, and who can afford the expense; however, most of the fastest growing jobs in the United States between 2016 and 2026 will not require a bachelor's degree (Doyle, 2019b). Trade school can be an excellent alternative to traditional college, especially for students who like to work with their hands (Farrington, 2014). A hands-on learner looking to get out of high school and start working may find trade school a relatively inexpensive option (Hamm, 2019). Trade school focuses on the skills essential for the job and the curriculum emphasizes practical, hands-on training, knowledge, and mentoring for a skilled career rather than the general education of a traditional college (Doyle, 2019b).

Trade School Resources Include:

- https://www.trade-schools.net/
- https://careerschoolnow.org/careers/trade-school-vs-traditional-college
- https://blog.prepscholar.com/what-is-a-trade-school

Apprenticeship

Another way to learn a trade is through apprenticeship—an industry-driven, high-quality career pathway where employers can develop and prepare their future workforce. They provide an affordable pathway to lucrative skill jobs and careers without incurring the student debt that is associated with college (U.S. Department of Labor, Employment and Training Administration, 2019). Apprenticeships, according to the U.S. Department of Labor, combine paid on-the-job training with classroom instruction and mentorship to prepare workers for highly skilled jobs and careers (U.S. Department of Labor, n.d.a).

Formal apprenticeship programs connect students, or workers, who are seeking to develop a marketable skill with employers who want to train workers for jobs that require those skills (Torpey, 2013) The length of these programs varies, most take approximately four years to complete, while some may take up to six years and others only a year. Upon completion of a registered apprenticeship program, apprentices receive a portable nationally recognized certificate of completion as proof of their skills (Torpey, 2013).

The U.S. Bureau of Labor Statistics (Torpey, 2017) anticipates that many of the occupations with apprenticeships will grow "at least as fast as the average for all occupations—if not faster—from 2016–26" (n.p.). Some trades, such as carpentry and electricians, are expected to grow at an average rate of 6 percent to 8 percent; however, the demand for plumbers, pipefitters, and steamfitters is projected to grow much faster than average (Torpey, 2017). After completing an apprenticeship, 92 percent of the apprentices retain their employment (U.S. Department of Labor, n.d.c).

Apprenticeships are generally sponsored by employers, employer associations, and labor unions (Torpey, 2013). Apprentices work and train directly under an experienced worker—mentor—and generally earn approximately half of what a fully qualified worker makes, though their wages increase as their training advances (Torpey, 2013).

Advantages of an apprenticeship are many. First and foremost, apprentices receive a paycheck from the beginning of their training, while some programs may also provide health insurance or other employee benefits (Torpey, 2013). Practical skills are learned through hands-on training provided by experienced workers and mentors. By the completion of an apprenticeship, a worker will normally have had exposure to and experience with the major aspects of their occupation.

Apprentices also receive technical classroom instruction, provided by experienced workers. These classes may count toward a certification or licensure requirement and, in some cases, may earn college credits (Torpey, 2013). Upon completion of a formal, registered program, apprentices receive a certificate of completion issued by the U.S. Department of Labor or a state apprentice agency that is recognized and accepted by employers across the country (Torpey, 2013).

The expense and academic classroom may not be the best course for many high school seniors, while an apprenticeship may be a viable and lucrative option. Hundreds of skilled trade positions are available through apprenticeships for a high school senior, young adult, or worker looking to gain entrance to a skilled field (Doyle, 2019a). The process of obtaining an apprenticeship is very much like applying for a job—because that is just what the applicant is doing.

An interested student must decide on a skill he or she wishes to master, find a program, apply, often participate in interviews, and then qualify for selection (Torpey, 2013). For a potential apprentice, the benefits of a salary, hands-on training, and plenty of job prospects make this pathway much more appealing than a four-year degree from a university or college (Johnson, 2017).

Apprenticeship Resources Include:

- https://www.dol.gov/apprenticeship/#
- https://www.apprenticeship.gov/become-apprentice
- https://www.thebalancecareers.com/what-are-apprenticeship-programs-2061927
- https://www.careeronestop.org/FindTraining/Types/apprenticeships.aspx?frd=true
- https://www.bls.gov/careeroutlook/2013/summer/art01.pdf
- https://www.mynextmove.org/
- For specific state apprenticeship information: https://www.doleta.gov/oa/contactlist.cfm
- For additional information on trades and apprenticeships contact local trade unions.

Internship versus Apprenticeship

An apprenticeship is not an internship. Apprenticeships lead to a highly skilled trade and career, while an internship is usually short-term and focuses on entry-level work for a specific company (U.S. Department of Labor, n.d.b). According to the U.S. Department of Labor (n.d.b), there are several key differences between the two to include

- Length of Time: Internships are usually short term (1–3 months) and apprenticeships are longer term (1–3 years).
- Structure:
  - Apprenticeships include a structured training plan, with a focus on mastering specific skills an employer needs to fill an occupation within their organization.
  - Internships aren't structured and often focus on entry-level general work experience.
- Mentorship: Apprentices receive individualized training with an experienced mentor who walks them through their entire process. Internships do not always include mentorship.
- Pay: Apprenticeships are paid experiences that often lead to full-time employment. Internships are often unpaid and may not lead to a full-time job.
- Credential: Apprenticeships lead to an industry-recognized credential. Internships typically do not lead to a credential.
- College Credit: Internship and apprenticeship experiences may both lead to college credit, although some apprenticeship programs will lead to a debt-free college degree.

UNITED STATES MILITARY

Another excellent alternative for a young man who does not wish to go the college route after high school is to enlist in the military. The military is unrivaled in its ability to provide job security, promotional opportunities, and education (Farrington, 2014). Military service is certainly a way to see the world but, more importantly, enlistees learn skills that can prove valuable when they return to civilian life (Lewis, n.d.). Learning skills such as responsibility, focus, and discipline will benefit an enlistee for life. Veterans who do not pursue a college degree generally earn a higher wage than non-veterans who do not have a college degree as confirmed by Lewis (n.d.) who stated "even if they [veterans] don't earn more education, they certainly earn more money" (n.p.).

A young man looking to join the military must meet the age requirement, which varies by branch; pass a health screening; and pass the Armed Services Vocational Aptitude Battery (ASVAB) test (Military Advantage, 2019c; RethinkOldSchool, n.d.). ASVAB scores are used to determine if a candidate is qualified to enlist in the military and to assign them to an appropriate job in the military (ASVAB, n.d.).

Legal immigrants living in the United States are eligible to enlist; however, they must become citizens if they wish to reenlist (Lewis, n.d.). Approximately 8,000 non-citizens enlist each year and this population is more likely to remain in the service, often choosing it as their career (Lewis, n.d.).

The Army, Navy, Marines, Air Force, and Coast Guard comprise the five branches of the United States military. Each branch has a full-time, active duty component as well as a part-time component made up of reserves and national guard (Department of Defense, n.d.; Young, Michael, & Jean, 2019). Active duty servicemembers generally live on base and the military is their full-time job. While there are some differences across service branches, reserve and national guard servicemembers may live where they wish and earn a civilian salary and are required to participate in ongoing training (Department of Defense, n.d.; Military Benefits. 2019a). Regardless of service branch, all servicemembers are obligated to serve a minimum number of years before they can either reenlist or deactivate (Lewis, n.d.).

The National Security Act of 1947 revamped the military structure into what it is today, restructuring the War Department into the Department of Defense (Powers, 2019). With 1.4 million active duty servicemembers, 1.1 million reserve and national guard personnel and 700,000 civilian workers, the U.S. Department of Defense is the largest employer in the world (Greenspan, 2019). In addition to servicemembers currently serving in the military, there are 21.8 million veterans (Young, Michael, & Jean, 2018).

In descending order, the Army dominates the five branches with 36 percent of all active duty military personnel, followed by the Navy with 24 percent, the Air Force with 23 percent, the Marine Corps with 14 percent and the Coast Guard with 3 percent (Young, Michael, & Jean, 2018). While all five military branches continue to be male-dominated, the numbers of female servicemembers increased from 11 percent in 1990 to 15 percent in 2015 (Young, Michael, & Jean, 2018). Diversity in the Armed Services is a top priority for military leaders in recruiting for military service (United States Army, 2018).

The U.S. military has become more racially and ethnically diverse as has the country. In 1990, racial and ethnic minorities comprised 25 percent of active duty military; that number increased to 40 percent in 2015 (United States Army, 2018). Broken out by gender, white men make up 69.5 percent and white women 51.7 percent of all servicemembers followed by black women at 30.7 percent and black men at 17 percent (Young, Michael, & Jean, 2018). Male and female Hispanic servicemembers are nearly even at about 14 percent each, with all other ethnicities making up the remaining percentages (Young, Michael, & Jean, 2018). While each branch of the armed services has differing missions and focus, they are similar in many ways.

Army

Established by the Continental Congress on June 14, 1775, the Army is the oldest U.S. military service (Powers, 2019). The main ground force for the United States, its primary function, as described by Powers (2019), "is to protect and defend the country and its interests with ground troops, armor (such as tanks), artillery, attack helicopters, tactical nuclear weapons and other weapons" (n.p.). It is the largest of the military services, with over one million active duty and reserve servicemembers (Powers, 2019; Young, Michael, & Jean, 2018).

Full-time, active duty servicemembers numbered slightly less than 500,000 in 2015 (Young et al., 2018). Active duty members by and large live on base, receive a salary, are entitled to health insurance and retirement benefits (Young, Michael, & Jean, 2018). Reservists, totaling over 300,000 in 2015, usually hold down a full-time civilian job and are a part-time soldier (Young, Michael, & Jean, 2018). They may live and work where they wish, and earn their civilian salary, as well as a partial salary and some benefits in their role as reservist in the Army (Young, Michael, & Jean, 2018).

Navy

Also established by the Continental Congress in 1775, the Navy is responsible for maintaining and protecting the United States interests at sea (Powers, 2019). As part of its mission, the Navy augments the Air Force's air power with aircraft carriers that can, in many cases, deploy to areas where fixed runways are not feasible and also provides transportation for Marines to areas of conflict (Powers, 2019).

Navy active duty servicemembers numbered in excess of 323,000 in 2015 (Young, Michael, & Jean, 2018). Similar to the Army, active duty Navy sailors work full-time at their Navy job. Navy reservists, which in 2015 totaled slightly over 110,000, are part-time, training one weekend a month and two weeks each year. They must be prepared to be deployed when needed (Young, Michael, & Jean, 2018).

Air Force

The Air Force, which prior to 1947 was part of the Army, is the youngest branch of military service (Powers, 2019). Protecting the United States via air and space is the primary mission of the Air Force. All military satellites and the control of strategic nuclear ballistic missiles are also its responsibility (Powers, 2019).

Active duty Air Force servicemembers exceeded 300,000 in 2015 (Young, Michael, & Jean, 2018). As with the other services, these are full-time jobs where the men and women generally live on a base. The Air Force reserve in 2015 numbered over 100,000 men and women (Young, Michael, & Jean, 2018). As in the Navy, a reservist holds a civilian job and trains one weekend a month and two weeks a year and they must be prepared to deploy at any time (Young, Michael, & Jean, 2018).

Marines

The Continental Congress originally established the Marines on November 10, 1775, to be a landing force for the Navy (Powers, 2019). Several years later, in 1798, Congress separated the Marines from the Navy (Powers, 2019). Amphibious operations continue to be the Marines primary area of expertise; however, recently they have also extended their operations into ground-combat actions (Powers, 2019).

The 180,000 active duty Marines around the world endured twelve weeks of intense training which often utilized extreme training techniques (Young, Michael, & Jean, 2018). Marine reservists, numbering 110,000, frequently elect to enter the reserves when their Marine service contract is completed, as a way to stay involved and connected to the Marine Corps as they pursue civilian employment or education (Young, Michael, & Jean, 2018).

Coast Guard

The United States Coast Guard was originally established in 1790 as the Revenue Cutter Service. In 1915 the Revenue Cutter Service merged with the U.S. Life-Saving Service and was renamed the Coast Guard under the Treasury Department (United States Coast Guard, 2019). The Coast Guard was transferred to the Department of Transportation in 1967 and, most recently, in 2002 the Guard was transferred to the Department of Homeland Security (United States Coast Guard, 2019). The Coast Guard is the smallest of all the U.S. military branches (Powers, 2019).

During times of peace, the Coast Guard is generally tasked with law enforcement at sea, protecting the marine environment, guarding the nations coastline and ports and carrying out lifesaving missions (United States Coast Guard, 2019). In times of conflict, or at the discretion of the president, the Coast Guard serves under the Department of the Navy and, as with the four other services, defends the nation against terrorism and foreign threats (United States Coast Guard, 2019).

Active duty Coast Guard men and women number 56,000 working in an assortment of roles, which include maritime stewardship, maritime safety and maritime security (States Coast Guard, 2019; Young, Michael, & Jean, 2018).

Coast Guard reservists total 7,500, with an additional 30,000 auxiliary members known as guardians (Young, Michael, & Jean, 2018). Military service comes with numerous benefits some of which are outlined here.

Enlistment and reenlistment bonuses

Each of the services offers extra enlistment and reenlistment bonuses to meet the needs of the service. These incentives facilitate recruitment for jobs that are hard to fill, require higher qualifications or specialized training with high dropout rates. This bonus is in addition to the ordinary benefits offered to all recruits (Lewis, n.d.; Military Advantage, 2019a).

Basic pay

Active duty is a full-time job with guaranteed pay and cost of living adjustments. Enlistees normally enter the service at the E-1 service grade and typically advance to E-4 level within a few years. Earnings are based on these levels and the longer a servicemember serves and advances in rank the more they can earn. (Lewis, n.d.; Military Advantage, 2019a).

Special pay

Some service members may receive special and incentive pay. The amount will vary according to their assignment, location or skills. This pay includes hazardous duty, the ability to speak a needed foreign language, or special duty assignments, among others. An additional benefit is that in some cases, such as serving in a combat zone, basic pay, and special payments are tax exempt (Lewis, n.d.).

Free room, board, and uniforms

Unmarried enlisted servicemembers without children generally live in barracks on base. A tax-free housing allowance is provided to servicemembers who live off base. While on active duty, servicemembers are eligible for free dining at base dining facilities or a tax-free allowance if dining facilities are unavailable. During basic training, all recruits are provided a complete set of uniforms and, thereafter, receive a clothing allowance to replace worn out items (Lewis, n.d.; Military Advantage, 2019a).

Health and dental care

All active-duty servicemembers receive free health and dental care. Veterans who served more than two years of active duty and sustained a service-related injury leading to a disability may qualify for related health care through lifetime Veterans Administration benefits (Lewis, n.d.).

Disability benefits

In addition to the health care benefit, veterans with a service-related disability may qualify for monthly disability payments for life (Lewis, n.d.).

Education benefits

Enlisting in the military does not deprive a recruit of a college education—far from it. The military encourages its servicemembers to pursue further education with its tremendous assortment and variety of education benefits available to active duty members, reserve, and veterans. It can assist in paying for college or paying off college loans (Lewis, n.d.; Military Advantage, 2019b).

Here is a summary of benefits and a link for further information:

- Tuition Assistance—Pays tuition and some fees. For virtually all active duty servicemembers. Criteria determined by each branch.
  https://www.military.com/education/money-for-school/tuition-assistance-ta-program-overview.html
- Tuition Assistance "Top Up" Program—Supplements the tuition and fees not covered by the Tuition Assistance program. Available for active duty servicemembers who have served at least two full years, who are eligible for federal Tuition Assistance by a military department and are also eligible for GI Bill benefits.
  https://benefits.va.gov/gibill/tuition_assistance.asp
- Post-9/11 GI Bill—Provides up to thirty-six months of education benefits for college and a variety of other educational programs and courses. Available for servicemembers (Active Duty, Guard, & Reserve) and veterans who have served at least 90 days on active duty or were discharged with a service-connected disability after 30 days, since 9/10/2001.
  https://benefits.va.gov/gibill/post911_gibill.asp
- Montgomery GI Bill (MGIB-AD)—Provides up to thirty-six months of education benefits for college and a variety of other educational programs and courses. Available for active duty servicemembers and veterans who have served a minimum of two years on active duty.
  https://www.benefits.va.gov/gibill/mgib_ad.asp
- Montgomery GI Bill (MGIB-SR)—Provides up to thirty-six months of education benefits for college and a variety of other educational programs and courses. Available to all Reserve service members who commit to serve six years in the Selected Reserves.
  https://www.benefits.va.gov/gibill/mgib_sr.asp
- Test Fees—Covers the cost of certain tests to apply to college, a training course, or become licensed or certified.
  https://www.va.gov/education/about-gi-bill-benefits/how-to-use-benefits/test-fees/
- Work-Study Program—An "earn while you learn" program, students may earn an hourly minimum wage. Available to veterans who are full-time or 3/4-time students in a college degree program or a vocational or profes-

sional program. Must be studying or training under the Post-9/11 GI Bill, Montgomery GI Bill, or other specified educational benefit programs. https://benefits.va.gov/gibill/workstudy.asp
- GI Bill Kicker (also known as the Army, Navy, or Marine Corps College Funds)—An amount added to the monthly GI Bill payment from the VA. This benefit is offered through each service branch as part of an enlistment or reenlistment contract. Each service determines who receives the benefit and the amount received.
https://www.military.com/education/gi-bill/the-gi-bill-kicker.html
- GI Bill Buy-up Program—By making monthly contributions to this program a servicemember can increase their total benefit by as much as $5,400. Available to veterans who are enrolled in the Montgomery Bill program. Veterans who elect the Post-9/11 GI Bill are not eligible.
https://www.military.com/education/gi-bill/gi-bill-buy-up-program.html
- Student Loan Repayment—Partial or full repayment of college loans. Available for enlisted servicemembers. Eligibility depends on several factors including service branch, Military Occupational Specialties (MOS), a minimum of a three-year enlistment, and a written agreement not to utilize the Montgomery GI Bill.
https://www.military.com/education/money-for-school/army-student-loan-repayments.html

(Military Advantage, 2019b; (Young, Michael, & Jean, 2018).

Home financing

The VA helps servicemembers, veterans, and eligible surviving spouses purchase, build, repair, retain, or adapt a home for their personal use. A VA loan requires no money down and there is no limit to the number of times a veteran can use this benefit, although the maximum amount that can be outstanding at any time is limited. In addition to VA home loans and grants, many states offer resources to veterans, including property tax reduction to certain veterans (U.S. Department of Veterans Affairs, 2019).

Qualities sought by employers

The qualities that a human resource department seeks when hiring new employees can be found in applicants with a military service background. A partial list of those qualities includes:

- Experience: a servicemember spends between two and twelve intense months training for a particular Military Occupational Specialty (MOS)—an occupation. The servicemember then performs that job for at least two to three years to maintain that employment and if performed well, would be rewarded with promotions and awards (Rosser, 2012).

- Perseverance: a servicemember commits to a goal and succeeds. Basic training is tough and most people who join the service complete their contract "because it is their personal goal to serve their country honorably" (Rosser, 2012).
- Analytical skills: a servicemember may spend long periods of time on a deployment in frenzied and confusing situations. They needed to gather information and data, be able to discuss clearly the meanings and implications of that information and ways it could impact that and other situations. According to Rosser (2012), "when their analysis is correct military members achieve their goals and when they are incorrect people could die" (n.p.).
- Time management and multi-tasking: Servicemembers are expected to handle situations as they are presented, come up with a way to adapt to and overcome challenges, and achieve their goal (Rosser, 2012).

Being a military veteran

There are many benefits to military service, including some many veterans are unaware of, such as free tax preparation, life insurance and long-term care (Military Benefits, 2019b). One benefit not often mentioned is "membership into one of the world's oldest clubs" (The Military Wallet, 2019, n.p.). Veterans are a group in which it is easy to be accepted and to bond with, to join clubs and other groups with, to socialize with, to find support, and with which to network and find employment (The Military Wallet, 2019).

A key reason many more people don't give military service consideration is the perception of danger and the possibility of death. This perception is chiefly caused by the media. In actuality, many military occupations are as safe as their civilian equivalent (The Military Wallet, 2019). Given that only 1 percent of the population join the military, the public perception of the danger of military service may be "grossly exaggerated" (Lewis, n.d.). Figures provided by the Congressional Research Organization (CRO), "less than 1% of those on active duty between 1980 and 2010 have died while in service, and most of those deaths were accidental" (Lewis, n.d.).

The advantages of enlisting in the military can be considerable. The military may be the only path to a college degree or professional status for many people, while for other people, it may be the opportunity to test oneself, gain invaluable maturity, and see the world. Despite the possible dangers, military service may provide the life and security some people want (Lewis, n.d.). That said, military service is not for everyone:

> If after you've weighed your options, done your research, and talked to recruiters and admissions officers, and you still can't say that you're 110% committed and comfortable with military service, then walk away. Go to college or even take a gap year instead. Remember that this isn't a debate about what's "better." It's about doing what's right for you, and no matter what, you'll be happier and better off doing what's right for you. (Marquell, 2016, n.p.)

GAP YEAR, TRAVEL, OR VOLUNTEER

A young man who is unsure of what he wants to do or which direction to head may consider volunteering before choosing to follow another path or head to college (Farrington, 2014). Volunteering can be a great way to have some adventure before settling down and starting a family, to give back and do some some service in areas around the world, build character, and perhaps figure out what do to with the rest of your life (Anderberg, 2019; Farrington, 2014). Taking a break between high school and college or full-time employment is an option more and more students are choosing, either as a service year or gap year (Wang, 2017; Zanville, 2017).

In 2013, 40,000 Americans elected to take a gap year, up almost 20 percent from 2006 (Zanville, 2017). The Gap Year Association National Alumni Survey Report for 2015 (Hoe, 2015) lists the motivations survey participants gave for taking a gap year (the participants could select multiple motivations). The top six motivations for taking a service or gap year were to (1) gain experiences, personal growth—92 percent, (2) travel, see the world, other cultures—85 percent, (3) take a break from academics—81 percent, (4) explore academic pursuits—52 percent, (5) volunteer—48 percent, and (6) explore careers—44 percent (Hoe, 2015). A service-focused or volunteer service gap year can help students discover what is important to them, clarify the direction they would like to take in their life, what path to follow, and what career they would like to pursue (Zanville, 2017).

Travel/Gap Year

For young men unsure of their direction in life, travel offers an opportunity to see new places, meet an array of people, experience different cultures, learn a variety of skills, and become more independent (Constable, 2017). Although travel is an expensive proposition, "travel hacking" (Constable, 2017, n.p.) has made this endeavor more affordable. Travel hacking refers to an ability to find inexpensive deals, use couch surfing, and other techniques as well as "the art of collecting frequent flyer miles and points to travel for free" (Johnston, 2014, n.p.).

When considering travel as an option, young men need to be flexible and creative in thinking as a means to maximize money, time, and efforts (Eliot, 2019). Some travel options include teaching English in foreign countries, volunteering, house-sitting, carpooling or hitchhiking, crewing on a yacht or cruise ship, staying in hostels, flying or taking the train using budget methods, or working at each location visited (Gourgy, 2009).

Sometimes referred to as a "gap year" (Safier, 2017, n.p.), this time to travel can prove to be a turning point or a way to figure out next steps. A gap year, or travel in general, may lead to a two or four-year college experience and then a career, while other times it may lead to finding that just-right job either at home or overseas. Global Citizen Year (2019) lists pros to a gap year as (1) being better prepared for college and higher GPAs, (2) a better sense of the world and of self, (3) college and universities look favorably on well-spent gap years, (4) résumé booster, and (5) expands personal network. This same website offers cons to the gap year as including (1) being left behind by peers, a loss of momentum in schooling, and (3) the cost of some gap year programs and trips (Global Citizen Year, 2019). In any case, travel has the ability to clarify school, work, and life goals (Safier, 2017).

AmeriCorps

AmeriCorps is a national system of service programs across the country, comprising three primary programs that each take a different approach to improve lives and foster civic engagement (AmeriCorps, n.d.a). Over 75,000 Americans participate in these programs each year. The service opportunities range from the classroom to the outdoors. While there are several AmeriCorps programs, three will be focused on here, including two AmeriCorps NCCC programs and the AmeriCorps VISTA program.

AmeriCorps NCCC

NCCC's (National Civilian Community Corps) mission is to strengthen and develop leaders through team-based national and community service (AmeriCorps, n.d.b). It is a full-time residential program targeted toward young adults aged eighteen to twenty-four (AmeriCorps, n.d.b). Teams of eight to ten members work on and complete several projects during a ten-month service term, addressing vital community needs all over the United States. As part of their service benefits, members are given lodging, transportation, uniforms, and meals (AmeriCorps, n.d.b). Participating in and completing their service provides team members with leadership skills and fundamental, unique life experiences and they are also eligible to receive awards upon completion of their service (AmeriCorps, n.d.b). There are two programs under the AmeriCorps NCCC umbrella to include:

- AmeriCorps NCCC Traditional Corps focuses on natural and other disasters, infrastructure improvement, energy conservation, and more (AmeriCorps, n.d.b). Examples of specific team projects range from filling and placing sandbags in local communities to lessen the impact of flooding, constructing, and rehabilitating low-income housing to educating citizens on sustainability and energy conservation (AmeriCorps, n.d.b).

- AmeriCorps NCCC FEMA Corps focuses on strengthening the federal government's disaster preparedness and response. NCCC-FEMA Corps teams "train and complete projects related to disaster preparedness, mitigation, response and recovery" (AmeriCorps, n.d.b, n.p.). Projects may take place in many different settings, including active disaster areas, recovery sites, and FEMA regional offices. Specific team projects range from training the public on disaster preparedness, preparing disaster kits to planning evacuation routes, and recovery plans (AmeriCorps, n.d.b).

AmeriCorps VISTA

Volunteers in Service to America was founded in 1965 and incorporated with AmeriCorps in 1994 (AmeriCorps, n.d.c). Its mission is to

> engage members in a year of full-time service to strengthen organizations that eliminate or alleviate poverty through the mobilization of community volunteers and resources. VISTA members establish systems, institutionalize knowledge, and develop community relationships to better generate resources, encourage volunteer service at the local level, and empower individuals and communities to lift themselves out of poverty. (AmeriCorps, n.d.c, n.p.)

Each year over 8,500 members, totaling 220,000 members since 1965, serve in VISTA in over 4,500 sites throughout the United States (AmeriCorps, 2018).

AmeriCorps VISTA supplies many benefits. It is a volunteer program and does not provide a salary to members. VISTA is not a residential program; however, it does provides a living allowance that will allow the member to live very frugally, similar to the community being served. An end-of-service award is made available either as an education award such as the Segal AmeriCorps Education Award or the end-of-service cash stipend (AmeriCorps, n.d.d).

AmeriCorps VISTA offers two healthcare options; one for VISTA members who already have coverage and one for those who do not. Travel assistance is offered to offset the cost of relocation, a settling-in allowance, service-related transportation reimbursement, and close-of-service travel (AmeriCorps, n.d.d).

The AmeriCorps VISTA program focuses on four main areas:

- Economic opportunity—members assist their community's access to knowledge about economic welfare through encouragement of financial literacy, job skills training, and safe and sound housing options, among other measures (AmeriCorps, n.d.e).

- Education—members work to improve literacy and encourage learners of all ages. Members working in this area may design and implement a GRE-preparedness class or make plans for a summer program for youth (AmeriCorps, n.d.e).
- Healthy Futures—VISTAs assist communities become happy and healthy by participating in programs that develop sustainable well-being practices. Potential activities might include implementing a program to help adults navigate healthcare options or search for resources and volunteers to build a community garden (AmeriCorps, n.d.e).
- Veterans and military families—VISTA's work to support veterans and military families through programming and outreach. They might develop outreach programs to homeless veterans or implement a program for children of deployed service members (AmeriCorps, n.d.e).

Peace Corps

Peace Corps is an international volunteer organization that was created in 1961 in response to an impromptu speech on October 14, 1960, by President John F. Kennedy at the University of Michigan in Ann Arbor (Peace Corps, n.d.b). The mission of the Peace Corps is to promote world peace and friendship (Peace Corps, n.d.a). While most of the volunteer assignments require a college degree, some will look for corresponding or equal experience in a desired field (Anderberg, 2019). Options for people with only a high school degree are limited; however, they do exist and require some research to find (Anderberg, 2019).

A volunteer, service, or gap year may help a student figure out what to do after high school, search for a new path, or look for and gain new skills and experience (Service Year, n.d.). Along with providing critical assistance to people in need, worthwhile causes and the community, volunteering has additional advantages for a student to consider (Top 10 Online Colleges, n.d).

Volunteer resources include:

- https://www.nationalservice.gov/programs/americorps
- https://www.nationalservice.gov/programs/americorps/americorps-programs/americorps-nccc
- https://www.peacecorps.gov/about/
- https://www.peacecorps.gov/volunteer/other-volunteering-opportunities/?_ga=2.152122809.1635502004.1556725503-148530208.1556725503
- https://serviceyear.org/about/what-is-service-year/
- https://gapyearassociation.org/about.php

FINAL THOUGHTS

Young men have many options moving forward after receiving their high school diploma or GED or, in some situations, simply leaving school. With guidance, these newly minted men will find the path that meets their needs. Whether they choose to go right to work in an entry-level job, start a business, learn a trade, join the military, volunteer, or take a gap year, each individual must consider what makes sense for him. College may cause an undue monetary burden for some students, making a job, trade school, or the military a natural next step; while others may see a service year or gap year as a viable option.

Entry-level jobs offer newcomers a chance to learn from the bottom up, and these jobs often lead to management positions for the hardworking individual. Starting a business takes some financial risk and hard work; yet it is doable if the individual is ready for the challenge as they often fail before they succeed. Going to a trade school, becoming an apprentice, or interning are all options for young men wishing to learn a craft. This hands-on method is often the preferred learning style for boys and men and sometimes provides benefits such as pay and insurance as well as a position upon graduation.

For some, volunteering or service work fill the void in their life as they search for what is next in their lives. These opportunities place young men in new and sometimes unusual circumstances where they are able to learn new skills, help others, and find out what they really want from life. There are both private and public organizations that can assist in finding a location for service work. A gap year can be either service or travel oriented. For those lucky enough to have travel as an option, finding ways to make it affordable is often the challenge. In the end, young men have many options for next steps if they decide college is not for them; however, guidance and support is key.

POINTS TO REMEMBER

- According to the Department of Labor, in 2019 more than 1 million young men aged sixteen to twenty-four were unemployed but looking for work while 9.6 million young men were employed with part- or full-time work.
- Young men can take on an entry-level job that may lead to managerial advancement. Starting at the bottom and working their way up to more responsibilities is often the key to success. This work requires soft skills such as leadership, problem solving, motivation, interpersonal communication, positivity, and efficiency, while also requiring hard skills such as computer and social media knowledge.

- Learning a trade through an apprenticeship or trade school offers the interested young man a chance to learn through a hands-on process. Some classroom time is necessary; however, the majority of work is completed on the job with a mentor.
- Joining the military offers young men a chance to see the world, build a résumé with both soft and hard skills, gain life experience, and amazing benefits that last a lifetime. The five branches of the military include the Army, Navy, Marines, Air Force, and Coast Guard, and all offer similar options in both part- and full-time work.
- Taking a gap year to travel or volunteer is another option. Those who travel may find it expensive and need to plan accordingly; however, the traveler may find a new location that interests him. Taking a volunteer year may help him to find new abilities or at the least provide a service to others.

Chapter Six

The Myth of Being a Macho Man

Aggression, Competition, Bullying, and Violence in Contemporary Society

In the past several years, increasing attention has been paid to masculinity and aggression (Berdahl, Cooper, Glick, Livingston, & Williams, 2018; Parent, Gobble, & Rochlen, 2018). Several movements have tried to address overly aggressive behaviors ranging from sexual assault to bullying; however, these efforts have met with pushback in the form of counter-movements that pressed back against anti-rape activism and feminism (Johnson & Cousineau, 2018). In the face of a society adopting changing beliefs regarding what constitutes acceptable masculinity, many college-aged men have taken to joining online communities in order to support their existing beliefs about masculinity.

Some men have come to think of themselves as victims and have coalesced into movements such as Gamergate (Salter, 2017). In some cases, they have found leaders and a national voice in the form of men like Yiannopoulous, an activist who perpetuated Gamergate; however, not all men have responded to this cultural change by retreating into groups that support their views (Ford, 2019). In other cases, some men have struggled to integrate multiple views and construct their own definition of masculinity. Defining masculinity and gender norms is important as it underlies aggressive behavior, which manifests in several contexts from sexual aggression to bullying; however, addressing gender norms is complicated by the ease with which young men can now find communities that reject the cultural changes currently occurring (Ford, 2019).

SEXUAL AGGRESSION

Consent has become an increasingly important concept in modern sexual relations between men and women (Brogaard, 2018). The concept of sexual consent refers to an active agreement between two partners, each letting the other know that sex is, or is not, wanted (Brogaard, 2018). If there is no consent, then the sexual activity is considered either rape or sexual assault (Brogaard, 2018). There are several principles that form the basis of sexual consent. When relations are desired between two consenting adults, then the decision is made without manipulation, and each partner can feel free to change his or her mind at any point during the act (Brogaard, 2018). Consent also requires honesty between both partners, and each partner should be specific about what they want. A person, for example, may want to perform certain acts of foreplay but not want full sexual intercourse. Consent requires two adults who can make fully informed decisions about what they want to do.

The importance of consent has only grown in an era of #MeToo, a movement originally founded in 2006 to help survivors of different types of sexual violence (MeToo, 2018). Although founded in 2006, its popularity grew in later years thanks to advocacy efforts of celebrities and the ability of social media networks to bring together rape and assault survivors (Johnson & Hawbaker, 2019). The #MeToo movement was conceived as a means of providing resources to all survivors and building supportive communities as well as to help remove the stigma surrounding survival, with the hope of encouraging more people to come forward and share their stories of survival (Johnson & Hawbaker, 2019). By doing this, the #MeToo movement was meant to make the issue of sexual violence more prominent and educate the public about the importance of consent.

An important part of the growing prominence of consent is that understanding of the concept plays a strong role in influencing sexual aggression among college males (Warren, Swan, & Allen, 2015). A critical issue facing college campuses is that of sexual assault. Data drawn from the Sexual Victimization of College Women Study (Morgan & Kena, 2018) indicated that there were 27.7 attempts or completed rapes for every 1,000 female students in a single academic year; however, this statistic should also be considered alongside the fact that rape is underreported. Several reports found that rape, specifically, went unreported in up to 80 percent of all cases (Morgan & Kena, 2018). This was not a new finding. Underreporting trends were also found in an analysis of violent crime that was conducted in 2016 (Truman & Morgan, 2018). As such, even well-conducted surveys run a risk of underestimating just how prevalent sexual assault is on college campuses.

At a minimum, the Sexual Victimization of College Women Study (Morgan & Kena, 2018) put a rough number on how many women were raped, or nearly raped, on college campuses, and consent seemed to play a role in whether men committed these acts (Warren et al., 2015). The issue of why men commit sexual assault has been studied for decades, with many theorizing that sexual assault acts were committed by those who lacked concern for the rights of others or out of disregard for boundaries (Murphy, 2017). These individuals may want to assert dominance over others. In other cases, individuals might commit acts of sexual assault because they misinterpreted cues when they were with another person and, consequently, disregarded their rights (Shpancer, 2016). Men who perpetrated sexual assault were more likely to have misunderstood cues from women and to have perceived them as being open to having sex versus those men who did not commit acts of sexual violence (Murphy, 2017; Shpancer, 2016).

An understanding of consent requires individuals to come to a better-developed understanding about the boundaries and rights of others (Warren et al., 2015). Those men who committed sexual assault tended to hold beliefs that supported rape, sexually aggressive behavior, and a misunderstanding of masculine norms (Shpancer, 2016). They often surrounded themselves with peer groups that reinforced those beliefs. Researchers found in their studies of college men, that as their beliefs shifted, and specifically when their comprehension of sexual consent improved, they were less likely to become perpetrators of sexual assault (Warren et al., 2015). College men who responded to a study of sexual behavior reported a variety of beliefs about sexual behavior; however, when the lack of understanding regarding the concept of consent was low, men were far more likely to have committed some sort of sexual assault in just the previous four months (Warren et al., 2015).

Such a study is indicative of the importance of the #MeToo movement and the role that informing the public of consent could play in influencing sexually aggressive behaviors. The growing role of movements like #MeToo has emboldened victims of sexual assault to come forward. For instance, the FBI reported an almost 20 percent increase in reported rapes between 2013 and 2018 (U.S. Department of Justice, 2018). Consequently, the culture has slowly changed to become more receptive to victims telling their stories. College-age men who have integrated the principles of consent are least likely to commit acts of sexual assault; yet there continue to be those men who hold beliefs that support acts of sexual assault, and who have peers who support their position (Warren et al., 2015). These beliefs have partially coalesced under the banner of the men's rights movement which, though not strictly limited to college-aged males, is present and active on college campuses (Gotell & Dutton, 2016).

Men's rights websites often attempt to reframe the existing discussions on consent, and definitions of rape, to take the focus off men or explicitly reject feminist issues and current ideas regarding consent (Gotell & Dutton, 2016). Men who subscribe to the movement often frame discussions surrounding rape as a false panic perpetuated by feminists, and that false allegations of sexual assault are widespread. These claims are made despite official statistics pinning false accusations at no more than 10 percent of all claims and also being as low as 2 percent of these claims (National Sexual Violence Resource Center, 2018).

The antifeminism reaction typified by men's rights activists has pushed back against the anti-rape messaging sent by feminists (Gotell & Dutton, 2016). Men's rights proponents, for instance, have tried to undermine anti-sexual violence campaigns hosted on college campuses. At the University of Edmonton, a campaign was launched using ads to challenge norms that encouraged feelings that men were entitled to sex in various circumstances (Gotell & Dutton, 2016). This message was spread through posters across the campus to counter this anti-sexual violence message. Men's rights activities made copycat posters that distorted these messages and played up the notion that women often made false allegations of sexual misconduct against men (Gotell & Dutton, 2016). These posters were also shared among men's rights websites and their followers (Gotell & Dutton, 2016).

This initial pushback against the University of Edmonton's anti-sexual violence campaign launched further research into how men's rights activists were responding to messages about consent (Gotell & Dutton, 2016). Researchers became victims of the activists who created misleading articles or messaged the researchers in attempts to intimidate and silence them. This was part of a larger movement that pushed back against anti-rape feminism. A common tactic was to exaggerate the position of feminists in an attempt to make those positions seem ridiculous (Gotell & Dutton, 2016).

The men's rights movement has shifted its focus to young, college-aged men (Gotell & Dutton, 2016). Where it previously focused on older men and fathers, particularly focusing on the issue of parental custody following divorce, men's rights activists have now begun to recruit male students from colleges (Gotell & Dutton, 2016). The primary topic discussed by these activists is no longer fatherhood and parental custody, but male sexual behavior and false accusations of rape (Gotell & Dutton, 2016). The movement has found fertile ground for discussing these issues among college-going men because so much discussion has been occurring on college campuses about rape and the responsibilities that men have to respect the boundaries of others. Part of the focus of men's rights groups has been on shifting definitions of sexual assault (Gotell & Dutton, 2016).

By restricting the definition of sexual assault to the strictest definitions of rape, these activists attempt to downplay how pervasive sexual assault really is; however, assault by physical force is not the only means of committing sexual assault. Sexual assault is defined as forced contact of a sexual nature inflicted upon another who has not given consent (Basile, Smith, Breiding, Black, & Mahendra, 2014). Men who employ sexual assault tactics are likely to use a variety when attempting to acquire sex (Zinzow & Thompson, 2014). Longitudinal research indicated that 13 percent of sexual assaults among college men consisted of verbal coercion, 16 percent consisted of taking advantage of incapacitated women, and only 5 percent used physical force (Zinzow & Thompson, 2014). By attempting to eliminate the definition of sexual assault that includes verbal coercion and sex with incapacitated individuals, men's rights activists try to make the issue seem smaller than it actually is (Zinzow & Thompson, 2014).

This focus has caused the spread of many erroneous ideas (Gotell & Dutton, 2016). Rape is not very rare, and men and women are not roughly equivalent in their victimization (Basile et al., 2014). By the numbers, women are overwhelmingly targeted and victimized by sexual assailants, while men, in contrast, are disproportionately the assailants (Basile et al., 2014). This pushback against feminism and issues of consent framed men as targets and the real victims. Such notions were mirrored by men who claimed that feminism led to double standards that held men to certain standards that women were not (Hackman, 2016).

In interviews, men reported feeling that women were granted unfair advantages and anecdotal testimonies indicated they felt that women could commit acts of violence against men that they would not be held accountable for (Hackman, 2016). Others complained that they felt society was somehow angry at them for being born male, while still others reported feeling bad for men, or feeling as if women were taking over the world (Hackman, 2016). Such opinions, which indicated that women were in more advantageous positions than men, flew in the face of statistical evidence demonstrating that men occupied a privileged position. Men's opinions ranged from them being held to a double standard to women who were actually privileged over men (Hackman, 2016). Such beliefs reflected the kind of frustration and framing of men as victims that men's rights activism mirrored.

Education efforts are ongoing as activists continue to try to teach the public about sexual assault and rape; yet reducing attitudes that are supportive of sexual violence may be difficult to deal with. Researchers have identified a boomerang effect that occurs in men, in which exposure to materials designed to teach them about women's preferences actually demonstrated increased sexual aggression (Bosson, Parrott, Swan, Kuchynka, & Schramm, 2015). This phenomenon occurred among men who already demonstrated hostile sexist attitudes rather than those who had non-hostile attitudes (Bosson et al., 2015). As such, it remains an open question concerning just how effective education efforts might be in reducing those attitudes among college-going men.

It should be noted that the pushback against discussions surrounding consent did not occur in a vacuum; rather, they were part of broader discussions happening in the culture regarding feminism and what role men occupied in the world (Kalra & Bhugra, 2013). Many of the same issues raised by men regarding consent were also raised against feminism as a whole, and young men found a unified voice with which to reinforce their existing ideas of masculinity, thanks to the internet (Schmitz & Kazyak, 2016).

ANTI-FEMINISM

The dialogue surrounding consent and rape is bound up in a larger discussion of men pushing back against feminism. Part of this pushback was made evident in the Gamergate controversy that emerged in 2014 (Ford, 2019). Outwardly, Gamergate claimed to be about honesty in videogame reporting; however in practice, the movement involved the harassment of women in the video game industry (Ford, 2019). Gamergate proponents harassed women in the gaming industry; most notably it targeted two developers, Zoe Quinn and Brianna Wu as well as media critic Anita Sarkeesian as the most prominent victims of the controversy (Valenti, 2017).

This controversy began in response to a series of feminism-related events that occurred almost simultaneously beginning in 2013. That year, Quinn released a video game that depicted depression in gaming, drawing from her own real-life experiences (Kidd & Turner, 2016).

This sparked pushback from those who claimed it was an attempt to politicize games and an effort to reduce the need for skills or violence in gaming. Following the game's release, Quinn was harassed, with violent threats made against her, her family, and her supporters (Valenti, 2017). Those who harassed her falsely believed that her game had received favorable reviews from a game reviewer that she was in a sexual relationship with at the time (Valenti, 2017). This was targeted harassment that occurred over chat software and using online forums.

Simultaneously, Anita Sarkeesian was also targeted. Sarkeesian had previously been a subject of harassment due to her work describing women's tropes in gaming, with a specific emphasis on how women were often portrayed in sexist stereotypes (Kolhatkar, 2014). The threats leveled against Sarkeesian became so overwhelming that she was forced to cancel public speaking engagements (Kolhatkar, 2014). Threats of mass violence against the crowd of attendees listening to Sarkeesian forced these cancellations.

Gamergate also involved independent game developer Brianna Wu, who was also targeted with threats of rape and violence (Wingfield, 2014). Critics of Gamergate were also targeted with threats and harassment (Hern, 2015). These threats forced the victims to withdraw from public engagements out of security concerns. Some women noted that they feared even voicing support for people like Wu, Sarkeesian, and Quinn (Hern, 2015; Ito, 2015). Actress Felicia Day voiced these fears and immediately had her private information posted online in retaliation, leading to threatening phone calls (Hathaway, 2014a).

The actions of Gamergate proponents have been part of the normalization of cultural violence against women (Gray, Buyukozturk, & Hill, 2017). Video gaming was, for decades, a male-dominated industry with products created for men. Women portrayed in video games fit into stereotypical gender norms and were often in need of saving while men were portrayed as strong saviors equipped with extensive weaponry (Gray at al., 2017). The structure of gaming was such that women were portrayed in places of unequal power. Attempts to disrupt this narrative created a backlash, thereby reinforcing the notion that women should occupy established spaces rather than move out of those spaces (Gray et al., 2017).

To varying degrees, the pushback against feminism in gaming has found an audience among college men. This is exemplified in Yiannopoulous, who was one of the earliest journalists to cover the Gamergate controversy (Ford, 2019). This coverage was largely in favor of those who were pro-Gamergate, and Yiannopoulous (2014) argued that video gaming culture was being invaded by "sociopathic feminist programmers" (n.p.). His coverage of the movement included the publication of private discussions used by game journalists in an attempt to discredit journalists who were anti-Gamergate (Ford, 2019).

As part of his efforts, Yiannopoulous also began speaking on college campuses. Often hosted by College Republican organizations, he was skilled at harnessing the anger of young men (Rouner, 2017). Yiannopoulous legitimized the positions of these individuals and gave them a collective voice. After becoming an editor at Breitbart, he was able to give more of a voice to these individuals and broadcast their views even further (Bernstein, 2017). To further consolidate his appeal among his college fans, Yiannopoulous established a college grant for white men, stating that they were underprivileged (Wojcik, 2017). In this statement, Yiannopoulous also blended the anti-feminist position he had become famous for with elements of racism (Bernstein, 2017; Wojcik, 2017). While Gamergate launched Yiannopoulous's career on an anti-feminism position, he integrated racial elements to specifically appeal to white males on college campuses. Yiannopoulous's argument was that men made up only 43 percent of the college population and yet women unfairly portrayed themselves as victims (Nash, 2017). This mirrored sentiments among college men that women were actually privileged and increasingly dominating society, placing men as the true victims (Hackman, 2016).

The importance of gaming to the constructions of masculinity should not be underestimated, given that games seem to have a significant influence on views of what is masculine (Blackburn & Scharrer, 2018). Both men and women who favor violent video games are more likely to characterize masculinity using aggressive traits, including toughness, dominance, and the suppression of feelings and emotions (Blackburn & Scharrer, 2018). It may be that this influence is why gaming culture has lent itself to the development of hypermasculinity. Young men, faced with violations of these norms, have retreated to groups such as the Gamergate movement that endorse beliefs that support aggressive masculine traits (Blackburn & Scharrer, 2018).

Consent and feminism are only two areas in which gender norms influence male behavior. Although not clearly obvious at first, gender norms and constructions of masculinity actually impact aggressive behaviors in several ways. The role of masculine identity, therefore, cannot be separated from bullying.

BULLYING AND AGGRESSION

The discussion surrounding gender norms often involves discussion about consent and feminism; however, gender norms also play a role in the act of bullying (Horn, 2007). Studies on tenth and twelfth grade adolescents revealed that if a person adhered to gender norms, this predicted whether they were considered acceptable to their peers (Horn, 2007). Gay and lesbian individuals were considered more acceptable when their appearance and mannerisms adhered to gender norms. Deviation from those norms was considered less acceptable. Notably, even when a boy was straight, he was rated as less acceptable than both gender conforming and non-conforming homosexual boys (Horn, 2017). This indicated the role of gender conformity to boys being considered acceptable among their peers (Horn, 2007). This was consistent with reports by boys of being bullied more often than girls (PREVNet, 2019). In studies across forty countries, and among multiple age groups, boys were more likely to become bullies, and more likely physically victimized (PREVNet, 2019).

One form of bullying, and specifically using the word "fag" to describe others, was also associated with conformity to gender norms (Rosenberg, Gates, Richmond, & Sinno, 2017). Not only did perceptions of male gender norms affect how acceptable people found the word "fag" to be, but also those same perceptions affected whether people believed teachers or peers should intervene when the word was used (Rosenberg et al., 2017). This suggested a connection between ideas of what constituted masculinity and homophobic responses (Rosenberg et al., 2017).

Given that homosexual individuals report being bullied at a higher rate than their heterosexual peers, addressing gender norms and stereotypes held by individuals may help address bullying of others (Rosenberg et al., 2017). Understanding gender norms may be important not only for understanding their role in sexual assault, but also in bullying. There are online communities where these norms can be reinforced; therefore, it may be difficult to address the underlying factors supporting aggressive behaviors toward both men and women (Gotell & Dutton, 2016).

Men sometimes act in ways that they are socialized to. Hegemonic masculinity suggests that there are ways men are socialized to believe they should feel and act, since such thoughts and behaviors are associated with the male gender (Leone & Parrott, 2019). They learn these acceptable behaviors and thoughts from numerous sources and then they are reinforced through the praise of their peers. Behaviors and thoughts that are not accepted as typical of masculinity are punished through disapproval, leaving only a few emotions and reactions available as acceptable; anger becomes the emotion considered acceptable by many men (Leone & Parrott, 2019). Hegemonic masculinity has been associated with numerous forms of aggression, ranging from aggression toward intimate partners to a variety of forms of psychological aggression (Leone & Parrott, 2019).

Gender norms, and how individuals conceive of masculinity, affect how they treat others. This effect is particularly prominent among boys, who find it less acceptable when other boys do not conform to gender norms. Adherence to those norms also impact how acceptable young men find it to be aggressive; however, masculinity is not a concrete concept. Young men are constantly defining masculinity as they try to combine examples set for them by role models with information they get from the media and other sources in a complex negotiation process.

NEGOTIATING MASCULINITY

The response to a changing world in which the definition of masculinity is being negotiated does not always result in college men retreating into groups that push back against consent advocates or feminists. In some cases, men become interested in creating a masculine identity that shifts away from characteristics that are violent and aggressive (Derraugh, 2018). For many men, family figures form the first role models for what defines masculinity. Fathers, grandfathers, uncles, and brothers all fill this role.

Older role model figures have an influence; not only because of how they conduct themselves, but also because of the "entertainment" they allow young boys access to; consequently, young men draw upon the patterns established by older men to define their masculinity (Derraugh, 2018). One study looked at how masculinity was defined and included identifying times when aggressive behavior was acceptable (Derraugh, 2018). Young men arrived at their answers by drawing upon the examples set by older men and examples they saw in the media (Derraugh, 2018).

These negotiations of masculine identities did not always go smoothly; for instance, men sometimes demonstrated frustration with arguments surrounding rape culture, demonstrating a lack of understanding between rape and hook-up cultures (Derraugh, 2018). This phenomenon occurred even among young men who wanted to move away from violent masculine identities, revealing additional clarification and understanding may sometimes be all that is necessary to support these young men in the establishment of their masculine identities (Derraugh, 2018).

Family members are among the earliest influencers on masculinity and identity; however, college men are influenced highly by their peers (Derraugh, 2018; Snyder, 2018). Individuals may become more receptive to new messages when a peer influences them. Interviews revealed that young men often became more receptive to hearing even difficult messages when their preconceived ideas about tough issues, such as sexual assault, were challenged by members of their peer group (Snyder, 2018).

The impact of peers was magnified when the individual speaking out or wielding influence carried increased social capital, indicating the outsized influence that an influential male peer could have on the attitudes of others (Snyder, 2018). It should not be surprising that respected elders had a key influential role in the lives of these younger men; for instance, young men reported the influence of their sports coaches (Snyder, 2018). These coaches carried the social capital and respect necessary to influence younger men, encouraging their participation in various events and even influencing their beliefs. For young men negotiating their masculinity, positive influence from peers and respected superiors may play an important role (Snyder, 2018).

FINAL THOUGHTS

Male aggression is rooted in a number of sources. Role models, peers, media, and existing stereotypes all exert an influence on how individuals construct their masculinity; however, how college-aged men respond in the face of these influences varies greatly. There are young men who work toward constructing forms of masculinity that eschew violence, even if they struggle to fully understand cultural shifts happening around them.

There are communities into which a segment of young men can retreat. These communities marginalize the positions of feminists and reinforce the importance of traditional gender norms of masculinity. With the support of these communities, young men adhere to gender norms that encourage aggression. These same communities support these men in pushing back against anti-rape activism and feminist activists. This pushback can become quite hostile, which is consistent with findings that hegemonic masculinity is tied to many different forms of aggression. Shifting beliefs regarding what construes masculinity may help to address this aggression; however, doing so may be difficult given that online communities are available that can reinforce existing beliefs regarding masculinity and the appropriateness of aggression.

POINTS TO REMEMBER

- Consent is a concept that refers to an agreement between two people; thus, sexual assault occurs when one person is being forced into an act they have not agreed to. As male aggression at college becomes a critical issue, rates of sexual assault rise.
- The men's rights movement is focusing on male sexual behavior and falsified rape allegations at the college level. Activists have launched campaigns to challenge the norms that currently exist surrounding the entitlement of sex by college men.
- Women gamers have been bullied and harassed by their male counterparts who see them as a threat to the video game being played. This bullying has extended to family members and friends and can be found in online forums and other means.
- Gender norms play a role in bullying as those who are gay or lesbian and appeared more like their gender were likely to be accepted by their peers; whereas, those who were more flamboyant or acted against gender appearance norms were more likely to be bullied.
- Hegemonic masculinity suggests that men are socialized to feel and act a particular way that is associated with the male gender. Atypical behaviors may lead to aggressive behaviors.
- Older men play a pivotal role in guiding young men to become more positive and accepting of the attitudes and actions of others.

Chapter Seven

Being Batman

Media Portrayals of Masculine Behavior

Men and boys receive almost constant messages about masculinity from all types of media. A leading source of influence, the media system is powerful, pervasive, and provides a steady stream of images that connect dominance, power, and control with being a man (Jhally et al., 1999). Although this cuts across all ethnic and social groups, it is more noticeable for men of color due to a lack of "diversity of image for them, to begin with—for example, Latino men are almost always presented as boxers, criminals, or tough guys in the barrio, and Asian-American men are disproportionately portrayed as martial artists and violent criminals" (Jhally et al., 1999, p. 4).

Over the course of time, men have been pigeonholed as one type of individual or another. Each period in time placed a different set of gender expectations on the unsuspecting male who was expected to conform to a set of metrics he may or may not have felt able or comfortable adhering to. These gender expectations brought to light the strong man (pre-industrial revolution), the absent man (industrial revolution), the money man (post–World War II), the emotional man (the sexual revolution and 1960s), the wonderful man (1980s), the modern man (2000), and most recently the grounded male (Ferebee, 2018). What is clear, though, is that each time frame also placed the male as the leader and provider, although this looked very different for each one.

For the most part, though, men in the media have been portrayed as macho, metrosexual, or overly amorous; yet a 2012 study of over 2,000 men aged eighteen to forty-nine proved that the male species has been misrepresented (Casserly, 2012). While the modern "grounded" man is willing to trade career advancement for family time and shop successfully unassisted in the grocery store, media portrayal continues to pigeon-hole men as being inept at relationships and family pursuits (Casserly, 2012). Men in the study listed their top three characteristics as being well rounded, a good friend, and good-hearted (Kassan, 2012). Break Media, the author of the study and, "the largest creator and distributor of male targeted content online" (Kassan, 2012), called this new breed of man "modern mensches" a term that means having character, dignity, and honor (Merriam-Webster, 2019).

The Acumen study (Kassan, 2012) found that at least half the men surveyed were "participating in traditionally non-male dominated tasks" (n.p.). These men felt no threat to their masculinity and, in fact, 55 percent of respondents would have welcomed a situation where they were the full-time caregiver (Kassan, 2012). This is a departure from the traditional perceived portrayal of men, and it is occurring on the big screen, the small screen, the internet, and on paper. In order to see the future of men in the media, it is necessary to look back and understand the beginnings of how gender norms took hold.

IT ALL BEGAN WITH THE AMERICAN COWBOY

The film industry began in in the 1830s with images seen in rapid succession, and although it was very rudimentary, it made quite an impression on the masses. Almost fifty years later, live action was added to movies and the first image was a horse galloping (Cook & Sklar, 2019). Every ten years or so, a novel idea would be added to the mix to include celluloid roll film and light (Cook & Sklar, 2019). By the late 1890s, Edison and his team had developed the Kinetoscope, a "continuous 47-foot (14-metre) film loop [that] ran on spools between an incandescent lamp" (Cook & Sklar, 2019, n.p.). There were continuous adaptations and changes made to Kinetoscope over time.

The early 1900s became a hotbed for cinematic creations and there were approximately "20 motion-picture companies operating in the United States" (Cook & Sklar, 2019, n.p.). In order to ensure dominance, the largest companies merged into the Motion Picture Patents Company and gave Eastman Kodak an exclusive contract for raw film (Cook & Sklar, 2019). It was after this that silent movies were introduced to the world. Even in silent movies, male dominance was seen and perpetuated; however, the advent of the American cowboy clearly solidified the concept (Modello, 2014).

The American cowboy could be seen in a multitude of movies made between 1930 and the late 1990s. During the 1930s, the film industry had banned drunkenness, sex, immorality, and revenge, leaving the filmmaker with the American cowboy (Manhas, 2018). Although industry control slowly died by the 1950s, John Wayne, Clint Eastwood, and the like provided the macho behavior that defined the male gender role of the times (Metcalf,

2017). These cowboys were not just visions of working men, they offered a lens into conflict between men and the social implications of being a man (Leith, 2002; Metcalf, 2017).

John Ford, director, and John Wayne, actor, created more than twenty movies together, including three deemed as "the best and most important Hollywood films ever made" (Metcalf, 2017, n.p.). According to Schoenberger (2017), Ford and Wayne defined "an ideal of American masculinity that dominated for nearly half a century" (p. 16). What is questionable, however, is if this ideal actually existed in real life or if this was a fabricated vision that men could not ascribe to (Metcalf, 2017).

Men did not cry in movies during this time period either. The stoic man was "characterized by . . . emotional impenetrability and solidification in their masculine identities" (Lotterhos, 2015). These men, portrayed by actors such as Humphrey Bogart and Sylvester Stallone, chose violence over tears in each character they played on screen (Lotterhos, 2015). If men were to be the ones with power and control, surely women were the weaker more passive species. This notion of the strong man, therefore, is perpetuated in film and other media over and over again leading to a "myriad of social problems, injustices, and hurtful behavioral tendencies" (Lotterhos, 2015, p. 4).

Each generation of the film industry has its own version of the toxic male (Lotterhos, 2015). For the most part, these men optimize the "white, heterosexual, perfectly sculpted, heroic, stoic, hyper-masculine character who faces conflict, doesn't give up, saves the day, gets the girl, and 'seals the deal' through procreation or marriage" (Lotterhos, 2015). It should come as no surprise that the majority of these films are created and directed by white, heterosexual men, and so the problem persists. There are a multitude of movie examples in which toxic masculinity is clearly portrayed and modeled; however, a sampling would include:

- John Wayne made a number of films, including *The Searchers*, in which he played a macho cowboy who used violence to solve issues (Metcalf, 2017).
- Movies such as *Rocky*, *Raging Bull*, and *The Terminator* all have main characters who embody the hyper-masculine stereotype.
- In *Back to the Future*, the main character is sent back in time to re-masculinize his father who has been continuously bullied by another character (Lotterhos, 2015).
- *Mad Max: Fury Road* in which toxic masculinity is directly at odds with a productive and healthy masculine lead and where the heroes "use their strength to support and build" (Han, 2015, n.p.).
- *Brokeback Mountain* gives legitimacy to men falling in love with each other (Bradshaw, 2006). Rejecting patriarchal ideas, the main characters

are able to "love, lose, win, fail, and be proud in spite of troubling stereotypes" (Manhas, 2018, n.p.).

Even Disney movies pose a threat to masculinity as they portray men in a variety of negative ways. All Disney movies involve heterosexual men who are either interested in finding a woman to share their life with, or they want no woman at all and are perceived as selfish as in the character Kuzco in *The Emperor's New Groove* (Kritselis, 2014). Men are expected to save women from a myriad of conditions from coma to personal calamity; and then women magically love them even if they are cruel as in *Snow White* or the Beast from *Beauty and the Beast* (Kritselis, 2014; Rosenberg, 2011).

Men are tasked with being in superhuman shape; however, if they are not "exquisitely handsome physical specimens" (Kritselis, 2014, n.p.) they are buffoons or evil characters with no redeeming qualities such as Hercules or Chien-Po from *Mulan* (Chen, 2017; Rosenberg, 2011). Fathers, for the most part, are mean and tyrannical, or fat and useless—the sultan father from *Aladdin* (Chen, 2017; Kritselis, 2014). The cards are clearly stacked against portraying men in a positive light with attainable qualities and all at the expense of the next generation of Disney movie watchers.

AND THEN CAME TELEVISION

The modern television was first demonstrated in 1927 when a screen projected an image of a single line that had come from radio waves (Stephens, n.d.). By the early 1940s two networks were showing rudimentary pictures including "two 15-minute newscasts a day" (Stephens, n.d., n.p.). Television gave all of America a lens into traditional masculine roles and responsibilities soon after it aired in 1947 (Stephens, n.d.; Thompson & Allen, 2017). Within five years, shows that had once graced the radio waves were on the screen showing strong male leads such as *The Lone Ranger* and *Man Against Crime* (Thompson & Allen, 2017).

At about the same time, the sitcom was born, which brought a bevy of characters—some of whom exuded toxic masculinity, while others were mensch worthy (Thompson & Allen, 2017). Today's male lead characters in television shows are a mix of buffoonery, masculinity, and common sense.

- *All in the Family* covered "controversial themes such as race relations, homosexuality, and feminism" (Cohen, 2018, n.p.); yet the main character, Archie Bunker, was extremely bigoted.

- *Last Man Standing* and *Modern Family* both portray the men as inept and the women as all-knowing. These examples only serve to solidify the societal mores in which women are viewed as "ruling the roost" and men viewed as bumbling fools (Casserly, 2012).

These examples identify sitcoms on current television programming that attempt to showcase the grounded male; that is, one who lives with balance and purpose, equal parts empathy and grit (Ferebee, 2018).

- *A Different World* and *Family Matters* offer examples of positive masculine characters (Smith, 2014).
- *Parenthood* introduces the viewer to a single man who fancies himself a playboy and suddenly finds out he is a father. He struggles with doing what is right (Casserly, 2012).
- In *Guys with Kids*, three men with children try to navigate fatherhood.

These are baby steps toward honest depictions of men in the twenty-first century and they help to create new expectations for both men and women in terms of work, relationships, and parenting (Casserly, 2012).

Cartoons and children's programming also depict men in unfavorable light and promote gender stereotypes (Knorr, 2017). Citing a report by Common Sense Media, Campbell (2017) explains that "male characters are depicted as strong, emotionally restrained, risk-taking leaders (who also get to be funny), while females are agreeable, virtuous, demure, and primarily concerned with their physical appearance (and much more likely to be shown crying" (n.p.).

These sexist shows produce another generation of boys and girls who are at risk for "developing sexist attitudes" (Campbell, 2017). Examples of gender stereotyped shows include the *Smurfs* in which there is only one female character, and *Paw Patrol* where out of the six main characters, only one is female and although the mayor is female, "she comes off as bumbling and inept" (Campbell, 2017).

As counters to these sexist and male dominated shows, Campbell (2017) offers up developmentally appropriate shows such as *Daniel Tiger's Neighborhood* (a spin-off of *Mr. Rogers' Neighborhood*), *Sesame Street*, *Little Einsteins*, and *Doc McStuffins*. These programs portray mixed gender groups, stay-at-home dads, female doctors, adopted children, and much more. In addition to appropriate viewing, discussions with children surrounding gender stereotypes is vital in the fight against toxic masculinity. At least one study found that these types of conversations led to a "greater acceptance of non-traditional gender roles" (Nathanson, Wilson, McGee, & Sebastian, 2006).

ADVERTISING: PRINT AND MEDIA

When looking at gender norms in the media, it is important to remember that so-called masculine traits will focus on achievement and assertiveness, while female traits will focus on modesty and cooperation (Maestripieri, 2012). A study by Goffman (1979), showed that there were gender representations in advertising that fell into six distinct groups to include:

- Relative size: Women are shown to be smaller or shorter than men;
- Feminine touch: Refers to a loose touch of an object or a man by the woman, also includes self-touch; for example, when a women puts her hand loosely to her neck or collar bones;
- Function ranking: In pictures, where individuals are placed shows hierarchy, for example, the children may be in the background while the father figure is front and center;
- Family: Relationships are drawn on gender lines; therefore, fathers and sons are shown doing things together as are mothers and daughters;
- Ritualization of subordination: Men are shown to be larger, on top, or of more importance then women; and
- Licensed withdraw: Women are not shown completely and/or they may be looking into the distance as if uninterested.

Signoretti (2017) took this study from the 1970s, updated it using advertisements from 2006, and asked if Goffman's (1979) strongest gender stereotypes had survived or disappeared.

For the most part, between 1979 and 2006 gender stereotypes still existed in advertisements, although some female stereotypes vanquished (Signoretti, 2017). More importantly, the overall message from this study was that both men and women should be critical decoders of the subliminal messages that advertising subjects them to on a daily basis (Signoretti, 2017).

One source of hidden clues, implicit information, that influences children's knowledge of gender presentation and behavior through media is television commercials. The vocabulary used in these commercials differs greatly according to the targeted gender. After analyzing the most commonly used words in children's toy ads, Smith (2011b) developed word clouds with the most commonly used words in television ads for children's toys by gender. The difference in word usage is striking in its reinforcement of traditional, stereotypical gender roles. Boys chose words such as battle, power, heroes, transform, and stealth; while girls opted for words such as love, magic, friendship, change, and fun (Smith, 2011b).

The average adult is assaulted by more than 4,000 advertisements in an average day (Simpson, 2017). For men, this may be cologne, clothing, cars and trucks, food and beverage, or sports; while for women this may be perfume, clothing, hair products, and diet foods (Kailing & Cantrell, 2014). Advertising, therefore, creates a cyclical effect where masculinity is modeled for viewers and then exhibited by the same men who watched the advertisements to begin with. This further cements toxic masculinity in the very being of the unsuspecting male. Regardless of whether the advertisement is in print, on the television, or the internet, considering gender norms and masculinity is necessary.

Although print ads have become somewhat passé, magazines, newspapers, and the like have had a prominent role in the perpetuation of toxic masculinity. As far back as the Marlboro man, who "epitomized resilience, self-sufficiency, independence, and free enterprise" (Shirk, 2015, n.p.), print ads held the power to dictate what it meant to be male. This was further influenced by advertising that placed the female squarely in a domestic setting such as cleaning the floor or washing the dishes (Catt, 2014). The dichotomy was stark and undeniable, and it was perpetuated over and over again for several decades.

TV commercials provide a view into both masculinity and femininity. Most recently, Gillette Corporation aired a commercial titled "We Believe" based off their tagline of "the best men can get" (Dryfuss, 2019; Mitovitch, 2019). It spends an uncomfortable amount of time shining light on toxic masculinity only to say at the end,

> Something has finally changed, and there will be no going back, because we believe in the best in men . . . to say the right thing, to act the right way . . . Some already are, in ways big and small . . . but some is not enough. Because the boys watching today . . . will be the men of tomorrow. (Gillette, 2019, n.p.)

This statement, then, becomes the battle cry of the twenty-first-century male with a new definition of what it means to be a good man. Taking it further, as part of "The Best Men Can Be" campaign, Gillette will be donating substantial funds to organizations that "inspire, educate and help men of all ages achieve their personal 'best' and become role models for the next generation" (Mitovitch, 2019, n.p.).

Advertising has not, however, kept up with the need for male representation in all arenas as there is a visible absence of transgender and gay people, which is clearly exacerbated by the beer drinking, shaving, perfect male (Exon & Arrow, 2015). In a recent study from Omnicom Management Group (Marketing Charts, 2018), 39 percent of consumers reported that "advertising does not accurately represent all genders," while "30% felt that brands misrepresent them and their gender" (n.p.). These statistics describe the struggles of advertising where stable brands may risk alienating current customers in order to appeal to potential customers and appease a variety of gender groups (Marketing Charts, 2018).

At least four Snickers commercials boast a whiny female who changes into a man when he eats a Snickers chocolate bar. The slogan is, "You're not you when you're hungry" (Haymarket Media Group, 2016). In each commercial the whiny female is either deemed dopey, weak, or cranky and needs the chocolate bar to turn into a "real" man. Miller, the global head of strategy for Mars, went so far as to exclaim, "there are universal symptoms that can prevent a man from living up to the male code" (Haymarket Media Group, 2016, n.p.). This suggests that the male code includes characteristics such as boundless energy, superhuman strength, and unbridled social skills; yet those skills can be attributed to any human who possesses them (Haymarket Media Group, 2016).

In another example, a recent deodorant advertisement for Old Spice shows a seemingly naked cowboy covered in bubbles sitting on a horse while a woman wrapped only in a towel looks on from the side (Barber & Bridges, 2017). In this particular case, the "advertisement identifies a potentially deficient man and offers a solution to shore up his masculinity" (Barber & Bridges, 2017, p. 39). The problem, however, is that who is to say this man, or any man for that matter, is deficient and why must his masculinity be bolstered? Perhaps he is as comfortable as the next man.

THE MASCULINE WORLD AS SEEN THROUGH THE INTERNET AND VIDEO GAMES

There is evidence that the internet gender gap actually favors men and leaves 12 percent of women lacking the possible benefits of using the internet in OECD countries, and as many as 32 percent in less developed countries (Chakravorti, 2017). This number translates into approximately 200 million fewer women on the internet at any time (World Wide Web Foundation, 2015). When they are connected, they are often the victims of threats of violence, personal defamation, sexualized hate speech, and other atrocities (Chakravorti, 2017). This would lead to the belief that men fair far better on the World Wide Web; yet it appears that this medium consistently reinforces traditional gender norms (Samuels, 2018).

Gender lines are clearly reproduced and solidified by online groups such as Pinterest and Facebook, shopping sites, and movements such as Gamergate

(Hathaway, 2014b, Samuels, 2018). Boys themselves search out websites that establish and reinforce interest in male society, using celebrity females as their visual ideal (Durham, 2001). Some websites and video games, however, use a newer term "beta-male" to define a man who is more withdrawn and less dominant than their alpha-male peers (Nagle, 2016). This new term is used to identify both a man who belongs to the group or one who feels personal disdain (Nagle, 2016).

Despite this conventionality of masculinity, the internet offers boys and men the opportunity to create new content that more accurately represents who they really are (Samuels, 2018). Often, males use social media to build their persona using photos that include others and doing things that fit their personal view of themselves or showing off their best attributes; whereas females are more likely to take selfies and show themselves as "overly seductive" (Atanasova, 2016, p. 3).

Video games are perpetuating the traditional male gender norms as boys no longer go outside to play and instead are often confined to the house and, by association, video screen time (Sims, 2014). Hegemonic role models in video games lead boys to believe that if they want to be a "real man" they need to engage in risk behaviors that could injure themselves or others and act macho, up to and including violence (Gosse, 2012). New games, however, come on the scene weekly that reinvent what it means to be male, and where there is a deliberate "break with the constraints of traditional masculinity" (Samuels, 2018, n.p.). This offers boys and men the chance to reaffirm new ways of thinking of themselves that are more in line with reality.

FINAL THOUGHTS

Gender norms and toxic masculinity are prevalent in all forms of media; therefore, it behooves the industry to become more in tune with the expectations and needs of male viewership in order to present a more realistic view of men in the twenty-first century. Ferebee (2018) calls this new breed the grounded male and believes he is a mixture of "power, grit, compassion, and empathy [who can] live a life of balance and purpose" (n.p.). If there is hope for this new male, gender stereotypes must take a backseat to current thinking and expression.

Throughout the history of film, television, internet, and all forms of advertising, toxic masculinity is front and center; rarely do these media forms show equality between men and women. The macho, metrosexual, and overly amorous male is vibrant in many movies, television shows, and video games; however, the grounded male or modern mensche is what the public is looking for and so, it is necessary for all media forms to be amenable to reevaluate their programming and provide more equality in gender roles.

Educators and families have an obligation to discuss gender stereotypes with their students and children. According to Campbell (2017) and Nathanson et al. (2006), even kindergarten students can understand how to create equality between the genders and spot inequality in shows, videos, and print media. With this in mind, Teaching Tolerance (2019) and GLSEN (2019) offer lessons that educators can easily replicate that discuss gender stereotypes, gender identity, and the implications of both. Families who need assistance with the conversation can also use these lessons as well as other helpful tools such as the tip sheet provided by Media Smarts (2016).

POINTS TO REMEMBER

- Toxic masculinity is rampant in all forms of media and is expressed primarily by showing men who are macho, metrosexual, or overly amorous.
- Gender stereotypes pigeonhole men into roles that do not reflect current thinking and being for a majority of men in society today.
- The modern mensch or grounded man is one who has empathy, grit, honor, character, dignity, and compassion. These traits should be the focus of how all forms of media represent man.
- Children, especially, should be exposed to television, movies, and video games that portray men and women in equal ways. Men and women are not the same, but they can certainly be seen as equal.

Chapter Eight

Does Father Know Best?

The Many Paths to Contemporary Fatherhood Among Young Males

One of the most powerful influences, either positive or negative, in young males' journey to healthy male adulthood is their relationship with their fathers. Young boys start to search for a masculine model to form a tentative sense of self when they are about three years old (Osherson, 1986; Bergman, 1995). This marks the time that they express the wish to "be like daddy" and when they start to segregate by gender. Society pressures young boys to begin the separation from their primary relationship with their mother so that they can start to fashion an early sense of male self; thus, they face what Osherson (1986) described as a "crucial dilemma" in that they must separate from the nurturing mother but often do not have a clear idea of what the male gender is all about because of the absence—physical, geographical, or emotional—of their father.

Fathers are so often on the fringes of their families' lives, Osherson (1986) argued, that boys often have idealized, distorted, mythologized, or misidentified relationships with them; this leads young men to be influenced throughout their lives by what has been termed the "wounded father" image. Osherson (1986) discovered that males described their fathers most frequently as "rejecting, incompetent, or absent" (p. 6). In that same study, Osherson (1986) pointed out that on average, fathers are in direct relational contact with their children a mere thirty-seven minutes a day when the children are three months or younger, and only one hour a day when they are nine months or older. Bergman (1995) wrote of similar geographical, emotional, or physical father-absence that leaves sons struggling to figure out just who this father figure is. The result, sadly, is that they usually create a father image that is either larger than life (a hero) or smaller than life (a wimp).

Many fathers create wonderful relationships with their sons; yet some fathers do not have a unique developmental role to play in their sons' healthy growth and well-being over the years. There is, however, much pressure on these fathers to stress individuation, independence, and action-orientation, even in the early years. Bergman (1995) also stressed that most fathers themselves have not been socialized to be fluent in the language of emotions and relationships so that they are not skilled at or comfortable with initiating their boys into these domains.

Researchers of male development have discovered four prominent father images in their studies that characterize the father–son relationship: the angry and disappointed father, the all-suffering father, the saintly or heroic father, and the secretly vulnerable father (Berman, 1995; Osherson, 1986). While it appears to be essential that sons work out their relationships with their fathers early on if they are to enter emerging and young adulthood with a healthy internalized image of masculinity, a large number of men become adults without having done so (Osherson, 1986).

Many of Osherson's (1986) participants had to experience adulthood by separating from their fathers in order to sort out their intense, usually highly charged and confusing feelings about them. This distance resulted in a 'father hunger" that haunts men in adulthood and has the power to hamper their parenting of their own sons. Osherson (1986) cited Vaillant's (1977) famous Grant Study of successful Harvard attendees by citing the fact that more than 95 percent of them saw their fathers as either negative examples or not influential in their development.

Both Bergman (1995) and Osherson (1986) characterized adult relationships with fathers as ones colored by the emotions of shame, anger, or confusion. Some grown men felt ashamed that they had not lived up to the heroic image they had of their fathers, whether these images were accurate or not; others were openly avoidant of their fathers' failures to be "real men" and often overcompensated for what they saw as ineffectiveness or passivity by opting for hypermasculinity as they matured. Still others were angry in their adult lives, feeling lost or abandoned as boys. A common theme in the research was that young males' emotional development was frequently impeded by fathers, who themselves did not receive intimacy, nurturance, or emotional care from their fathers and therefore did not know how to instruct their sons in those areas (Bergman, 1995; Osherson, 1986).

Osherson (1986) spoke of the "wounded father" and wrote of the damage that this can result in for the son. The son may remember the father as being wounded, and evaluate his father by his deep sadness, incompetence, or anger (Osherson, 1986). He may also experience his father as wounding, with the son damaged by his rejection or feelings of having disappointed his father or the son may internalize images of the father that are distorted or idealized, leading to his own struggles to consolidate his identity as a man (Osherson, 1986).

FATHERING IN TWO-PARENT FAMILIES

Previous research has suggested that fathers are far less engaged in childrearing on a daily basis than are mothers; however, other studies show that they wish to incorporate this role into their repertoire (Coles, 2002; 2015). Their parenting styles tend to be more authoritarian and they have been portrayed as being less intimately involved in their children's personal interests and day-to-day activities (Bronte-Tinkew et al., 2010). Sharing in daily care, household work, and childrearing is beginning to increase as has time spent in direct contact and care of children (Berger, Carlson, Bzostek, & Osborne, 2008; Doucet 2004; Johansson & Klinth, 2008; Riina & Feinberg, 2012). As the time that fathers spent involved with their children increased, they reported greater self-efficacy, more positive feelings about their role as a father, and better outcomes (Riina & Feinberg, 2012).

Shows and Gerstel's (2009) research on class and gender revealed that working class fathers assisted more readily in the division of household labor and participated more in the traditional constellation of daily childcare chores than did higher SES fathers but that those fathers were more apt to take part in specialized activities such as school events or athletics.

PARENTING IN SINGLE-PARENT FAMILIES

Single parenting research and literature is mainly centered on single mothers, especially those from lower economic statuses (Kotchick, Dorsey, & Heller, 2005; Olson & Banyard, 1993); middle- and upper-class single mothers and single fathers from all economic groups have essentially been ignored in the literature. Only recently have single fathers become an object of scholarly interest as their numbers rise in this and other countries.

Parenting research does reveal that there are specific gender role associations that impact the lives of both parents and children (Castillo & Sarver, 2012; Chesley, 2011; Coles, 2002, 2015). The results of this research translate into more specific findings about how roles are carried out by gender in single-parent households. Bronte-Tinkew et al. (2010) found gendered differences in how parents carried out their parental roles and responsibilities in single parent households, remarking that single mothers and single fathers conducted daily tasks, play activities, and household labor in different ways.

YOUNG MALES AS TEEN FATHERS

There are many negative images that come to mind when contemplating teen fatherhood. According to one website (DoSomething.org, n.d.), about 750,000 women younger than twenty become pregnant each year and 80 percent of teen fathers do not marry the mother. Teen fathers are less likely than their peers to finish high school, and absent teen fathers contribute less than $800 per year to support their children (DoSomething.org, n.d.). Young fathers in their teens and emerging adulthood face economic and career challenges that lead them to be more likely to be economically disadvantaged. If they do not live with their children, those children are five times more likely to live in poverty (DoSomething.org, n.d.). They are more likely to be black and they are three times more likely to come from low SES families (DoSomething.org, n.d.).

Scott, Steward-Streng, Manlove, and Moore (2012) reported that 66 percent of teen fathers had their first child at eighteen or nineteen; and 62 percent had a partner nineteen or younger at the time of conception. Almost half had at least one more child by the age of twenty-two to twenty-four, often with a different mother (Scott et al., 2012). Fifty percent were of ethnic and racial minorities and only 3 percent had been born outside of this country (Scott et al., 2012). Less than a half lived with their first child at the time of the birth and their residential status at the birth of their first child is correlated with whether they live with their children during emerging adulthood (Scott et al., 2012).

While unmarried young fathers have legal rights and responsibilities involving their children, they must take action in order to obtain custody or visitation rights (DoSomething.org, n.d.). There are few services established specifically for young fathers and even if they wish to be involved in their children's lives, they often do not have the support to do so. At least one organization has tracked recent statistics about the crisis of father absence in our country and the impact is staggering (Brown, 2014).

Children raised in father-absent homes are more likely to face abuse and neglect, seven times more likely to become pregnant themselves as a teen, more likely to have behavioral problems, more likely to commit crimes, are more likely to engage in risky sexual behavior, more likely to become incarcerated, twice as likely to be obese, 279 percent more likely to carry weapons and deal drugs, and twice as likely to drop out of school (Allen & Lo, 2012; Brown, 2014). Perhaps even more unbelievable is that 92 percent of all parents in prison are fathers. The effects are noticeable even in gestation; fathers' involvement during pregnancy leads to better health for mother, father, and baby and lower rates of infant mortality (Brown, 2014).

Despite the grim statistics, there are many young fathers who wish to be involved in their children's lives; however, there are few supports in place to help them know how to do so successfully. Breiding-Buss, Guise, Scanlan, and Voice (2003) compiled one of the more comprehensive reports on the support needs of teenage fathers. The research team found that while many young fathers wanted to be involved, they gradually lost contact with their children and their mothers due to a lack of structured intervention and lack of committed support from grandparents and the mothers themselves. The research participants cited mothers' reluctance to involve them and give them more or continued access to their children after their births and maternal grandmothers also were cited as impediments (Breidling-Buss et al., 2003).

One informant summed up the struggles he faced, despite his desire to do the right thing

> A lot of people think we're [teen fathers] just running from our responsibilities because we don't want to take care of our children. There might be some like that, but I know that I'm not one of them. I want to be a good father, but there's only so much I can do. I know I need to be able to buy Kenis what he needs, but I'm just 15. I know I need to get a job, but I'm in school. Should I drop out? I know they don't want me to drop out. . . . I almost feel like I'm an uncle or something—you know someone that just drops by or gives you something every now and then. I don't feel like a good father, or a real father for that matter. (Paschal, Lewis-Moss, & Hsaio, 2011, p. 69)

Teen fathers who were most disinterested in remaining engaged were less likely to care about their education, less likely to have wanted a child, less economically secure, and more lacking in knowledge about child development and care (Breidling-Buss et al., 2003; Paschal et al., 2011). There were also gendered differences in perceptions of parenting roles. Mothers felt that beyond economic contributions to the child, fathers should also be more emotionally involved and share the basic work of childcare with the mother (Breidling-Buss et al., 2003; Paschal et al., 2011). Fathers, on the other hand, felt that they should be involved in fun activities with the children and develop quality relationships (Breidling-Buss et al., 2003; Paschal et al., 2011). They did not report feeling that their relationship with the mother needed to be a strong and positive one, although they did believe that they should not argue or fight with the mothers in front of the children (Breidling-Buss et al., 2003; Paschal et al., 2011).

Paschal et al. (2011) found that the young fathers they studied (ranging in age from fourteen to seventeen) constructed a number of different roles that they related to fatherhood. The provider role was the most common, attended by a sense of financial responsibility (at least to some degree) for their children. The autonomous role indicated a lack of responsibility for the child in any way, often accompanied by bitterness toward the mother whom the young men saw as having trapped them or punished them with the pregnancy. The most poignant theme, and the least represented, was that of the nurturer role, expressed here by a sixteen-year-old father:

> I mean spending quality time with my girl. Being a key part of her life. When she gets older, I want her to know that she can count on her daddy. I don't want her to think that I'm just there to give her money whenever Carlissa can't, I want her to know that I'm there for her when she needs someone to talk to. I want her to know that I'll be there. (p. 70)

Breiding-Buss et al. (2003) noted other obstacles to engaged parenting. Low self-esteem, marginalization during the pregnancy and birth, poor parenting during their own childhood, and low SES all contributed to absent or part-time parenting (Breidling-Buss et al., 2003). Participants also had difficulty in establishing suitable independent housing for themselves and having stable enough employment to provide adequately for their children (Breidling-Buss et al., 2003). Their young age and status made them feel unwelcome at the few family support groups that they were aware of.

The researchers found many lost opportunities from their interviews with teen fathers and sought to locate what components of programming the young males felt would be most useful to their successful engagement. While many wished this engagement, they reported feeling "useless," not wanted, marginalized, not appreciated, and not supported (Breidling-Buss et al., 2003). Systems meant to support them discouraged them or made them feel judged negatively instead.

Young fathers reported the need for different kinds of support (Breidling-Buss et al., 2003). The first was emotional support, which might include mentoring, young fathers' groups, dedicated advocates, and interactions that were positive and encouraging. The young men also needed structural support, including education, jobs that provided more money than the welfare system, career advice, help with housing, and legal advice (Breidling-Buss et al., 2003). The young men needed networking opportunities, and one suggestion that emerged from the research was that the most effective personnel in these programs would be young males who had been teen fathers themselves (Breidling-Buss et al., 2003).

Young fathers and the mothers needed counseling to recognize the importance of maintaining a good relationship in order to model cooperation to their children (Breidling-Buss et al., 2003). Support programs for young fathers cannot operate effectively if they are in isolation from supports for young mothers. Both need information on child development, as well as maintaining their own mental health and well-being.

Weber (2012) chronicled the stories of teen fathers and wrote that these young males must negotiate the possible stigmas of teen pregnancy while they are simultaneously trying to negotiate their identities as men. If the teens subscribe to traditional norms of masculinity, they are more apt to navigate the stigma by denying responsibility for the pregnancy and for constructing a self that is more likely to contain elements of toxic masculinity. Weber (2012) acknowledged that teen fathers are more at risk in social and academic areas but that these facts reveal little about how they make sense of their experience of coming to teen fatherhood.

Weber's (2012) narrative approach to the research sought to tease out the themes relevant to this meaning-making and revealed that not one of the informants took responsibility for the pregnancy, with most blaming the mother or circumstances such as not being able to obtain contraception or using alcohol the night of conception. Their gendered assumptions that it was women's responsibility for preventing pregnancy, that males are sexually uncontrollable, and that it is a sign of masculinity to impregnate feed into cultural tropes that they are constantly witness to (Weber, 2012).

The interviewees often blamed the females for wanting to get pregnant and talking the male into the pregnancy or not taking the responsibility for being on the pill and using it regularly (Weber, 2012). The young men also stated that their partners told them not to use condoms, but also admitted that they themselves didn't like them because they were not comfortable (Weber, 2012). There was a distinct belief that sex enhances a male's masculinity while it compromises a woman's femininity and her moral character. Weber (2012) saw blame and general lack of empathy for women in the narratives, with the teen fathers seeing themselves as powerless or blameless because sexuality is a natural part of being a male and family planning and pregnancy prevention are the sole domain of females.

The interviewees were also characterized by a "heat of the moment/boys will be boys" sort of narrative that again divested them of responsibility for the pregnancy (Weber, 2012). As one young man stated, "I mean . . . I'm a guy, you know . . . I'm like, I just wanna have sex. And, when you're a man and your hormones are raging, and it's like you can't think about anything else besides having sex . . . so you just do it" (Weber, 2012, p. 912). The phrase "I can't help it" was echoed throughout the narratives and the fact that they subscribed to a defense that male biology made it impossible for them to control their urges gave them an easy out for denying responsibility for their part in the pregnancy (Weber, 2012). Many of the informants blamed the females for being with other young men as justification for the pregnancy, even though they admitted to wanting sex and not using any means of contraception (Weber, 2012).

One informant reinforced a dominant belief—that having multiple sexual partners is all right for men because it is equated with sexual prowess that reinforces masculinity; yet that it is wrong for women. He stated, "Cause you know how they say it looks worse for a girl than a boy? Yeah, that's how I think about it. With a boy, there ain't too much wrong with it, really. But like a girl . . . that's just nasty" (Weber, 2012, p. 913).

Many of the men referred to their sexual partners as "sluts" and others tried to shun responsibility by casting doubt on whether the child was even theirs. While allowing the teens to avoid responsibility for their actions and claim masculine identities, they unfortunately found themselves stigmatized as irresponsible, reckless, selfish, and negative male stereotypes.

Weber (2012) also found themes of love and romance in the study. Love has become the province of women, who are supposed to be the ones responsible for understanding and teaching men about love and relationships and intimacy. Women should know better is one aspect of the theme and women should also be flattered if men display romance or affection. Interviewees equated not using contraception with having a special bond with a woman and shared that being with one particular young lady felt comfortable and different than the others (Weber, 2012). Having that special feeling was a justification for unprotected sex that might lead to pregnancy; the males equated not using a condom with complimenting the girl and showing her how special she was to him (Weber, 2012). Some of the young men located the pregnancy within the love they had and a desire for a future together that might include having a child at a young age.

In the study conclusion, Weber (2012) remarked that most attempts to combat teen pregnancy are located in sex education reform as well as enforced mandates around paternity and child support. These generally ignore the cultural influences on masculinity construction and identity formation and are thus doomed to fail. Failing to confront stereotypes that make pregnancy and childrearing a woman's responsibility and that reinforce hegemonic constructions of masculinity among young men will not address the outcomes for young women and their children. The repercussions extend well beyond bad reputations into poverty, lack of resources, and lack of support in rearing and providing for these children once they are born.

Moloney, Mackenzie, Hunt, and Joe-Laidler (2009) revealed an interesting side effect of fatherhood among the young gang members in San Francisco that they studied. For many, fatherhood, even if unexpected, proved to be a catalyst for positive change if accompanied by changes in the amount of time they spent on the streets and the ability to secure legally sourced income to support their family (Moloney et al., 2009). The study looked at young males for whom gang membership was their career prior to fatherhood. It served as a financial opportunity, a "family," and a masculine identity; yet for many of the young fathers, the transition was transformative and in some cases lifesaving (Moloney et al., 2009).

For some, their time and lifestyle had to be completely reorganized to meet the needs of the child(ren) and demands of their mothers. As their lives became busier and less random in terms of activities, they moved away from a lifestyle that presented them with too much time for trouble (Moloney et al., 2009). Non-residential fathers appeared to be a change agent, and the threat of being incarcerated and away from their children was also a deterrent (Moloney et al., 2009). Some mentioned that they wanted to be the positive role models for their children that their own fathers had not been (Moloney et al., 2009).

The constraining effects of fatherhood were similar to a curfew for the young males. There were identity and emotional transformations; for example, now many identified as a father as primary identity, while others spoke of becoming more mellow (Moloney et al., 2009). Their badass images were shed and fatherhood provided them with something to care about. This led to priorities in their lives, which most admitted to never having had previously, and they shifted from a fundamental orientation to the here-and-now to a more future-oriented view of life (Moloney et al., 2009).

Now that they had children to live for, they could not afford the reckless behaviors that they had previously embraced; thus, they began to desist from crime and acts that could put them in physical danger (Moloney et al., 2009). Some of the participants began to change their behaviors as soon as they learned of the pregnancy, while for others the actual physical presence of their child served as the trigger (Moloney et al., 2009). Some of the gang members had sired children previously so maturation was a factor in finally recognizing that they needed to engage with the most recent child's life (Moloney et al., 2009).

Perhaps most poignantly, fatherhood served to alter their definitions of masculinity. Whereas gang involvement meant masculinity as measured by violence, aggression, or substance use, fatherhood defined masculinity in roles of caregiver, breadwinner, teacher, and mentor; however, it was often perilous negotiating the difference between displays of masculinity in private and on the streets, and many were threatened by their own fellow gang members or had to "knife off" from those who had been their former fellows (Moloney et al., 2009). It was also difficult for some to leave behind the hustling that had provided a good income, especially if they did not have skills to find legitimate jobs. Those who continued to hustle often were cut off from their children by the mothers (Moloney et al., 2009).

Along with losing friendships and bonds in the gang, new fathers who did knife off often struggled to find alternatives to the security and sense of belonging that the gang had provided (Moloney et al., 2009). This pointed out the need for more interventions and resources for young fathers so that they can network, work, pursue their education, or access necessary supports to break the gang connection and be present and effective fathers to their children (Moloney et al., 2009).

What is the experience of other young males who themselves become fathers as teens or emerging adults? The popular image is that they are absent fathers or unskilled in the competencies that they need to support their offspring; yet as with many of the studied gang members turned fathers, becoming a young father is not necessarily a negative occurrence (Moloney et al., 2009).

> Becoming a father at such a young age is something I don't regret at all! I love my life and I'm tremendously happy. I want to say that I've been blessed indeed. My son is the best thing that has happened to me, and it's he who makes me a whole person. It's him I live for and will always live for! I look forward to every year we will have together and I look forward to seeing how he grows and develops. My life is absolutely wonderful. There are people who think I'm pathetic and have a pathetic life as a young father, but they could not be more wrong! It's the best thing that's happened to me and it's just made my life better. . . . When I was young I did all kinds of stupid things. . . . I spent time with the wrong kind of people, and got stuck in bad crowds of people. I was close to burning my candle at both ends, and it could have ended badly. I was not a good person, at all, and I didn't respect people, not even my parents. I let people down, and was first and foremost an egoist, an idiot, cold and arrogant. Thinking back on this time makes me very sad: Becoming a father really saved me, and made me a better person. (Johansson & Hammaren, 2014, Blog 2)

Johansson and Hammaren (2014) analyzed a Swedish blog where emerging adult fathers who were between eighteen and twenty-two and had posted a minimum of thirty times wrote about "my life as a dad" in order to see how they portray their roles and identities. Their identities, the researchers found, were "under construction"; yet definitely pointed to a chipping away at traditional definitions of masculinity in favor of more pluralistic and inclusive definitions of what it means to be a man.

They compensated for their marginalized societal position and young ages through caring fatherhood that gave them a defined masculinity and an adult alibi (Johansson & Hammaren, 2014).

The blogs also illustrated that these young men saw fatherhood as a way to rectify some of the challenges and previous personal difficulties they may have gone through as children (Johansson & Hammaren, 2014). By embodying the ethic of engaged and nurturing fatherhood, they were able to replace hate or anger from prior abuse or neglect through the intimate love of their children; therefore, for them, parenthood had a healing quality. Like the gang members previously described, they also credit fatherhood from turning them away from dangerous behaviors, finding a purpose in life, and growing forward into healthy adulthood (Johansson & Hammaren, 2014).

The Fatherhood Project (2016) identified teen fathers as "the forgotten partner in teen pregnancies" and works to provide them with resources, fathering skills, and emotional support. Sporty duffle bags filled with materials needed to parent a young child—ranging from books to diapers to wipes—are given to all participants in the program and they are taught about their importance in healthy child development (The Fatherhood Project, 2016). Given that so many are isolated in their experience, the all-dads group serves as a chance to compare notes, ask questions, and share strategies. The "curriculum" is augmented by fathering skills-building exercises, practical parenting tips, virtual visits with child experts, and information about co-parenting effectively (The Fatherhood Project, 2016).

Kiselica (1999) wrote one of the most extensive chapters on counseling teenage fathers, and later augmented that work with additions that are more multicultural in their approach. The technique begins with avoiding stereotypes of teen fathers and looking to build rapport right from the start of counseling. A series of seminal questions are asked to determine how best to support each teen client (Kiselica, 1999). The first set of questions looks at the circumstances that led to the young man's condition; how can these situations be mitigated; who might be effective mentors and role models to teach the young male what it means to be an effective father; and what other forms of support does the young man need in order to fulfill his responsibilities as a father (Kiselica, 1999).

Taking care to observe relational and cultural styles and preferences, the therapist then attempts to build trust by assuring the young man that he is a primary advocate for his success (Kiselica, 1999). Counseling attends to the stages of fatherhood, beginning in the prenatal stage. Pregnancy counseling involves a good deal of education and in some cases can involve the mother if the parents are willing and can communicate effectively. There is a great deal of work to prepare for fatherhood, and beyond necessary information about what to expect in labor, birth, and infancy, there are economic, career, and educational decisions to be made (Kiselica, 1999).

Degges-White and Colon (2012) identified the combination of the typical stressors in emerging adulthood as pregnancies (which are generally unplanned), and the need to be a provider as a set of dynamics that threaten to overwhelm young fathers. This can lead to complex psychological problems or extend existing ones. This is especially true for those young men on the margins and those who have grown up without or who lack positive males in their lives. School counselors, who are often the closest to the situation in terms of teen fathers, are much less likely to steer teen fathers toward resources to help them than they do with teen mothers; yet the fields of human services, social work, and counseling tend to be female-dominated (Degges-White & Colon, 2012).

Group counseling has been found to be important and effective in that it can bring young fathers together in a safe environment, and under the supervision of a skilled leader, can assist them in discussing personal responsibility, child health and welfare, family-of-origin issues, fundamental parenting and discipline skills, and how to establish healthy co-parenting (Degges-White & Colon, 2012). This combination of psychoeducational and therapeutic approaches in the group helps build confidence as well as a network of others with similar experiences (Degges-White & Colon, 2012).

Some therapeutic approaches also involve reflection and writing. One such program, reported Degges-White and Colon (2012), involved having the young males write three letters—one to their own father; one to themselves telling what they wished their father had said to them when they were younger; and one to their child. They then actively made a commitment to engagement and appear to be influenced to do just that after these assignments.

Another approach is to help young fathers set goals and adopt a future orientation. They are urged to develop a ten-year plan for themselves and that plan must include their child(ren) in each year of the plan (Degges-White & Colon, 2012). After the plans are shared in group, counselors can then work with individuals to coach them to success in meeting step-by-step goals.

Kiselica (1999, 2008) found that the most effective programs to prepare young males for impending fatherhood are those run by veteran fathers themselves and that take a very active, hands-on approach to teaching skills. Young males, especially from marginalized groups, generally do not trust government authorities and other state and local agencies; therefore, the need for local solutions that involve, as much as possible, respected male mentors and role models, as well as recent teen fathers who have successfully overcome the odds is extremely important Kiselica (2008).

Kiselica (2008) cited a program in Bridgeport, Connecticut, that is headquartered at the local YMCA. The program links other youth service organizations such as the health center and a spiritual center as two of the many resources that are connected to the program and therefore is able to meet the social, spiritual, and physical needs of teenage fathers from the greater Bridgeport area (Kiselica, 2008). In order to replicate this kind of multipronged approach service, service coalitions should be headed by a board of directors that sets policy and guides all members. Its population should be comprised of residents from the local community, professionals from local, county, state, and national agencies serving youth, and representatives from the juvenile justice system (Kiselica, 2008).

Kiselica (2008) stressed the importance of the board having at least one current or former teen father to provide firsthand knowledge of the experience and needs of young fathers. It is also important to include well-respected role models, community catalysts, and those who have a genuine interest in listening and responding to young fathers' needs rather than subscribing to social stereotypes (Kiselica, 2008). Representatives from housing, health and human services, education, job training, and mental health agencies need to unite to tackle young fathers' challenges with the end result being healthier fathers and children.

Single Fatherhood

Historically, there has been little attention in the research literature given to the experience of single fathers. Recently, however, there has been an uptick in the exploration of this topic with some fascinating findings to add to our knowledge of this phenomenon. According to the United States Census Bureau (2016), there were two million single fathers in the United States, about 16 percent of the parent population and of these 40 percent were divorced, 38 percent never married, 16 percent were separated, and 6 percent were widowed.

ElHatage (2017) wrote that single fathers are more likely to be divorced than are single mothers but they are less likely to be in poverty. They are also more likely to be white, older, and better educated than single mothers, and are more apt to be cohabitating (ElHage, 2017). While studies generally show that children in single-father and single-mother homes fare just about equally, those children growing up in homes with single fathers cohabitating with a partner experienced fewer family routines and had lower levels of closeness with their fathers (ElHage, 2017).

Non-traditional families, including single-parent households, have become a common phenomenon in this country, and the diversity of those non-traditional families, including the growing number of single father households, bears examining. What little research exists explores the stories and experiences of fathers and seems to indicate their general lack of socialization to the role, some social stigmas and biases against different types of fathering, and possible class considerations—topics that need further scrutiny (ElHage, 2017; Taylor, 2014).

As Taylor (2014) described it, most men are not socialized to become full parents, let alone single parents. Single parenting is difficult for both genders; yet Taylor stated,

> I think it's tougher on us men, however, because we aren't raised to nurture and be empathetic. In fact, Western Society does its best through a culture of shaming, bullying, crass images of masculinity and dismal media portrayals of fathers to teach us men that we're just not going to be successful parents. We don't tote babies around when we're little, we aren't the one hired to babysit the twins down the street when we're in our teens, we're instead pushed to physical activities, sports, video games, and other activities that emphasize the testosterone factors rather than help us learn how to balance it with the more traditionally "feminine" aspects of humanity. (p. 2)

Early research on fathers and masculinity found that it was difficult for fathers to integrate the gendered notion that they must be the protectors and breadwinners with a more participatory and engaged definition of the role (Williams, 2009; Hatter et al., 2002). Given that so many men struggle over their identities as fathers, they come upon a challenge to prove themselves to be capable in both the feminine and masculine roles when faced with single fatherhood (Coles, 2009). For some, these gender role struggles fundamentally change their beliefs about themselves, but others ignore or dismiss the tension (Williams, 2009).

Some men alter the roles and insert far more risk-taking, physical activity, and looser discipline to replace what they consider more maternal (indoor play, safer activities, more arts and crafts). Feeling conflicted between being a nurturer and a provider is found in the research, and, interestingly, it is not a stressor that single mothers tend to experience (Coles 2009; Doucet 2004; Williams, 2009).

The 1980s and early 1990s produced a good deal of research on single fathers, probably because the population began to rise (Coles 2002; Greif, 1985). This early research eventually was augmented to include African Americans and other ethnic groups, stay-at-home fathers, homeless fathers, and gay fathers; which all brought other perspectives (Coles, 2002, 2009; Doucet, 2004; Schindler & Coley, 2006).

The previous research on single fathers did illustrate the struggles in adjusting to full-time parenting, grappling with new roles for which one might not be prepared, and general lack of knowledge about many elements of parenting and child development (Coles, 2002, 2015; Dufur et al., 2010; Hamer and Marchioro, 2002). The difficulty in adjustment occurs across all variables that relate to how a man came to be a single father—whether through the death of a spouse, mother's loss of parental rights, or personal decision (Coles, 2002; 2009; Hamer & Marchioro, 2002).

Among the more difficult aspects of the transition were the need to increase patience, to learn new means of communicating, to find a balance with the added roles and responsibilities that must be assumed, and to decide on things such as discipline, schedules, diet, and activities (Coles, 2002; 2009; Hamer & Marchiorio, 2002). Dufur, Howell, Downey, Ainsworth, and Lapray (2010) found that these difficulties were most pronounced when fathers had younger children whose demands were more constant.

Socialization to parenting and less active engagement by fathers throughout history left many single fathers looking for assistance when establishing a daily routine that incorporated discipline, developmentally appropriate practices, and boundaries (Kielty, 2006). Dufur et al. (2010) discovered that parenting practices in single father homes was different from that in single mother or dual parent homes, mainly due to the fact that single fathers were stricter on daily routines, less expressive emotionally, and more abrasive in disciplining their children. Some activities, such as arts and crafts and imaginary play, occurred less, but other activities such as sports, exploration, outdoor activities, building things, and doing puzzles or playing with other manipulatives occurred more frequently.

Studies such as those by Coles (2009; 2015) and Maupin et al. (2010) suggested that fathers are less likely to access social services designed to support them and their families. Whether this is due to socialization to greater independence, perceived or actual barriers to access, or social stigmas attached to the use of such services is not necessarily clear. Neither is their level of awareness of these resources; however, the fact that they may be offered in venues and manners that are not male-friendly is also a possibility (Coles, 2015). Rather than depend on assistance services, men are more apt to depend on their families of origin as their primary support network when dealing with parenting responsibilities and childcare issues (Maupin et al., 2010).

Esbensen (2014) conducted a qualitative study aimed at uncovering how single fathers maneuver daily life, how they balance work and family, how they use services and support networks, and how they view gender within their roles. Interviews explored these topics and conversations included discussions about daily life, scheduling, work and school balance, services and support networks; as well as gendered parenting, their perceptions about masculinity in this scenario, and social reactions (Esbensen, 2014). Single fathers in both the low-income and middle-class were interviewed to see if SES affected views and practices of parenting.

Esbensen's study (2014) revealed the logistical and emotional struggles that these fathers faced. It was difficult for them to balance daily life roles within the university of household, school, activities work, and their children's well-being. The fathers experienced stress and loneliness as well as feelings of inadequacy when they couldn't juggle all of their roles successfully (Esbensen, 2014). They underwent the feelings of overload, being overwhelmed, and questioned their decisions without another adult to bounce ideas and concerns off (Esbensen, 2014).

Several fathers expressed great concern that they might be failing their children in a variety of arenas such as behaviors, manners, dress, and everyday decisions they made alone (Esbensen, 2014). They missed the checks and balances that a partner might provide. Without a partner to share the daily stories and challenges of raising their children, they mentioned feeling like an island unto themselves (Esbensen, 2014).

While all of these fathers had adopted the daily lives of childrearing alone, even within that main caregiver role they were influenced by gendered expectations. Their inherited concepts of what parenting entailed left them in a state of constant doubt about whether they were doing the "right thing" and they feared that they were not devoting enough time to engaging with their children. All of the findings cut across class lines (Esbensen, 2014).

Even though the fathers reconfigured their work or education to accommodate their children's schedules, they still struggled with finding and keeping dependable and sustainable childcare and they often made sacrifices for their children that caused impediments to career success or advancement (Esbensen, 2014). Several of the fathers had even gone so far as to build self-run businesses to help manage their children and work schedules, giving them options such as working at home, staying at home with children during vacations or sick days or taking them to work if necessary; while others had left more demanding jobs to move to sites or organizations that were more family-friendly (Esbensen, 2014).

Clearly, all of these fathers were aiming for some sort of work/life balance while needing to be the primary breadwinner. To do so, they had to throw off some of their preconceived notions about what men were supposed to do or fatherhood was supposed to look like; therefore, they challenged the concepts of hegemonic masculinity that many were raised on in order to fulfill their children's needs.

Half of the fathers used or had used in the past some aspect of social or community assistance services (Esbensen, 2014). Those who did not use services mentioned their desire for autonomy and their feeling that they needed to provide for their children alone; and some expressed distrust or unfamiliarity with such institutions (Esbensen, 2014). Many had experienced problems as they attempted to access services; yet others had such strong support networks of family, friends, faith, or community that they were proud to be able to go it alone (Esbensen, 2014).

Single fathers who regularly accessed services found that they were extremely valuable in supporting their ability to work and balance their schedules as well as providing some respite from caring for their children (Esbensen, 2014). Services could provide mental and emotional support for the fathers, lessening their stress and isolation and boosting their sense of well-being. The men who reached out to service providers were able to overcome the stigma of male help-seeking. One of the most useful services was communication with other single fathers, facilitated by media, as well as face-to-face groups (Esbensen, 2014).

Esbensen (2014) found that many of the interviewees had grown up with rigid ideas about the role of a mother versus a father; yet when they became single fathers, they generally viewed parenting as a more fluid process with roles blurred. In many cases, they abandoned or modified the earlier views in order to incorporate more feminine nurturing and emotional expression in their children. These young fathers viewed their own masculinity positively, as a strong expression of manhood, because they had been capable of providing for both kinds of needs (Esbensen, 2014).

The men wanted to raise boys who were strong but also wanted to encourage their children to express their emotional side as well. Since so many of the fathers had not been encouraged to do this, they were proud of their ability to rise above limitations that resulted from societal stigmas around males and emotionality (Esbensen, 2014). The fathers felt that in many ways they had been forced to grow beyond hegemonic male images inherited from their youth and had grown into "whole" men in order to meet their children's needs (Esbensen, 2014).

Schafer (2018) highlighted the fact that single fathers are vulnerable to mental health issues. Getting to the heart of the reasons for this fact, just like single mothers, single fathers often are impacted by the loss of two household incomes if they come by single parenthood through death, divorce, or other debilitating conditions to the mother (Schafer, 2018). This often means moving to a less attractive dwelling or to a less safe neighborhood. They may also be fearful that because of social stigmas about the accommodations necessary to parent children, they may be hampered in career advancement (Schafer, 2018). If employers do not provide flexibility to new fathers or fathers dealing with life transitions, they risk either losing them or taxing them with additional stressors that may impact their physical and emotional health.

Many men subscribe to the equation that to be male is to show toughness and not let others know when they are struggling. They also may have been socialized to see asking for help as a sign of vulnerability. Further, they are less likely to be as adept at reading and reacting to children's emotions. Single fathers who have lost a partner most often have lost their main confidante, putting them at further risk (Schafer, 2018).

Media portrays dads in sitcoms and movies as inept and many men may take these images to heart. They also are less likely to practice healthy habits such as fruit and vegetable consumption, avoiding binge drinking, maintaining a healthy weight through exercise, and practicing stress reduction through meditation, tai chi, or social networking (Schafer, 2018). Single dads need to build some of the safety nets that women have, asking for help and relief at times, talking with other single dads to normalize feelings, or talking honestly with a counselor if stress levels rise (Shafer, 2018).

Gay and a Single Father

Scher (2018) began his *New York Times* article on gay single fathers with an anecdote about one of his interviewees, who grew up poor and in a homophobic environment and eventually decided to have and raise his own children through the surrogacy process

> Julius Ybañez Towers was taking a walk around the Harlem Meer in Central Park with his twin 10-month-old sons and two dogs. A woman stopped to compliment him for giving his wife a break. "There's no wife," he told the woman. "I'm a single gay dad from surrogacy." He smiled at the confused look on her face. (n.p.)

For many gay men who have felt discrimination in the adoption process, surrogacy is now the avenue to fulfilling their dreams of fatherhood. Scher (2018) illustrated this point in his discussion with one of his informants who had his son via surrogacy four years ago. This single father, who is forty-six and black, said he chose surrogacy because the prospect of persuading a woman to allow him to adopt was daunting. "As a single, gay black man," he said, "I figured I'd be at the bottom of the list for most women" (Scher, 2018, n.p.). Despite the difficulties in arranging for surrogacy and dealing with people's reactions to his choice, Williams found that the decision to have children completed something in him and "he felt as if he finally fit in with his big family in Kansas, where he grew up" (Scher, 2018, n.p.).

MOTIVATIONS FOR BECOMING A FATHER

The motives for becoming a single, full-time father have been illustrated in research such as Coles's (2002) ethnographic study of black, single birth fathers. The participants in that study relayed that they were driven to their decision by a sense of responsibility and personal duty. They wanted to be positive role models for what being an engaged father looked like (Coles, 2002; 2015). In most cases, they also expressed the desire to make up for their own fathers' absences, whether those were physical or emotional, and that they wanted to act as fully engaged fathers should act (Coles, 2002; 2009). A June 2016 meeting of the Society for Research in Child Development, which involved an interdisciplinary group of scholars, came to the same conclusion about motivation for fatherhood; they found that these same motives were articulated to a wide array of men, including both gay and straight, seeking either to foster or adopt children (Seeman, 2018).

Possible Biases Against Fathers

In the United States, it is now possible for single adults to adopt in any state as long as they meet the state-specific criteria for adoption. Recent additions to many state statutes have even protected the rights of individuals with disabilities, including ones that are psychiatric in nature, from discrimination in creating and maintaining their families (Seeman, 2018). Yet statistics show that the vast majority of single adoptive parents are female and there appears to be suspicion of would-be fathers (Seeman, 2018). Seeman (2018) termed this a form of anti-male sexism and it is a view that, unfortunately, is held by many childcare professionals.

This same bias is displayed in many childcare proceedings, and it includes such omissions of males as the failure to include fathers in the case planning about their children, ignoring birth fathers as placement options for children, and in conducting home visits when fathers are not present (Seeman, 2018). As one might expect, gay fathers reported more barriers, especially if they lived in a state with fewer legal protections (Rapaport, 2019; Seeman, 2018). In states that had greater protection for gay parents, they were more likely to form their family through surrogacy, whereas they became fathers through heterosexual relationships in more restrictive states (Seeman, 2018).

Overall, about 35 percent of the families in the study were formed through adoption or foster care, 15 percent with the assistance of a pregnancy carrier or surrogate, and 39 percent through a heterosexual relationship (Seeman, 2018). About 40 percent encountered difficulties in the adoption process and 33 percent in custody arrangements in heterosexual relationships (Seeman, 2018). Gay fathers were far more likely than other adoptive parents to be willing to adopt harder-to-place children, such as those of color, older children, sibling groups, or those with disabilities or at risk (Seeman, 2018).

Despite their willingness to adopt more difficult to place children, single men, in general, are in the minority of those who adopt. Childcare agencies, it seems, are still more reluctant to place children with single fathers, as evidenced by a 2015 estimate that only 3 percent of such children were adopted by single men, most often gay men (Seeman, 2018).

There was also discrimination within the ranks of non-traditional dads. Blum (2018) spoke to the lack of inclusivity that can infect even queer parenting communities:

> Marginalized queer dads have to contend with their own unique challenges, including prejudice from other gay dads, lack of resources, and cultural invisibility. Single dads, for example, often encounter heterosexist assumptions in public (like the dreaded "Is it Mom's day off?"), forcing them to come out to strangers again and again. Gay dads of color, meanwhile, report feeling caught between their sexual and ethnic identities. (p. 3)

Divorced gay dads, thought to comprise a majority of gay households, aren't embraced with open arms at gay parent groups (Rapaport, 2019). Likewise, gay fathers with children from previous heterosexual relationships may feel socially ostracized from the broader queer dad community.

THE EVOLUTION OF A FATHER

In a review of the literature on gender differences in parenting styles, Seeman (2018) noted that there have been historical stereotypes about males' style of parenting. They have been seen as being more comfortable in traditional masculine parenting roles, such as the disciplinarian or the supporter and less so in more feminine roles such as comforter and emotional support. "Male" ways of parenting have conformed to more restricted roles such as engaging their children in active or physical play, teaching life lessons, coaching, exploring the great outdoors, or making things (Seeman, 2018). Studies of fathers, however, who stay at home with their children a good deal or all of the time show that the more time they spend, the more fathers branch out into other kinds of activities and build relationships not just on activities, but also on emotional and relational expressions of love (Seeman, 2018). In identical situations male and female ways of parenting grow more similar the more single parents become alike as brain "plasticity" is influenced by parenthood, raising the level of vigilance and socio-emotional engagement by fathers (Seeman, 2018).

While Seeman (2018) found that such changes are triggered hormonally in mothers, it is interesting to note that brain changes can occur in fathers as well, and are activated by ongoing and engaged childcare. Taking part in relationships with children, it is postulated, provides emotional feedback to male brains and shapes the paternal brain to becoming more attuned to children's needs and feelings (Seeman, 2018).

THE SUCCESS OR STRUGGLES OF CHILDREN OF SINGLE-PARENT FATHERS

There is not much specific research on the outcomes of those children who are adopted by single fathers who are not their biological parents; however, Biblarz and Stacy (2010) reported that, despite some earlier research findings that adolescents who lived with single mothers were more securely attached, had fewer behavioral problems, earned higher academic test scores and achieved higher educational and occupational status than those living with comparable single fathers, most contemporary literature reached the conclusion that gender of the parent makes little difference. They found that if the size of a family were controlled, the frequency and severity of children's behavioral problems were similar regardless of a single parent's gender (Biblarz & Stacy, 2010). Although children in single-father or single-mother families perform less well academically, on average, than children in two-parent families and while parenting behaviors, on average, may be slightly different between single mothers and single fathers, Dufur et al. (2010) found no long-term effects on children's outcomes.

FINAL THOUGHTS

Fathers and fatherhood are two of the most important and complicated facets of coming to be an adult male in this country; yet it is not an easy business. Each of the different populations of young fathers described faced myriad daily struggles, challenges, barriers, and stress in their roles as fathers. Some of the challenges came in the form of social struggles to define new roles that rejected or moved away from traditional hegemonic masculinity. In other cases, there were few role models or mentors or even opportunities to interact comfortably with other young fathers in a supportive setting; quite clearly, the path was one that not many had walked upon and that left the young males looking for signs of how to successfully parent along the way.

Other fathers faced personal struggles due to the fathering that they had received as children. Their construction of what defined good parenting was created as much in opposition to what they had experienced as it was born from personal values; yet, despite early adverse experiences, many rose to the challenge and raised their children successfully, seeing fatherhood as their primary role and deriving joy and pride in the undertaking.

The experience of becoming a father was transformative for many young males, even if they had not planned for the pregnancy. For gang members, it served as the catalyst for life changes, and that theme was repeated for other teens and emerging adults. Those who had suffered in their own childhoods often were able to heal through their own positive parenting; yet there still were too many young males who subscribed to offshoots of toxic masculinity, denying responsibility for their part in pregnancies, blaming young women for not being responsible for birth control, excusing their "boys will be boys" attitudes, or justifying sexual behaviors due to male sex drive.

Services to support young fathers need to take into consideration male socialization around help-seeking and autonomy. They also must be constructed in male-friendly ways, run by males who themselves have experienced parenting at a young age, be free of bias and misconceptions about young fathers and their desire to be involved in their children's lives, and sensitive to issues of race, ethnicity, social class, and sexual orientation. Young fathers need to have the safety of communicating with each other and counseling methods need to be tailored to more male-centric preferences for therapeutic interventions.

All young males should be included in family education and family planning education that should stress the importance of fathers in their children's health, well-being, and prosocial development. Transitional support and counseling as young men prepare for fathering roles is essential. So are counseling and advocacy for learning how to maintain productive relationships with birth mothers, whether the fathers are residential or not. Learning the skills to co-parent effectively is vital in presenting children with a secure and united front in parenting.

As with the needs of young mothers, young fathers need access to education, job and career counseling, training, and opportunities, adequate health care for them and their children, and sufficient housing to be able to care for their children. Reliable, quality childcare permits further education and the ability to access job training and career paths; thus, promoting the likelihood of better-paying and secure jobs that can lessen dependence upon social services.

Confronting stereotypes about traditional masculine roles and traditionally female gendered roles around childrearing and family planning is a delicate, but necessary, task at this point in history. It is highly unlikely that young males can address these charged topics and be open to examination, reflection, and possible reconfiguring of their ideas about what it means to be a man without the guidance of other men who have "been there."

Using peer counseling and education and respected mentors is far more apt to bring about results than canned curriculum or lectures or presentations by outsiders, and one of the most powerful ways that star athletes, the media, entertainers, and other well-respected figures could use their wealth and fame is to contribute to initiatives and public outreach programs that stress the importance of healthy masculinity and the role of fathers in promoting positive development and prosocial behaviors in their children. In the words of a fifteen-year-old father, "Being a father means being a real man. A real man will do what he has to do. He takes care of his own . . . He gets a job. He goes to work. He provides for his kids . . . He does what he has to do" (Paschal et al., 2011, p. 68).

POINTS TO REMEMBER

- Fathers play an incredibly important role in their children's development; yet, depending upon their absence or active engagement, the outcomes of that role are drastically different.
- Fathers who are actively engaged with their children reduce many developmental risk factors and increase the likelihood of protective factors, academic achievement, and better mental and emotional health in their children.
- Fatherhood has taken on many different shapes and forms in our contemporary society and children in many different constellations of fathering thrive if their fathers are actively engaged in single parenting or co-parenting effectively.
- Young fathers—those in adolescence and emerging adulthood—are less likely to be engaged with their children, provide adequate financial support to them, be able to co-parent well with children's mothers, advance their educations, and be on career paths that lead to economic stability.
- Young fathers and single fathers are at higher risk for mental and emotional health threats to their well-being.
- Fathers tend to view and practice parenting in manners that are different from mothers but if they take on the role of single parent, their styles tend to become more androgynous as time passes.
- Young fathers are stereotyped as reckless, driven by hormones, selfish, and subscribing to toxic images of masculinity; however, there are many young males who eschew these stereotypes in favor of other definitions of masculinity that embrace the nurturing and caregiving roles.
- There are biases against young fathers that can be expressed by birth mothers, grandparents, and social service agencies, and these biases may work against young fathers as they seek access to their children.

- Our society must rethink the best ways to support young fathers, stress the essential link between their involvement with their children and future outcomes, advocate for them to continue their education, career training, and developing their parenting skills and help them to find resources such as adequate housing and transportation so that they can actively engage with their children right from birth, even if they are not residential parents.
- For some young males, becoming a father is a transformative experience that helps them shed destructive behaviors, set goals, adopt a more future-oriented perspective, heal childhood wounds, and redefine what it means to be a man.

References

Adelman, H. S., & Taylor, L. (2010). *Mental health in schools: Engaging learners, preventing problems, and improving schools.* Thousand Oaks, CA: Corwin.

Allen, A. N., & Lo, C. C. (2012). Drugs, guns, and disadvantaged youths: Co-occurring behavior and the code of the street. *Crime & Delinquency, 58*(6), 932–953. DOI: 10.1177/001128709359652.

American Foundation for Suicide Prevention (2019). *Risk factors and warning signs.* Retrieved from https://afsp.org/about-suicide/risk-factors-and-warning-signs/.

American Psychiatric Association (n.d.). *What is schizophrenia?* Retrieved from https://www.psychiatry.org/patients-families/schizophrenia/what-is-schizophrenia.

American Psychological Association (2013). *Diagnostic and statistical manual of mental disorders.* Washington, DC: American Psychiatric Association.

AmeriCorps (2018). *The VISTA review—the impact edition.* Retrieved from https://www.nationalservice.gov/sites/default/files/documents/VISTA%20Review%20-%20Spring%202018%20508d.pdf.

———. (n.d.a). *What is AmeriCorps?* Retrieved from https://www.nationalservice.gov/programs/americorps.

———. (n.d.b). *AmeriCorps NCCC.* Retrieved from https://www.nationalservice.gov/programs/americorps/americorps-programs/americorps-nccc.

———. (n.d.c). *VISTA's mission and program goals.* Retrieved from https://www.vistacampus.gov/vistas-mission-and-program-goals.

———. (n.d.d). *Benefits of service.* Retrieved from https://www.vistacampus.gov/in-service/benefits-service#healthcare_benefit.

———. (n.d.e). *VISTA program areas.* Retrieved from https://www.vistacampus.gov/about/vista-program-areas.

Amin, A., Kågesten, A., Adebayo, E., & Chandra-Mouli, V. (2018). Addressing gender socialization and masculinity norms among adolescent boys: Policy and programmatic implications. *The Journal of Adolescent Health: Official Publication of the Society for Adolescent Medicine, 62*(3S), S3-S5. DOI: 10.1016/j.jadohealth.2017.06.022.

References

Anderberg, J. (2019). *Is college for everyone? 11 alternatives to the traditional 4-year college.* Retrieved from https://www.artofmanliness.com/articles/is-college-for-everyone-10-alternatives-to-the-traditional-4-year-college/.

Anderson, M. (2016). *Here's how schools can support students' mental health.* Retrieved from https://www.npr.org/sections/ed/2016/09/20/459843929/heres-how-schools-can-support-students-mental-health.

Arbeit, M. R., Hershberg, R. M., Johnson, S. K., Lerner, J. V., & Lerner, R. M. (2017). "I mean, we're guys": Constructing gender at all-male trade school. *Journal of Adolescent Research. 32*(2), 227–58. DOI: 10.1177/0743558415590659.

Arminio, J., Grabosky, T. K., & Lang, J. (2015). *Student veterans and service members in higher education.* New York: Routledge.

Armstrong, T. (2018). *Multiple intelligences in the classroom.* (4th ed.). Alexandria, VA: Association for Supervision and Curriculum Development.

Arnett, J. J. (2015). *Emerging adulthood* (2nd ed.). New York: Oxford University Press.

———. (2017). *Adolescence and emerging adulthood* (6th ed.). New York: Pearson.

Arnett, J. J., Kloep, M., Hendry, L. B., & Tanner, J. L. (2011). *Debating emerging adulthood: Stage or process?* New York: Oxford University Press.

Arnett, J. J. & Murray, J. L. (2019). *Emerging adulthood and higher education: A new student development paradigm.* New York: Routledge.

Ashford, K. (2017). *Parents of only boys are prioritizing college more than parents of only girls.* Retrieved from https://www.forbes.com/sites/kateashford/2017/09/30/boys/#4059a19c2724.

ASVAB. (n.d.). *ASVAB fact sheet.* Retrieved from http://official-asvab.com/docs/asvab_fact_sheet.pdf.

Atanasova, A. (2016). Gender-specific behaviors on social media and what they mean for online communications. *SocialMediaToday.* Retrieved from https://www.socialmediatoday.com/social-networks/gender-specific-behaviors-social-media-and-what-they-mean-online-communications.

Balis, T., & Postolache, T. T. (2008). Ethnic differences in adolescent suicide in the United States. *International Journal of Child Health and Human Development: IJCHD, 1*(3), 281–96. Retrieved from https://www.ncbi.nlm.nih.gov/pmc/articles/PMC2845977/pdf/nihms-86201.pdf.

Banerjee, P. A. (2016). A systematic review of factors linked to poor academic performance of disadvantaged students in science and math in schools. *Cogent Education, 3*(1), 1–17. DOI: 10.1080/2331186X.2016.1178441.

Barber, K. & Bridges, T. (2017). Marketing manhood in a "post-feminist" age. *Contexts: The American Sociological Association, 16*(2), 38–43. DOI: 10.1177/1536504217714257.

Basile, K. C., Smith S. G., Breiding, M. J., Black, M. C., & Mahendra, R. (2014). Sexual violence surveillance: Uniform definitions and recommended data elements, version 2.0. *Centers for Disease Control and Prevention and the National Center for Injury Prevention and Control.* Retrieved from https://www.cdc.gov/violenceprevention/pdf/sv_surveillance_definitionsl-2009-a.pdf.

Bem, S. L. (1981). Gender schema theory: A cognitive account of sex typing. *Psychological Review, 88*(4), 354–64. DOI: 10.1037/0033-295X.88.4.354.

Berdahl, J. L., Cooper, M., Glick, P., Livingston, R. W., & Williams, J. C. (2018). Work as a masculinity contest. *Journal of Social Issues, 74*(3), 422–48. DOI:10.1111/josi.12289.

Berger, L. M., Carlson, M. J., Bzostek, S. H., & Osborne, C. (2008). Parenting practices of resident fathers: The role of marital and biological ties. *Journal of Marriage and Family, 70*(3), 625–639. DOI: 10.1111/j.1741-3737.2008.00510.x.

Bergman, S. J. (1995). Men's psychological development: A relational perspective. In R. F. Levant & W. S. Pollack (Eds.). *A New Psychology of Men*, (pp. 68–90). New York: Harper Collins.

Berk, L. E. (2017). *Child Development* (9th ed.). Saddle River, NJ: Pearson Education.

Bernstein, J. (2017). *Here's how Breitbart and Milo smuggled white nationalism into the mainstream.* Retrieved from https://www.buzzfeednews.com/article/joseph bernstein/heres-how-breitbart-and-milo-smuggled-white-nationalism.

Biblarz T. J., & Stacy J. (2010). How does the gender of parents matter? *Journal of Marriage and the Family, 72*(1). 3–22. DOI: 10.1111/j.1741-3737.2009.00678.x.

Birch, E. R. & Miller, P. W. (2007). The characteristics of "gap-year" students and their tertiary academic outcomes. *Economic Record, 83*(262), 329–44. DOI: 10.1111/j.1475-4932.2007.00418.x.

Blackburn, G., & Scharrer, E. (2018). Video game playing and beliefs about masculinity among male and female emerging adults. *Sex Roles, 80*(5–6), 310–24. DOI: 10.1007/s11199-018-0934-4.

Blum, S. (2018). *Is it Mom's day off?* Retrieved from https://slate.com/human-interest/2018/02/the-queer-parentings-community-sidelines-diverse-gay-dads.html.

Boon, K. A. (2005). Heroes, metanarratives, and the paradox of masculinity in contemporary western culture. *Journal of Men's Studies, 13*(3), 301–12. DOI: 10.3149/jms.1303.301.

Bosson, J. K., Parrott, D. J., Swan, S. C., Kuchynka, S. L., & Schramm, A. T. (2015). A dangerous boomerang: Injunctive norms, hostile sexist attitudes, and male-to-female sexual aggression. *Aggressive Behavior, 41*(6), 580–93. DOI:10.1002/ab.21597.

Bosson, J. K. & Vandello, J. A. (2011). Precarious manhood and its links to action and aggression. *Current Directions in Psychological Science, 20*(2), 82–86. DOI: 10.1177/0963721411402669.

Bowman, J. M., & Filar, D. C. (2018). *Masculinity and student success in higher education.* New York: Routledge.

Bradshaw, P. (2006). *Brokeback Mountain.* Retrieved from https://www.theguardian.com/film/2006/jan/06/3.

Branker, C. (2009). Deserving design: The new generation of student veterans. *Journal of Postsecondary Education and Disability, 22*(1), 59–66. Retrieved from https://eric.ed.gov/?id=EJ844252.

Breiding-Buss, H., Guise, T., Scanlan, T., & Voice, T. (2003). *The support needs of young fathers.* Retrieved from fatherandchild.org.nz/papers/the-support-needs-of-teenage-fathers/.

Bremmer, P. (2017). *Anti-male environment driving men away from campus.* Retrieved from https://www.wnd.com/2017/06/anti-male-environment-driving-men-away-from-college/.

Brogaard, B. (2018). Why agreement to sex is not consent. *Psychology Today.* Retrieved from https://www.psychologytoday.com/us/blog/the-mysteries-love/201803/why-agreement-sex-is-not-consent.

Bronk, K. C., & Baumsteiger, R. (2017). The role of purpose among emerging adults. In L. M. Padilla-Walker & L. J. Nelson (eds.), *Flourishing in emerging adulthood: Positive development during the third decade of life,* (pp. 45–69). New York: Oxford University Press.

Bronte-Tinkew, J., Scott, M. E., & Lilja, E. (2010). Single custodial fathers' involvement and parenting: Implications for outcomes in emerging adulthood. *Journal of Marriage and Family, 72*(5), 107–1127. DOI: 10.1111/j.1741-3737.2010.00753.x.

Brooks, G. R. (1998). *A new psychotherapy for traditional men.* San Francisco, CA: Jossey-Bass.

———. (2017). Counseling, psychotherapy, and psychological interventions for boys and men. In R. F. Levant & Y. J. Wong (eds.). *The Psychology of Men and Masculinities,* (pp. 317–345). Washington, DC: American Psychological Association.

Brooks, D. (2007). *The odyssey years.* Retrieved from https://www.nytimes.com/2007/10/09/opinion/09brooks.html.

Brooks, G. R. (2017). Counseling, psychotherapy, and psychological interventions for boys and men. In R. F. Levant & Y. J. Wong (eds.). *The Psychology of Men and Masculinities,* (pp. 317-345). Washington, DC: American Psychological Association.

Brooms, D. R., Clark, J. S., & Smith, M. (2018). *Empowering men of color on campus.* New Brunswick, NJ: Rutgers University Press.

Brooms, D. R. (2018). "Building us up": Supporting Black male college students in a Black male initiative program. *Critical Sociology, 44*(1), 141–55. DOI: 10.1177/0896920516658940.

Brown, C. A. (2014). *The proof is in: Father absence harms children.* Retrieved from https://www.huffpost.com/entry/the-proof-is-infather-abs_n_4941353.

Calvert, S. L., Staiano, A. E. & Bond, B. J. (2013). Electronic gaming and the obesity crisis. *New Directions in Child Adolescent Development,* 2013(139), 51–57. DOI: 10.1002/cad.20031.

Campbell, O. (2017). *Why gender stereotypes in kids' shows are a really big deal.* Retrieved from https://www.refinery29.com/en-us/kids-shows-gender-roles-stereotypes.

Carberry, D. (2017). Masculinities, attachment theory and transformative learning: A discussion of some theoretical considerations for developing an emotionally secure teaching praxis. *Journal of Prison Education and Reentry, 4*(2), 82–97. DOI:10.15845/jper.v4i2.883.

Career Now Brands. (2019). *Trade school vs. traditional college.* Retrieved from https://careerschoolnow.org/careers/trade-school-vs-traditional-college.

Carnevale, A. P., Hanson, A. R., & Fasules, M. (2018). *The career-ready high-school graduate exists only in your imagination.* Retrieved from https://www.marketwatch.com/story/the-career-ready-high-school-graduate-exists-only-in-your-imagination-2018-01-03.

Cartreine, J. (2016). *More than sad: Depression affects your ability to think.* Retrieved from https://www.health.harvard.edu/blog/sad-depression-affects-ability-think-201605069551.

Casserly, M. (2012). Are men the latest victims of media misrepresentation? *Forbes Magazine.* Retrieved from https://www.forbes.com/sites/meghancasserly/2012/11/14/are-men-the-latest-victims-of-media-misrepresentation/#92c26fd2caf0.

CAST (2019). *About universal design for learning.* Retrieved from http://www.cast.org/our-work/about-udl.html#.XFjm4lxKg2w.

Castillo, J. T., & Sarver, C. M. (2012). Non-resident fathers' social networks: The relationship between social support and father involvement. *Personal Relationships, 19*(4), 759–74. DOI: 10.1111/j.1475-6811.2011.01391.x.

Catt, C. (2014). *Trapped in the kitchen: How advertising defined women's roles in 1950s America.* Retrieved from https://baylor-ir.tdl.org/handle/2104/8951.

Celli, L. & Young, N. D. (2014). *Learning style perspectives: Impact in the classroom* (3rd ed.). Madison, WI: Atwood Publishing.

Centers for Disease Control and Prevention: Division of Adolescent and School Health (2017). *Youth risk behavior survey: Data summary & trends report: 2007–2017.* Retrieved from https://www.cdc.gov/healthyyouth/data/yrbs/pdf/trendsreport.pdf.

Chakravorti, B. (2017). *There's a gender gap in internet usage. Closing it would open up opportunities for everyone.* Retrieved from https://hbr.org/2017/12/theres-a-gender-gap-in-internet-usage-closing-it-would-open-up-opportunities-for-everyone.

Chaplin, T. M. (2015). Gender and emotion expression: A developmental contextual perspective. *Emotion Review: Journal of the International Society for Research on Emotion, 7*(1), 14–21. DOI: 10.1177/1754073914544408.

Chen, T. (2017). *The issue of masculinity in Disney princes.* Retrieved from https://www.stuyspec.com/ae/film/the-issue-of-masculinity-in-disney-princes.

Chen, X. (2005). *First-generation students in postsecondary education: A look at their college transcripts.* U.S. Department of Education, National Center for Education Statistics. Retrieved from https://nces.ed.gov/pubs2005/2005171.pdf.

Chen, Y. C. & Curtner-Smith, M. (2013). Hegemonic masculinity in sport education: Case Studies of experienced in-service teachers with teaching orientations. *European Physical Education Review, 19*(3), 360–80. DOI: 10.1177/1356336X13495631.

Chen, J., Moran, S., & Gardner, H. (2009) *Multiple intelligences around the world.* San Francisco, CA: Jossey-Bass.

Chesley, N. (2011). Stay-at-home fathers and breadwinning mothers: Gender, couple dynamics, and social change. *Gender and Society, 25*(5), 642–64. DOI: 10.1177/0891243211417433.

Chickering, A. W. (1969). *Education and identity*. San Francisco, CA: Jossey-Bass.
Chickering, A. W. & Reisser, L. (1993). *Education and identity* (2nd ed.). San Francisco, CA: Jossey-Bass.
Chu, J. Y. (2014). *When boys become boys: Development, relationships, and masculinity*. New York: New York University Press.
Cleveland, K. C. (2011). *Teaching boys who struggle in school: Strategies that turn underachievers into successful learners*. Alexandria, VA: ASCD.
Cohen, S. (2018). *How Archie Bunker forever changed the American sitcom*. Retrieved from https://www.smithsonianmag.com/arts-culture/history-working-class-families-american-sitcom-180968555/.
Coles, R. L. (2002). Black single fathers: Choosing to parent fulltime. *Journal of Contemporary Ethnography, 31*(4), 411–39.
———. (2009). Just doing what they gotta do: Single black custodial fathers coping with the stresses and reaping the rewards of parenting. *Journal of Family Issues, 30*(10), 1311–1338.
———. (2015). Single-father families: A review of the literature. *Journal of Family Theory & Review, 7*(2), 144–66. DOI: 10.1177/0891241602031004002.
Collins, K., Connors, K., Davis, S., Donohue, A., Gardner, S., Goldblatt, E., Thompson, E. (2010). *Understanding the impact of trauma and urban poverty on family systems: Risks, resilience, and interventions*. Baltimore, MD: Family Informed Trauma Treatment Center. Retrieved from https://www.nctsn.org/sites/default/files/resources/resource-guide/understanding_impact_trauma_urban_poverty_family_systems.pdf.
Connell, R. (2008). Masculinity construction and sports in boys' education: A framework for thinking about the issue. *Sport Education and Society, 13*(2), 131–45. DOI: 10.1080/13573320801957053.
Connell, R. W. & Messerschmidt, J. W. (2005). Hegemonic masculinity: Rethinking the concept. *Gender and Society, 19*(6), 829–59. DOI: 10.1177/0891243205278639.
Constable, K. (2017). *8 reasons to choose travel over going to college*. Retrieved from https://www.huffpost.com/entry/8-reasons-to-choose-trave_n_6282714.
Cook, D. A. & Sklar, R. (2019). *History of the motion picture*. Retrieved from https://www.britannica.com/art/history-of-the-motion-picture.
Cortiella, C. & Horowitz, S. H. (2014). *The State of Learning Disabilities: Facts, Trends and Emerging Issues*. New York: National Center for Learning Disabilities, 2014. Retrieved from www.ncld.org/wp-content/uploads/2014/11/2014-State-of-LD.pdf.
Cote, J. (2000). *Arrested adulthood: The changing nature of maturity and identity*. New York: New York University Press.
Crawford, C. & Cribb, J. (2012). *Gap year takers: Uptake, trends and long term outcomes*. Department for Education: Institute for Fiscal Studies through the Centre for Analysis of Youth Transitions (CAYT). Retrieved from https://assets.publishing.service.gov.uk/government/uploads/system/uploads/attachment_data/file/219637/DFE-RR252.pdf.
Dalley-Trim, L. (2007). "The boys" present . . . Hegemonic masculinity: A performance of multiple acts. *Gender and Education, 19*(2), 199–217. DOI: 10.1080/09540250601166027.

Daloz, L. A. P. (2011). Mentoring men for wisdom: Transforming the pillars of manhood. New *Directions for Adult and Continuing Education, 2001*(131), 75–83. DOI: 10.1002/ace.423.

Davies, A. W. J. (2018). Boys do cry: Why conversations about gender are crucial in schools. *Education Canada.* Retrieved from https://www.edcan.ca/articles/boys-do-cry/.

Degges-White, S., & Colon, B. (Eds.) (2012). Counseling boys and young men. New York: Springer Publishing Company.

Department of Defense. (n.d.). *Types of military service.* Retrieved from https://www.myfuture.com/military/joining/types-of-military-service.

Derman-Sparks, L. (2012). *Stages in children's development of racial/cultural identity and attitudes.* Retrieved from https://www.uua.org/sites/live-new.uua.org/files/documents/derman-sparkslouise/1206_233_identity_stages.pdf.

Derraugh, L. S. (2018). Hegemonic masculinity and rape culture: Negotiating manhood at a Canadian university (Unpublished doctoral dissertation). Memorial University of Newfoundland. Retrieved from https://research.library.mun.ca/13251/1/thesis.pdf.

DeSilver, D. (2016). *10 facts about American workers.* Pew Research Center. Retrieved from http://www.pewresearch.org/fact-tank/2016/09/01/8-facts-about-american-workers/.

DiPrete, T. A., & Buchmann, C. (2013). *The rise of women: The growing gender gap in education and what it means for American schools.* New York: Russell Sage Foundation.

DiRamio, D., & Jarvis, K. (2011). *When Johnny and Jane come marching to campus: Veterans in higher education.* Hoboken, NJ: Wiley Periodicals Inc.

DoSomething.org (n.d.). *11 facts about teen dads.* Retrieved from https://www.dosomething.org/us/facts/11-facts-about-teen-dads.

Dos Santos, J. P., Tavares, M., & Barros, P. P. (2016). More than just numbers: Suicide rates and the economic cycle in Portugal (1910-2013). *SSM–Population Health, 2,* 14–23. DOI:10.1016/j.ssmph.2015.11.004.

Doucet, A. (2004). "It's almost like I have a job, but I don't get paid": Fathers at home reconfiguring work, care, and masculinity. *Fathering, 2*(3), 277–303. DOI: 10.3149/fth.0203.277.

Doyle, A. (2018). *Soft skills list and examples.* Retrieved from https://www.thebalance.com/list-of-soft-skills-2063770.

———. (2019a). *Certificate programs that lead to high-paying jobs.* Retrieved from https://www.thebalancecareers.com/certificate-programs-that-lead-to-high-paying-jobs-4171913.

———. (2019b). *Top 10 fastest growing careers.* Retrieved from https://www.thebalancecareers.com/top-fastest-growing-jobs-2059649.

Dreher, R. (2018). *The lost boys.* Retrieved from https://www.theamericanconservative.com/dreher/lost-boys-millennial-male-unemployment/.

Drew, A. (2019). *Guys, let's talk about mental health.* Retrieved from https://thriveglobal.com/stories/guys-lets-talk-about-mental-health/.

Dryfuss, E. (2019). *Gillette's ad proves the definition of a good man has changed.* Retrieved from https://www.wired.com/story/gillette-we-believe-ad-men-backlash/.

Dufur, M. J., Howell, N. C., Downey, D. B., Ainsworth, J. W, & Lapray, A. J. (2010). Sex differences in parenting behaviors in single-mother and single-father households. *Journal of Marriage and Family, 72*(5), 1092–1106. DOI: 10.1111/j.1741-3737.2010.00752.x.

Durham, M. (2001). Adolescents, the internet, and the politics of gender: A feminist case analysis. *Race, Gender & Class, 8*(4), 20–41. Retrieved from http://www.jstor.org/stable/41674993.

Dwyer, R. E., Hodson, R. & McCloud, L. (2013). Gender, debt, and dropping out of college. *Gender & Society, 27*(1), 30–55. DOI: 10.1177/0891243212464906.

Eisler, R. M. (1995). The relationship between masculine gender role stress and men's health risks: The validation of a construct. In R. F. Levant & W. S. Pollack (Eds.). *A New Psychology of Men,* (pp. 207-228). New York: Harper Collins.

ElHatage, A. (2017). Five facts about today's single fathers. Retrieved from https://ifstudies.org/blog/five-facts-about-todays-single-fathers.

Eliot, L. (2009). *Pink brain, blue brain: How small differences grow into troublesome gaps and what we can do about it.* New York: First Mariner Books.

Elliot, C. (2019). *The smartest and cheapest ways to travel.* Retrieved from https://www.listenmoneymatters.com/cheapest-ways-to-travel/.

Erikson, E. H. (1968). *Identity: Youth and crisis.* New York: W.W. Norton & Company.

Esbensen, H. R. (2014). *Illuminating the experiences of single fathers.* Retrieved from https://pdxscholar.library.pdx.edu/cgi/viewcontent.cgi?article=2963&context=open_access_etds.

Exon, M. & Arrow, M. (2015). *Eight ads that shatter tired gender stereotypes.* Retrieved from https://www.theguardian.com/media-network/2015/may/26/eight-ads-shatter-gender-stereotypes.

Farrington, R. (2014). *5 proud alternatives to going to college.* Retrieved from https://www.forbes.com/sites/robertfarrington/2014/11/10/5-proud-alternatives-to-going-to-college/#7a893c7354e7.

The Fatherhood Project. (2016). Teen dads: The forgotten parent. Retrieved from www.thefatherhoodproject.org/teen-dads-forgotten-parent/.

Ferebee, A. (2018). *Why has masculinity in men declined over generations?* Retrieved from https://www.quora.com/Why-has-masculinity-in-men-declined-over-generations.

Fleming, M. C., & Englar-Carlson, M. (2008). Examining depression and suicidality in boys and male adolescents. In M. S. Kiselica, M. Englar-Carlson, & A. M. Horne (Eds). *Counseling Troubled Boys: A Guidebook for Professionals*, (pp. 125–61). New York: Taylor & Francis.

Ford, C. (2019). *Boys will be boys: Power, patriarchy and toxic masculinity.* London, UK: Oneworld Publications.

Ford, M. (2018). *Should I enter college or start working after high school?* Retrieved from https://www.businessadministrationinformation.com/education/should-i-enter-college-or-start-working-after-high-school.

Froschl, M. & Sprung, B. (2005). *Raising and educating healthy boys: A report on the growing crisis in boys' education.* Retrieved from https://files.eric.ed.gov/fulltext/ED500855.pdf.

Gap Year Association (2019). *Gap year data & benefits.* Retrieved from https://gap yearassociation.org/data-benefits.php.

Gardner, H. (2006). *Multiple intelligences: New horizons.* New York: Basic Books.

Gentleman's Journal (n.d.). *20 of the most successful business men without degrees.* Retrieved from https://www.thegentlemansjournal.com/20-of-the-most-successful-businessmen-without-degrees/.

Gillette (2019). *We believe: The best men can be.* Retrieved from https://www.youtube.com/watch?v=koPmuEyP3a0.

Gilmore, D. D. (1990). *Manhood in the making: Cultural concepts of masculinity.* New Haven, CT: Yale University Press.

Global Citizen Year (2019). *About us: Global Citizen Year is launching a generation of leaders we can all be proud of.* Retrieved from https://www.globalcitizenyear.org/.

GLSEN (2019). *That's a (gender) stereotype!* Retrieved from https://www.glsen.org/article/thats-gender-stereotype.

Goffman, E. (1979). *Gender advertisements.* New York: Harper Row.

Gosse, D. (2012). Men, masculinities, and sexualities in education and society: A call for evolution! *Education Canada, 52*(1). Retrieved from https://eric.ed.gov/?id=EJ970549.

Gotell, L. & Dutton, E. (2016). Sexual violence in the "manosphere": Antifeminist men's rights discourses on rape. *International Journal for Crime, Justice and Social Democracy, 5*(2), 65–80. DOI:10.5204/ijcjsd.v5i2.310.

Gottman, J. W. & Gottman, J. M. (2015). *10 principles for doing effective couples therapy.* New York: W.W. Norton & Company.

Gourgy, A. (2009). 15 ways to travel for free (or at least cheap). Retrieved from https://www.vergemagazine.com/travel-intelligence/budget-travel/76-15-ways-to-travel-for-free-or-at-least-cheap.html.

Gray, K. L., Buyukozturk, B., & Hill, Z. G. (2017). Blurring the boundaries: Using Gamergate to examine real and symbolic violence against women in contemporary gaming culture. *Sociology Compass, 11*(3), 1–8. DOI:10.1111/soc4.12458.

Greenspan, J. (2019). *9 things you may not know about the U.S. Armed Services.* Retrieved from https://www.history.com/news/9-things-you-may-not-know-about-the-u-s-armed-forces.

Greer, S. (2017). *No campus for white men: The transformation of higher education into hateful indoctrination.* Washington, DC: WND Books.

Greif, G. L. (1985). Single fathers rearing children. *Journal of Marriage and the Family, 47*(1), 185–91. DOI: 10.2307/352081.

Griffin, K. W. & Botvin, G. J. (2010). Evidence-based interventions for preventing substance abuse disorders in adolescents. *Clinical Adolescent Psychiatric Clinics of North America, 19*(3), 505–26. DOI: 10.1016/j.chc.2010.03.005.

Griffith, D. M., Brinkley-Rubinstein, L., Bruce, M. A., Thorpe, R. J., & Metzl, J. M. (2015). The interdependence of African American men's definitions of manhood and health. *Family & Community Health, 38*(4), 284–96. DOI: 10.1097/FCH.0000000000000079.

Hackman, R. (September 5, 2013). *"I didn't choose to be straight, white and male": Are modern men the suffering sex?* Retrieved from https://www.theguardian.com/world/2016/sep/05/straight-while-men-suffering-sex-feminism.

Hadley, W. M. (2007). The necessity of academic accommodations for first-year college students with learning disabilities. *Journal of College Admission, 195*, 9–13. Retrieved from http://www.eric.ed.gov/?idEJ783943.

Hamer, J., & Marchioro, K. (2002). Becoming custodial dads: Exploring parenting among low-income and working-class African American fathers. *Journal of Marriage and Family*, 64, 116–129. DOI: 10.1111.j.1741-3737.2002.00116.x.

Hamilton, S. F., & Hamilton, M. A. (2006). School, work, and emerging adulthood. In J. J. Arnett & J. L. Tanner (Eds.), *Emerging adults in America: Coming of age in the 21st century* (pp. 257–77). Washington, DC: American Psychological Association.

Hamm, T. (2019). *Why you should consider trade school instead of college.* Retrieved from https://www.thesimpledollar.com/why-you-should-consider-trade-school-instead-of-college/.

Han, A. (2015). *The heroic masculinity of "Mad Max: Fury Road."* Retrieved from https://www.slashfilm.com/mad-max-masculinity/.

Hart Research Associates (2014). *Rising to the challenge: Are high school graduates prepared for college and work?* Retrieved from https://sites.ed.gov/underserved youth/files/2017/01/MS3-Lead-Higher-Initiative-Rising-To-The-Challenge.pdf.

Hathaway, J. (2014a). *Felicia Day says she's afraid of Gamergate, immediately gets doxxed.* Retrieved from https://gawker.com/felicia-day-says-shes-afraid-of-gamergate-immediately-1649790900.

———. (2014b). *What is Gamergate, and why? An explainer for non-geeks.* Retrieved from https://gawker.com/what-is-gamergate-and-why-an-explainer-for-non-geeks-1642909080.

Hatter, W., Williams, R. A., & Vinter, L. (2002). *Dads on dads: Needs and expectations at home and at work.* Manchester, UK: Equal Opportunities Commission.

Haymarket Media Group (2016). *Case study: How fame made Snickers' "you're not you when you're hungry" campaign a success.* Retrieved from https://www.campaignlive.com/article/case-study-fame-made-snickers-youre-not-when-youre-hungry-campaign-success/1413554#uwk7BvoaoC4REfJq.99.

Heathfield, S. M. (2018). *An entry-level job: A foot in the door.* Retrieved from https://www.thebalancecareers.com/what-is-an-entry-level-job-1918126.

Hern, A. (January 13, 2015). *Gamergate hits new low with attempts to send SWAT teams to critics.* Retrieved from https://www.theguardian.com/technology/2015/jan/13/gamergate-hits-new-low-with-attempts-to-send-swat-teams-to-critics.

Hess, A. (2018). *Massive survey finds 1 in 3 college freshmen struggle with mental health-here are 4 things you can do.* Retrieved from https://www.cnbc.com/2018/10/04/4-ways-to-be-proactive-about-your-mental-health-in-college.html.

Hirstein, W. (2013). *What is a psychopath?* Retrieved from https://www.psychology today.com/us/blog/mindmelding/201301/what-is-psychopath-0.

Hoe, N. (2015). *American gap year association national alumni survey report.* Retrieved from https://gapyearassociation.org/assets/2015%20NAS%20Report.pdf.

Hogan, A. & Roberts, B. (2015). Occupational employment projections to 2024. *United States Department of Labor: Bureau of Labor Statistics*. Retrieved from https://www.bls.gov/opub/mlr/2015/article/occupational-employment-projections-to-2024.htm.

Horn, S. S. (2007). Adolescents' acceptance of same-sex peers based on sexual orientation and gender expression. *Journal of Youth and Adolescence, 36*(3), 373. DOI:10.1007/s10964-007-9176-4.

Horowitz, S. H., Rawe, J., & Whittaker, M. C. (2017). *The state of learning disabilities: Understanding the 1 in 5.* New York: National Center for Learning Disabilities. Retrieved from https://www.ncld.org/wp-content/uploads/2017/03/Executive-Summary.Fin_.03142017.pdf.

Houshmand, S., Spanierman, L., & Tafarodi, R. W. (2014). Racial microaggressions targeting Asian students in Canada. *American Psychological Association, 20*(3), 377–88. DOI: 10.1037/a0035404.

Hymowitz, K. S. (2008). Child-man in the promised land. Retrieved from https://www.city-journal.org/html/child-man-promised-land-13063.html.

Institute for Community Inclusion (2017). What is Think College? Retrieved from https://thinkcollege.net/about/what-is-think-college.

Ito, R. (2015). In the documentary "GTFO," female video gamers fight back. *The New York Times*. Retrieved from https://www.nytimes.com/2015/03/08/movies/in-the-documentary-gtfo-female-video-gamers-fight-back.html.

Jhally, S., Ericsson, S., Talreja, S., Katz, J., Earp, J., & Media Education Foundation. (1999). *Tough guise: Violence, media, and the crisis in masculinity.* Retrieved from http://www.mediaed.org/transcripts/Tough-Guise-Abridged-Transcript.pdf.

Johansson, T., & Hammeren, N. (2014). "Imagine, just 16 years old and already a dad!" The construction of young fatherhood on the internet. DOI: 10.1080/02673843.2012.747972.

Johansson, T., & Klinth, R. (2008). Caring fathers: The ideology of gender equality and masculine positions. *Men and Masculinities, 11*(1), 42–62. DOI: 10.1177/1097184X06291899.

Johnson, H. (2017). *Earn and Learn: 10 great jobs that start with an apprenticeship.* Retrieved from https://www.thesimpledollar.com/apprenticeship-programs/.

Johnson, C. W. & Cousineau, L. S. (2019). Manning up and manning on: Masculinities, hegemonic masculinity, and leisure studies. In D. C. Parry (ed.), *Feminisms in Leisure Studies: Advancing a fourth wave*, (pp. 126–48). New York: Routledge.

Johnson, C. A. & Hawbaker, K. T. (2019). #MeToo: A timeline of events. *Chicago Tribune*. Retrieved from https://www.chicagotribune.com/lifestyles/ct-me-too-timeline-20171208-htmlstory.html.

Johnston, J. H. (2012). *The trouble with boys: Observations about boys' post-secondary aspirations, attendance, and success.* Retrieved from https://files.eric.ed.gov/fulltext/ED538697.pdf.

Jordan E. (1995). Fighting boys and fantasy play: The construction of masculinity in the early years of school. *Gender and Education, 7*(1), 69–86. DOI: 10.1080/713668458.

Kailing, D. & Cantrell, P. (2014). *Traditional masculinity & advertising image approval.* Retrieved from https://dc.etsu.edu/cgi/viewcontent.cgi?referer=https://www.google.com/&httpsredir=1&article=1204&context=honors.

Kalra, G. & Bhugra, D. (2013). Sexual violence against women: Understanding cross-cultural intersections. *Indian Journal of Psychiatry, 55*(3), 244–49. DOI: 10.4103/0019-5545.117139.

Kassan, M. (2012). *Break Media debuts the Acumen Report: The modern "mensch" and the power of insight.* Retrieved from https://www.mediavillage.com/article/break-media-debuts-the-acumen-report-the-modern-mensch-and-the-power-of-insight-michael-kassan/.

Kennedy-Moore, E. & Watson, J. C. (1999). *Expressing emotion: Myths, realities and therapeutic strategies.* New York: The Guilford Press.

Kerr, S. P., Kerr, W. R., & Xu, T. (2017). Personality traits of entrepreneurs: A review of recent literature. *Harvard Business School.* Retrieved from https://www.hbs.edu/faculty/Publication%20Files/18-047_b0074a64-5428-479b-8c83-16f2a0e97eb6.pdf.

Kidd, D., & Turner, A. J. (2016). The #GamerGate Files: misogyny in the media. In A. Novak & I. J. El-Burki, *Defining identity and the changing scope of culture in the digital age* (pp. 117–39). Hershey, PA: IGI Global.

Kids Count Data Center (2017). *Child population by race and age group.* Retrieved from https://www.kidsdata.org/topic/7/demographics/summary.

Kielty, S. (2006). Similarities and differences in the experiences of non-resident mothers and non-resident fathers, *International Journal of Law, Policy and the Family, 20*(1). 74–94. DOI: 10.1093/lawfam/ebi033.

Kiselica, M. S. (1999). Counseling teen fathers. In A. M. Horne & M. S. Kiselica (Eds.). *Handbook of Counseling Boys and Adolescent Males: A Practitioner's Guide* (pp. 179–97). Thousand Oaks, CA: Sage Publications, Inc.

Kiselica, M. S. (2008). When boys become fathers: Adolescent fatherhood in America. New Brunswick, NJ: Rutgers University Press.

Kleinfeld, J. (2009). No map to manhood: Male and female mindsets behind college gender gap. *Gender Issues, 26*(3–4), 171–82. Retrieved from http://www.judithkleinfeld.com/ar_nomap.html.

Knorr, C. (2017). *What media teach kids about gender can have lasting effects, report says.* Retrieved from https://www-m.cnn.com/2017/06/29/health/gender-stereotypes-media-children-partner/index.html?r=https%3A%2F%2Fwww.google.com%2F.

Koenig, R. (2019). *25 best jobs that don't require a college degree.* Retrieved from https://money.usnews.com/money/careers/slideshow/25-best-jobs-that-dont-require-a-college-degree.

Kolhatkar, S. (November 26, 2014). *The gaming industry's greatest adversary is just getting started.* Retrieved from https://longform.org/posts/the-gaming-industry-s-greatest-adversary-is-just-getting-started.

Korte, L. (2017). *Youth suicide rates are rising: School and the internet may be to blame.* Retrieved from https://www.usatoday.com/story/news/nation-now/2017/05/30/youth-suicide-rates-rising-school-and-internet-may-blame/356539001/.

Kotchick, B. A., Dorsey, S., & Heller, L. (2005). Predictors of parenting among African American single mothers: Personal and contextual factors. *Journal of Marriage and Family, 67*(2), 448–60. DOI: 10.1111/j.0022-2445.2005.00127.x.

Kraemer, S. (2011). The mental health of boys. *Trends in Urology & Men's Health*, 9–11. Retrieved from https://onlinelibrary.wiley.com/doi/pdf/10.1002/tre.196.

Kreisman, D. & Strange, K. (2017). *Vocational and career tech education in American high schools: The value of depth over breadth.* Retrieved from https://aysps.gsu.edu/files/2017/10/17-12-Kreisman-VocationalTech.pdf.

Kritselis, A. (2014). *7 Problematic lessons Disney movies teach boys about masculinity.* Retrieved from https://www.bustle.com/articles/17264-7-problematic-lessons-disney-movies-teach-boys-about-masculinity.

Kroeger, T., Cooke, T., & Gould, E. (2016). *The class of 2016: The labor market is still far from ideal for young graduates.* Retrieved from https://www.epi.org/publication/class-of-2016/.

Kugelmass, H. & Ready, D. D. (2011). Racial/ethnic disparities in collegiate cognitive gains: A multilevel analysis of instructional influences on learning and its equitable distribution. *Research in Higher Education, 52*(4), 323–48. DOI: 10.1007/s11162-010-9200-5.

Kuh, G. D. (2001). Assessing what really matters to student learning: Inside the National Survey of Student Engagement. *Change: The Magazine of Higher Learning, 33*(3), 10–17. DOI: 10.1080/00091380109601795.

Kutner, M. (2018). Teen suicide is contagious, and the problem may be worse than we thought. *Newsweek Magazine.* Retrieved from http://www.newsweek.com/2016/10/28/teen-suicide-contagious-colorado-springs-511365.html.

Lang, N. (2018). *New study: Rates of anti-LGBTQ school bullying at "unprecedented high."* Retrieved from https://www.thedailybeast.com/new-study-rates-of-anti-lgbtq-school-bullying-at-unprecedented-high.

Langman, P. (2009). *Why kids kill: Inside the minds of school shooters.* New York: St. Martin's Griffin.

———. (2015). *School shooters: Understanding high school, college, and adult perpetrators.* Lanham, MD: Rowman & Littlefield.

Leadem, R. (2018). *Trade school vs. college: Which is right for you?* Retrieved from https://www.entrepreneur.com/article/316320.

Leaper, C., Farkas, T., & Starr, C. R. (2018). Traditional masculinity, help avoidance, and intrinsic interest in relation to high school students' English and math performance. *Psychology of Men & Masculinity*, 1–9. DOI: 10.1037/men0000188.

Lederman, D. (2018). Who is studying online (and where). *Inside Higher Ed.* Retrieved from https://www.insidehighered.com/digital-learning/article/2018/01/05/new-us-data-show-continued-growth-college-students-studying.

Leone, R. M. & Parrott, D. J. (2019). Misogynistic peers, masculinity, and bystander intervention for sexual aggression: Is it really just "locker-room talk?" *Aggressive Behavior, 45*(1), 42–51. DOI: 10.1002/ab.21795.

Levant, R. F. (1995). Toward the reconstruction of masculinity. In R. Levant & W. Pollack (Eds.), *A New Psychology of Men* (pp. 229–51). New York: Basic Books.

Lewis, M. (n.d.). *Joining the military after high school—Benefits & risks*. Retrieved from https://www.moneycrashers.com/joining-military-benefits-risks/.

Logan, J. E. & Mercy, J. A. (2018). Suicide, violence, and other forms of injury. *The CDC Field Epidemiology Manual*. Retrieved from https://www.cdc.gov/eis/field-epi-manual/chapters/other-injury.html.

Lotterhos, F. H. (2015). *Men cry: Embodiments of masculinity in western cinema circa 1999*. Retrieved from https://scholar.colorado.edu/cgi/viewcontent.cgi?article=2112&context=honr_theses.

Lynch, L., Long, M., & Moorhead, A. (2018). Young men, help-seeking, and mental health services: Exploring barriers and solutions. *American Journal of Men's Health, 12*(1), 138–49. DOI: 10.1177/1557988315619469.

Maestripieri, D. (2012). Gender differences in personality are larger than previously thought. *Psychology Today*. Retrieved from https://www.psychologytoday.com/us/blog/games-primates-play/201201/gender-differences-in-personality-are-larger-previously-thought.

Mahalik, J. R., Locke, B. D., Ludlow, L. H., Diemer, M. A., Scott, R. P. J., Gottfried, M., & Freitas, G. (2003). Development of the Conformity to Masculine Norms Inventory. *Psychology of Men & Masculinity, 4*(1), 3–25. DOI: 10.1037/1524-9220.4.1.3.

Mahnken, K. (2017). *The hidden mental health crisis in America's schools: Millions of kids not receiving services they need*. Retrieved from https://www.the74million.org/the-hidden-mental-health-crisis-in-americas-schools-millions-of-kids-not-receiving-services-they-need/.

Manhas, S. (2018). *How modern cinema is shifting ideas of masculinity*. Retrieved from https://goodmenproject.com/featured-content/how-modern-cinema-is-shifting-ideas-of-masculinity/.

Marcus, J. (2017). *Why men are the new college minority*. Retrieved from https://www.theatlantic.com/education/archive/2017/08/why-men-are-the-new-college-minority/536103/.

Marcus, J. (2018). *Facts about race and college admission*. Retrieved from https://hechingerreport.org/facts-about-race-and-college-admission/.

Marketing Charts. (2018). *Consumers: Gender roles have changed. Advertising hasn't*. Retrieved from https://www.marketingcharts.com/advertising-trends/creative-and-formats-82594.

Marquell, T. (2016). *The military or college? Insight from a veteran*. Retrieved from https://americanhonors.org/blog/article/military-or-college-insight-veteran.

Martino, W. (2011). Failing boys! Beyond crisis, moral panic and limiting stereotypes. *Education Canada, 51*(4). Retrieved from https://eric.ed.gov/?id=EJ946430.

Mascolo, M. F. & Fischer, K. W. (2010). The dynamic development of thinking, feeling and acting over the lifespan. Retrieved from https://www.gse.harvard.edu/~ddl/articlesCopy/Mascolo_Fischer_Dynamic_Development_072009_rvsdJul27.pdf.

Maslow, A. H. (1987). *Motivation and personality* (3rd ed.). Delhi, India: Pearson Education.

Matsuba, M. K., Alisat, S., & Pratt, M. W. (2017). Environmental activism in emerging adulthood. In L. M. Padilla-Walker & L. J. Nelson (eds.), *Flourishing in*

Emerging Adulthood: Positive Development During the Third Decade of Life (pp. 175–211). New York: Oxford University Press.

Maupin, A. N., Brophy-Herb, H. E., Schiffman, R. F., & Bocknek, E. L. (2010). Low-income parental profiles of coping, resource adequacy, and public assistance receipt: Links to parenting. *Family Relations, 59*(2), 180–94. DOI: 10.1111/j.1741-3729.2010.00594.x.

McConville, M. (July 26, 2018). How to help a teenager be college-ready. *The New York Times*. Retrieved from https://www.nytimes.com/2018/07/26/well/how-to-help-a-teenager-be-college-ready.html.

McGrath, E. (2016). *Teen depression-boys: Adolescent males face a unique set of pressures*. Retrieved from https://www.psychologytoday.com/us/articles/200207/teen-depression-boys.

McWhirter, K. (2019). *Mental health in college*. Retrieved from https://www.affordablecollegesonline.org/college-resource-center/college-student-mental-health/.

Media Smarts. (2016). *Talking to kids about gender stereotypes*. Retrieved from http://mediasmarts.ca/sites/mediasmarts/files/pdfs/tipsheet/TipSheet_Talking_Kids_Gender_Stereotypes.pdf.

Mehta, S. S., Newbold, J. J., & O'Rourke, M. A. (2011). Why do first-generation students fail? *College Student Journal, 45*(1), 20–35. Retrieved from https://www.researchgate.net/publication/313154576_Why_do_first-generation_students_fail.

Men's Health Month (2019). *June is men's health month!* Retrieved from http://www.menshealthmonth.org/.

Metcalf, S. (2017). How John Wayne became a hollow masculine icon. *The Atlantic*. Retrieved from https://www.theatlantic.com/magazine/archive/2017/12/john-wayne-john-ford/544113/.

MeToo (2018). *You are not alone: History & vision*. Retrieved from https://metoomvmt.org/about/.

Military Advantage (2019a). *Military benefits at a glance*. Retrieved from https://www.military.com/join-armed-forces/military-benefits-overview.html.

———. (2019b). *Overview of military educational benefits*. Retrieved from https://www.military.com/education/money-for-school/education-benefits-in-the-military.html.

———. (2019c). *The ASVAB test*. Retrieved from https://www.military.com/join-armed-forces/asvab.

Military Benefits (2019a). *Inactive ready reserves*. Retrieved from https://militarybenefits.info/irr/.

———. (2019b). *10 veterans benefits you may not know about*. Retrieved from https://militarybenefits.info/10-veterans-benefits-you-may-not-know-about/.

The Military Wallet (2019). *Should I join the military? 11 reasons the military is a good career option*. Retrieved from https://themilitarywallet.com/reasons-to-join-the-military/.

Mitovitch, M. W. (2019). *Gillette says it won't pull TV ad that targets "toxic masculinity" despite backlash*. Retrieved from https://portal.tds.net/news/read/article/

tvline-gillette_wont_pull_tv_ad_that_targets_toxic_mascul-rpenskemc/category/news.

Modello, B. (2014). *Who's the man? Hollywood heroes defined masculinity for millions.* Retrieved from https://www.npr.org/2014/07/30/336575116/whos-the-man-hollywood-heroes-defined-masculinity-for-millions.

Moloney, M., Mackenzie, K., Hunt, G., & Joe-Laidler, K. (2009). The path and promise of fatherhood for gang members. *The British Journal of Criminology, 49*(3), 305–25. DOI:10.1093/bjc/azp003.

Moore, E. (2018). *14 must-have skills for entry-level workers.* Retrieved from https://www.glassdoor.com/blog/must-have-entry-level-worker-skills/.

Morgan, R. E., & Kena, G. (2018). Criminal victimization, 2016: Revised. *U.S. Department of Justice, Office of Justice Programs, Bureau of Justice Statistics.* Retrieved from https://www.bjs.gov/content/pub/pdf/cv16.pdf.

Murphy, H. (2017). What experts know about men who rape. *New York Times.* Retrieved from https://www.nytimes.com/2017/10/30/health/men-rape-sexual-assault.html.

My Brother's Keeper Alliance and MENTOR: The National Mentoring Partnership (2016). *Guide to mentoring boys and young men of color.* Retrieved from https://www.mentoring.org/new-site/wp-content/uploads/2016/05/Guide-to-Mentoring-BYMOC.pdf.

Nagle, A. (2016). The new man of 4chan. *The Baffler,* (30), 64–76. Retrieved from http://www.jstor.org/stable/43959201.

Nash, C. (January 31, 2017). *Applications open for the Yiannopoulos privilege grant.* Retrieved from https://www.breitbart.com/social-justice/2017/01/31/applications-open-yiannopoulos-privilege-grant/.

Naskar, S., Victor, R., Nath, K., & Sengupta, C. (2016). "One level more:" A narrative review on internet gaming disorder. *Industrial Psychiatry Journal, 25*(2), 145–54. DOI: 10.4103/ipj.ipj_67_16.

Nathanson, A. I., Wilson, B. J., McGee, J., & Sebastian, M. (2006). Counteracting the effects of female stereotypes on television via active mediation. *Journal of Communication, 52*(4), 922–37. DOI: 10.1111/j.1460-2466.2002.tb02581.x.

National Academies of Sciences, Engineering, and Medicine (2016). *Parenting Matters: Supporting Parents of Children Ages 0-8.* Washington, DC: The National Academies Press. DOI: 10.17226/21868.

National Sexual Violence Resource Center (2018). *Get statistics: Sexual assault in the United States.* Retrieved from https://www.nsvrc.org/statistics.

Neighmond, P. (2007). *"Generation next" in the slow lane to adulthood.* Retrieved from https://www.npr.org/templates/story/story.php?storyId=17429734.

Neu, T. W. & Weinfield, R. (2007). *Helping Boys succeed in school: A practical guide for parents and teachers.* Waco, TX: Prufrock Press.

Nutt, A. E. (2018). *Suicide rates for black children twice that of white children, new data show.* Retrieved from https://www.washingtonpost.com/news/to-your-health/wp/2018/05/21/suicide-rates-for-black-children-twice-that-of-white-children-new-data-show/?noredirect=on&utm_term=.17a760ae7ccf.

Oesterle, S., Hawkins, J. D., Hill, K. G., & Bailey, J. A. (2010). Men's and women's pathways to adulthood and their adolescent precursors. *Journal of Marriage and the Family, 72*(5), 1436–1453. DOI: 10.1111.j.1741-3737.2010.00775.x.

Ogundele, M. O. (2018). Behavioural and emotional disorders in childhood: A brief overview for paediatricians. *World Journal of Clinical Pediatrics, 7*(1), 9–26. DOI: 10.5409/wjcp.v7.i1.9.

Olson, S. L., & Banyard, V. (1993). "Stop the world so I can get off for a while": Sources of daily stress in the lives of low-income single mothers of young children. *Family Relations, 42*(1), 50–56. DOI: 10.2307/584921.

O'Neil, J. M. (2015). *Men's gender role conflict: Psychological costs, consequences, and an agenda for change.* Washington, DC: American Psychological Association.

O'Neil, J. M., Helms, B., Gable, R., David, L., & Wrightsman, L. (1986). Gender role conflict scale: College men's fear of femininity. *Sex Roles, 14*(5–6), 335–50. DOI: 10.1007/BF00287583.

Oransky, M. & Marecek, J. (2009). "I'm not going to be a girl": Masculinity and emotions in boys' friendships and peer groups. *Journal of Adolescent Research, 24*(2), 218–41. DOI: 10.1177/0743558408329951.

Osherson, S. (1986). *Finding our fathers: The unfinished business of manhood.* New York: Free Press.

Özen, S., & Darcan, Ş. (2011). Effects of environmental endocrine disruptors on pubertal development. *Journal of Clinical Research in Pediatric Endocrinology, 3*(1), 1–6. DOI:10.4274/jcrpe.v3i1.01

Padilla-Walker, L. M., & Nelson, L. J. (2017). *Flourishing in emerging adulthood: Positive development during the third decade of life.* New York: Oxford University Press.

Page, D. & Johnstone, D. (2017). *Five things schools can do to help pupils' mental health.* Retrieved from https://theconversation.com/five-things-schools-can-do-to-help-pupils-mental-health-79376.

Parent, M. C., Gobble, T. D., & Rochlen, A. (2018). Social media behavior, toxic masculinity, and depression. *Psychology of Men & Masculinity.* DOI: 10.1037/men0000156.

Paschal, A. M., Lewis-Moss, R. K., & Hsaio, T. (2011). Perceived fatherhood roles and parenting behaviors among African American teen fathers. *Journal of Adolescent Research, 26*(1), 61–83. DOI: 10.1177/0743558410384733.

Patton, G. C., Darmstadt, G. L., Petroni, S., & Sawyer, S. M. (2018). A gender lens on the health and well-being of young males. *Journal of Adolescent Health, 62*(3S), S6–S8. DOI: 10.1016/jadohealth.2017.06.020.

PBS Parents (n.d.). *The Search for Masculinity: Understanding & raising boys: Growing up masculine.* Retrieved from http://nunu.pbs.org/parents/raisingboys/masculinity02.html.

Peace Corps (n.d.a). *About.* Retrieved from https://www.peacecorps.gov/about/.

———. (n.d.b). *History.* Retrieved from https://www.peacecorps.gov/about/history/.

Pearson, A., (n.d.). *Trade school vs. apprenticeship.* Retrieved from https://www.theclassroom.com/trade-school-vs-apprenticeship-33325.html.

Pendoley, R. (2017). Avoid the gap year mistake. *Psychology Today*. Retrieved from https://www.psychologytoday.com/us/blog/the-transition-college/201705/avoid-the-gap-year-mistake.

Phinney, J. S. (2003). Ethnic identity and acculturation. In K. M. Chun, P. B. Organista, & G. Marin (Eds.), *Acculturation: Advances in Theory, Measurement, and Applied Research* (pp. 63-81). Washington, DC: American Psychological Association.

———. (2006). Ethnic Identity Exploration in Emerging Adulthood. In J. J. Arnett & J. L. Tanner (Eds.), *Emerging Adults in America: Coming of Age in the 21st Century* (pp. 117–34). Washington, DC: American Psychological Association.

Pittman, F. (1993). *Man enough: Fathers, sons, and the search for masculinity*. New York: Pedigree Publishing.

Pleck, J. H. (1981). *The myth of masculinity*. Cambridge, MA: MIT Press.

———. (2003). The gender role strain paradigm. An update. In R. F. Levant & W. S. Pollack (eds.), *A new psychology of men* (pp. 11–32). New York, NY: Basic Books.

Pollack, W. S. (1998). *Real boys: Rescuing our sons from the myths of boyhood*. New York: Henry Holt and Company.

———. (2001). *Real boys' voices*. New York: Penguin Books.

———. (2005). "Masked men": New psychoanalytically oriented treatment models for adult and young adult men. In G. E. Good & G. R. Brooks (Eds.), *The New Handbook of Psychotherapy and Counseling with Men* (pp. 203–16). San Francisco, CA: Jossey-Bass.

Porpora, D. (1996). Personal heroes, religion, and transcendental matanarratives. *Sociological Forum, 11*(2), 209–29. DOI: 10.1007/BF02408365.

Powell, W. (n.d.). *Speaking of psychology: How masculinity can hurt mental health*. Retrieved from https://www.apa.org/research/action/speaking-of-psychology/men-boys-health-disparities.

Powers, R. (2019). *U.S. military 101—Army, navy, air force, marines and coast guard*. Retrieved from https://www.thebalancecareers.com/u-s-military-101-3331988.

Prescott, A. T., Sargent, J. D., & Hull, J. G. (2018). Metaanalysis of the relationship between violent video game play and physical aggression over time. *Proceedings of the National Academy of Sciences, 115*(40), 9882–9888. DOI: 10.1073/pnas.1611617114.

PREVNet (2019). *Bullying: Facts & solutions*. Retrieved from https://www.prevnet.ca/bullying/facts-and-solutions.

Purnell-Mack, R. D. (2017). *The college bound brotherhood: A regional movement to increase college opportunity and success for the black male youth*. Retrieved from https://www.marcusfoster.org/collegeboundbrotherhood.

Rampton, J. (2016). *12 of the most successful entrepreneurs who dropped out of college*. Retrieved from https://mashable.com/2016/09/22/12-entrepreneurs-who-dropped-out-of-college/.

Randolph, M. E., Torres, H., Gore-Felton, C., Lloyd, B., & McGarvey, E. L. (2009). Alcohol use and sexual risk behavior among college students: Understanding gender and ethnic differences. *American Journal of Drug and Alcohol Abuse, 35*(2), 80–84. DOI: 10.1080/00952990802585422.

Rapaport, L. (2019). Gay fathers face stigma as parents. Retrieved from https://www.reuters.com/article/us-health-lgbt-gay-dads/gay-fathers-face-stigma-as-parents-idUSKCN1P92TS.

Real, T. (1997). *I don't want to talk about it: Overcoming the secret legacy of male depression.* New York: Scribner.

Recovery Worldwide (2019). *Drinking and drugs: Combining alcohol and drugs.* Retrieved from https://www.alcoholrehabguide.org/alcohol/drinking-drugs/.

Reichert, M. & Hawley, R. (2010). *Reaching boys, teaching boys: Strategies that work—and why.* San Francisco, CA: John Wiley & Sons.

Reilly, D. (2019). Coddled kids crumble. Retrieved from https://www.lifezette.com/2019/03/coddled-kids-crumble/.

Reksodiputro, J. (2018). *Opinion: Mental health culture on college campuses needs to be more gender-inclusive.* Retrieved from https://www.statepress.com/article/2018/09/spopinion-mental-health-culture-gender-inclusive.

RethinkOldSchool (n.d.). *Military or college?* Retrieved from https://www.yourfreecareertest.com/college-prep/college-degrees/military-or-college/.

Rice, S. M., Purcell, R., & McGorry, P. D. (2018). Adolescent and young adult male mental health: Transforming system failures into proactive models of engagement. *Journal of Adolescent Health, 62*(3S), S9–S17. DOI: 10.1016/jadohealth.2017.07.024.

Riina, E. M., & Feinberg, M. E. (2012). Involvement in childrearing and mothers' and fathers' adjustment. *Family Relations, 61*(5), 836–50. DOI: 10.1111/j.1741-3729.2012.00739.x.

Riseman, D. (2016). *Why young men are dropping out of college.* Retrieved from https://www.lifezette.com/2016/03/why-young-men-drop-out-of-college/.

Robbins, A. (2019). *Fraternity: An inside look at a year of college boys becoming men.* New York: Dutton.

Roberts, C. (2013). *Men, sports, and the culture of masculinity.* Retrieved from https://menscenter.org/sports-culture-masculinity/.

Robertson, J. M., & Shepard, D. S. (2008). The psychological development of boys. In M. S. Kiselica, M. Englar-Carlson, & A. M. Horne (Eds). *Counseling Troubled Boys: A Guidebook for Professionals* (pp. 3–29). New York: Taylor & Francis.

Rochlen, A. B., Land, L. N., & Wong, Y. J. (2004). Male restrictive emotionality and evaluations of online versus face-to-face counseling. *Psychology of Men and Masculinity, 5*(2), 190–200. DIO: 10.1037/1524-9220.5.2.190.

Rochlen, A. B. Whilde, M. R., & Hoyer, W. D. (2005). The real men. Real depression campaign: Overview, theoretical implications, and research considerations. *Psychology of Men & Masculinity, 6*(3), 186–94. DOI: 10.1037/1524-9220.6.3.186.

Rock, A. (2017). *Report: Middle school suicide rates more than doubled since 2007.* Retrieved from https://www.campussafetymagazine.com/for-parents/middle-school-suicide-rates-middle-doubled/.

Rosenberg, A. (2011). *Disney movies are more subtle about masculinity than this documentary gives them credit for.* Retrieved from https://thinkprogress.org/disney-movies-are-more-subtle-about-masculinity-than-this-documentary-gives-them-credit-for-2a0c7c87c0d4/.

Rosenberg, A., Gates, A., Richmond, K., & Sinno, S. (2017). It's not a joke: Masculinity ideology and homophobic language. *Psychology of Men & Masculinity, 18*(4), 293–300. DOI:10.1037/men0000063.

Rosin, H. (2015). *The Silicon Valley suicides: Why are so many kids with bright prospects killing themselves in Palo Alto?* Retrieved from https://www.theatlantic.com/magazine/archive/2015/12/the-silicon-valley-suicides/413140.

Ross, M. & Bateman, N. (2018). *Millions of young adults have entered the workforce with no more than a high school diploma.* Retrieved from https://www.brookings.edu/blog/the-avenue/2018/01/31/millions-of-young-adults-have-entered-the-workforce-with-no-more-than-a-high-school-diploma/.

Rosser, L. (2012). *Bachelors degree vs. military experience—why do employers view one as less valuable?* Retrieved from https://thevalueofaveteran.wordpress.com/2012/06/03/bachelors-degree-vs-military-experience-why-do-employers-view-one-as-less-valuable/.

Rouner, J. (February 24, 2017). *Milo Yiannopoulos was only famous because of GamerGate.* Retrieved from https://www.houstonpress.com/arts/milo-yiannopoulos-was-only-famous-because-of-gamergate-9220643.

Safier, R. (2017). *8 important pros and cons of taking a gap year before college.* Retrieved from https://studentloanhero.com/featured/gap-year-disadvantages-important-pros-before-college/.

Salter, M. (2017). From geek masculinity to Gamergate: The technological rationality of online abuse. *Crime, Media, Culture: An International Journal, 14*(2), 247–64. DOI: 10.1177/1741659017690893.

Samuels, A. (2018). *Making men online.* Retrieved from https://daily.jstor.org/making-men-online/.

Santi, K. L., Hawkins, J. K., Antonelli, J. & Phipps, S. (2018). Valuing the workforce of tomorrow: Transition from secondary education. In N. D. Young, C. N. Michael, & T. A. Citro. *Turbulent Times: Confronting Challenges in Emerging Adulthood* (pp. 147–64). Madison, WI: Atwood Publishers.

Sax, L. (2016). *Boys adrift: The five factors driving the growing epidemic of unmotivated boys and underachieving young men.* New York: Basic Books.

Schafer, A. (2018). Single dads are vulnerable to mental health issues, so what can they do if they're struggling? Retrieved from https://www.huffingtonpost.ca/2018/06/18/single-dads-mental-health_a_23460211/.

Scher, A. (2018). Gay fathers, going it alone. Retrieved from https://www.nytimes.com/2018/10/25/nyregion/single-gay-fathers-through-surrogacy.html.

Schindler, H. S., & Coley, R. L. (2006). A qualitative study of homeless fathers: Exploring parenting and gender role transitions. *Family Relations, 56*(1), 40–51. DOI: 10.1111/j.1741-3729.2007.00438.x.

Schmitz, R. M. & Kazyak, E. (2016). Masculinities in cyberspace: An analysis of portrayals of manhood in men's rights activist websites. *Social Sciences, 5*(18), 1–16. DOI: 10.3390/socsci5020018.

Schoenberger, N. (2017). *Wayne & Ford: The films, the friendship, and the forging of an American hero.* New York: Penguin/Random House.

Schrock, D. & Schwalbe, M. (2009). Men, masculinity, and manhood acts. *Annual Review of Sociology, 35*(1), 277–95. DOI: 10.1146/annurev-soc-070308-115933.

Schwyzer, H. (2013). *Men are more likely to drop out of college than women because they can afford it.* Retrieved from https://jezebel.com/men-are-more-likely-to-drop-out-of-college-than-women-5985963.

Scott, M. E., Steward-Streng, N. R., Manlove, J., & Moore, K. A. (2012). The characteristics and circumstances of teen fathers: At the birth of their first child and beyond. *Trends in Child Research Brief. Publication #2012-19.* Retrieved from https://www.childtrends.org/wp-content/uploads/2013/03/Child_Trends-2012_06_01_RB_TeenFathers.pdf.

Seeman, M. V. (2018). Single men seeking adoption. *World Journal of Psychiatry, 8*(3): 83–87. DOI: 10.5498/wjp.v8.i3.83.

Semuels, A. (2017). *Poor girls are leaving their brothers behind.* Retrieved from https://www.theatlantic.com/business/archive/2017/11/gender-education-gap/546677.

Service Year. (n.d.). *What is a service year?* Retrieved from https://serviceyear.org/about/what-is-service-year/.

Seth, S. (2019). 5 characteristics of successful entrepreneurs. Retrieved from https://www.investopedia.com/articles/personal-finance/101014/10-characteristics-successful-entrepreneurs.asp.

Shain, B. (2016). Suicide and suicide attempts in adolescents. *Pediatrics, 138*(1). Retrieved from https://pediatrics.aappublications.org/content/pediatrics/138/1/e20161420.full.pdf.

Sheehy, G. (1986). *The victorious personality.* Retrieved from https://www.nytimes.com/1986/04/20/magazine/the-victorious-personality.html.

———. (1999). *Understanding men's passages: Discovering the new map of men's lives.* New York, NY: Rando House.

Shirk, A. (2015). *The real Marlboro man.* Retrieved from https://www.theatlantic.com/business/archive/2015/02/the-real-marlboro-man/385447/.

Shows, C., & Gerstel, N. (2009). Fathering, class, and gender: A comparison of physicians and emergency medical technicians. *Gender & Society, 23*(2), 161–87. DOI: 10.1177/0891243209333872.

Shpancer, N. (2017). Rape is not (only) about power; it's (also) about sex. *Psychology Today.* Retrieved from https://www.psychologytoday.com/us/blog/insight-therapy/201602/rape-is-not-only-about-power-it-s-also-about-sex.

Sifneos, P. E. (1987). *Short-term dynamic psychotherapy: Evaluation & technique* (2nd ed.). New York: Springer Science + Business Media.

Signoretti, N. (2017). *A study of gender advertisements: A statistical measuring of the prevalence of genders' patterns in the images of print advertisements.* DOI: 10.3390/proceedings1090947.

Simpson, J. (2017). *Finding brand success in the digital world.* Retrieved from https://www.forbes.com/sites/forbesagencycouncil/2017/08/25/finding-brand-success-in-the-digital-world/#412fb113626e.

Sims, C. (2014). Video game culture, contentious masculinities, and reproducing racialized social class divisions in middle school. *Signs, 39*(4), 848–57. DOI: 10.1086/675539.

Smiler, A. (2016). Man up . . . Whatever that means: Telling a guy to "man up" can be a powerful insult. *American Psychological Association.* Retrieved from https://www.apa.org/pi/about/newsletter/2016/04/man-up.aspx.

Smith, C. (2011a). Lost in transition: The dark side of emerging adulthood. Oxford University Press.

———. (2011b). *Most commonly used words in children's toys ads reinforce gender Stereotypes [infographic].* Retrieved from http://www.communicationstudies.com/most-commonly-used-words-in-childrens-toy-ads-reinforce-gender-stereotypes-infographic.

Smith, D. J. (2014). *Camille Paglia: The war on men, masculinity & the family.* Retrieved from https://www.souleticsresourcecenter.com/camille-paglia-the-war-on-men-masculinity-the-family/.

Snyder, M. (2018). *Men, masculinity and perceptions of higher education sexual violence programming: A qualitative analysis.* Retrieved from https://digitalcommons.hamline.edu/cgi/viewcontent.cgi?article=1086&context=dhp.

Snyder, T. D., De Brey, C. & Dillow, S. A. (2019). *Digest of education statistics 2017.* National Center for Education Statistics, Institute of Education Statistics, U.S. Department of Education. Retrieved from https://nces.ed.gov/pubsearch/pubsinfo.asp?pubid=2018070.

Sommers, C. H. (2013). How to make school better for boys. *The Atlantic.* Retrieved from https://www.theatlantic.com/education/archive/2013/09/how-to-make-school-better-for-boys/279635/.

Southern Poverty Law Center. (2012). *Misogyny: The sites.* Retrieved from https://www.splcenter.org/fighting-hate/intelligence-report/2012/misogyny-sites.

Statista (2019). *Percentage of the U.S. population who have completed four years of college or more from 1940 to 2017, by gender.* Retrieved from https://www.statista.com/statistics/184272/educational-attainment-of-college-diploma-or-higher-by-gender/#0.

Strayhorn, T. L. (2016). *Student development theory in higher education: A social psychological approach.* New York: Routledge.

Stephens, M. (n.d.). *History of television.* Retrieved from https://www.nyu.edu/classes/stephens/History%20of%20Television%20page.htm.

Stirling, A. E. & Kerr, G. A. (2015). Creating meaningful co-curricular experiences in higher education. *Journal of Education & Social Policy, 2*(6), 1–7. Retrieved from http://jespnet.com/journals/Vol_2_No_6_December_2015/1.pdf.

Swanson, N., Vaughn, A. L., & Wilkinson, B. D. (2015). First-year seminars: Supporting male college students' long-term academic success. *Journal of College Student Retention: Research, Theory & Practice, 18*(4), 386–400. DOI: 10.1177/1521025115604811.

Taylor, D. (2014). *The challenge of becoming a single father.* Retrieved from https://www.fatherhood.org/fatherhood/the-challenge-of-becoming-a-single-father.

Taylor, P., Funk, C., Craighill, P., & Kennedy, C. (2006). As family forms change, bonds remain strong: Families drawn together by communication revolution.

Pew Research Center. Retrieved from https://www.pewresearch.org/wp-content/uploads/sites/3/2010/10/FamilyBonds.pdf.

Teaching Tolerance (2019). *What are gender stereotypes?* Retrieved from https://www.tolerance.org/classroom-resources/tolerance-lessons/what-are-gender-stereotypes.

Thomas, P. (2018). *5 ways your campus can support men's mental health.* Retrieved from www.presence.io/blog/5-ways-your-campus-can-support-mens-mental-health/.

Thompson R. J. & Allen, S. (2017). *Television in the United States.* Retrieved from https://www.britannica.com/art/television-in-the-United-States.

Tinto, V. (1993). *Leaving college: Rethinking the causes and cures of student attrition.* Chicago, IL: University of Chicago Press.

Tinto, V. (2007). Research and practice of student retention: What next? *Journal of College Student Retention: Research, Theory & Practice, 8*(1), 1–19. DOI: 10.2190/4YNU-4TMB-22DJ-AN4W.

Tischler, A. & McCaughtry, N. (2011). PE is not for me: When boys' masculinities are threatened. *Research Quarterly for Exercise and Sport, 82*(1), 37–48. DOI: 10.1080/02701367.2011.10599720.

Top 10 Online Colleges (2019). *5 advantages of gap years.* Retrieved from https://www.top10onlinecolleges.org/list/5-advantages-of-gap-years/.

Toren, M. (2011). *Top 100 entrepreneurs who made millions without a college degree.* Retrieved from https://www.businessinsider.com/top-100-entrepreneurs-who-made-millions-without-a-college-degree-2011-1.

Torpey, E. (2013). *Apprenticeship: Earn while you learn.* Retrieved from https://www.bls.gov/careeroutlook/2013/summer/art01.pdf.

———. (2017). *Apprenticeships: Occupations and outlook.* Retrieved from https://www.bls.gov/careeroutlook/2017/article/apprenticeships_occupations-and-outlook.htm.

Truman, J. L., & Morgan, R. E. (2018). Criminal victimization, 2015. *U.S. Department of Justice, Office of Justice Programs, Bureau of Justice Statistics, 1–24.* Retrieved from https://www.bjs.gov/content/pub/pdf/cv15.pdf.

United States Army (2018). *Diversity in our nation's armed forces.* Retrieved from https://www.goarmy.com/advocates/advocates-news-and-events/diversity-army-life.html.

United States Census Bureau (2016). *Fathers in the United States.* Retrieved from https://www.census.gov/schools/resources/news/fathers.html.

———. (2018a). *Median age at first marriage: 1890 to present.* Retrieved from https://www.census.gov/content/dam/Census/library/visualizations/time-series/demo/families-and-households/ms-2.pdf.

———. (2018b). *Annual estimates of the resident population for selected age groups by sex for the United States, States, Countries, and Puerto Rico Commonwealth and municipios: April 1, 2010 to July 1, 2017.* Retrieved from https://factfinder.census.gov/faces/tableservices/jsf/pages/productview.xhtml?pid=PEP_2017_PEPAGESEX&prodType=table.

United States Coast Guard (2019). *The coast guard: America's oldest maritime defenders.* Retrieved from https://www.gocoastguard.com/about-the-coast-guard/learn-the-history.

University of Oregon (2010). Academic probation hits college guys harder. *ScienceDaily.* Retrieved from www.sciencedaily.com/releases/2010/05/100513093735.htm.

University of Washington (2012). *DO-IT prof: A project to help postsecondary educators work successfully with students who have disabilities.* Retrieved from https://www.washington.edu/doit/sites/default/files/atoms/files/prof.pdf.

———. (2017). *What can disabled student services offices do to help students with disabilities successfully transition from two- to four-year colleges?* Retrieved from https://www.washington.edu/doit/what-can-disabled-student-services-offices-do-help-students-disabilities-successfully-transition-two.

The Urban Dictionary (2013). *Big man on campus.* Retrieved from https://www.urbandictionary.com/define.php?term=big%20man%20on%20campus.

U.S. Bureau of Labor Statistics (2019). *Labor force statistics from the current population survey.* Retrieved from https://www.bls.gov/cps/cpsaat08.htm.

U.S. Department of Education (2011). *Students with disabilities preparing for postsecondary education: Know your rights and responsibilities.* Retrieved from https://www2.ed.gov/about/offices/list/ocr/transition.html.

U.S. Department of Health & Human Services, National Institutes of Health (n.d.). *NIMH's "Real men. Real depression." campaign.* Retrieved from https://www.nimh.nih.gov/health/topics/men-and-mental-health/men-and-depression/nimhs-real-men-real-depression-campaign.shtml.

U.S. Department of Justice (2018). *2017 Crime in the United States.* Retrieved from https://ucr.fbi.gov/crime-in-the-u.s/2017/crime-in-the-u.s.-2017/tables/table-1.

U.S. Department of Labor, Employment and Training Administration (2019). *Apprenticeships* Retrieved from https://www.careeronestop.org/findtraining/types/apprenticeships.aspx.

U.S. Department of Labor (n.d.a). *Apprenticeship.* Retrieved from https://www.dol.gov/general/topic/training/apprenticeship.

———. (n.d.b). *Frequently asked questions.* Retrieved from https://www.apprenticeship.gov/faqs.

———. (n.d.c). *Your one stop source for all things apprenticeship.* Retrieved from https://www.apprenticeship.gov/.

U.S. Department of Veterans Affairs (2019). *About home loans.* Retrieved from https://www.benefits.va.gov/homeloans/.

Vaillant, G. E. (1977). *Adaptation to life.* Cambridge, MA: Harvard University Press.

Valenti, J. (2017). *Zoe Quinn: After Gamergate, don't "cede the internet to whoever screams the loudest."* Retrieved from https://www.theguardian.com/technology/2017/sep/24/zoe-quinn-gamergate-online-abuse.

Violence Policy Center (2018). *Guns and suicide.* Retrieved from http://www.vpc.org/wp-content/uploads/2018/05/suicide-factsheet-2018.pdf.

Wang, A. X. (2017). *The complete guide to not going to college.* Retrieved from https://qz.com/1054087/the-complete-guide-to-not-going-to-college/.

Wang, W. & Parker, K. (2011). *By the numbers: Gender, race, and education.* Pew Research Center. Retrieved from http://www.pewsocialtrends.org/2011/08/17/iv-by-the-numbers-gender-race-and-education/.

Warren, P., Swan, S., & Allen, C. T. (2015). Comprehension of sexual consent as a key factor in the perpetration of sexual aggression among college men. *Journal of Aggression, Maltreatment & Trauma, 24*(8), 897–913. DOI: 10.1080/10926771.2015.1070232.

Watts, R. H., & Borders, L. D. (2005). Boys' perceptions of the male role: Understanding gender role conflict in adolescent males. *The Journal of Men's Studies, 13*(3), 267–80. DOI: 10.3149/jms.1302.267.

Way, N. (2013). *Deep secrets: Boys' friendships and the crisis of connection.* Cambridge, MA: Harvard College Press.

Weaver, A. G., Forte, D. J., & McFadden, C. (2017). Perceptions of higher education administrators regarding the role of club sports in recruitment and retention of male students. *Recreational Sports Journal, 41*, 42–54. DOI: 10.1023/rsj.2016-0023.

Weber, J. (2012). Becoming teen fathers: Stories of teen pregnancy, responsibility, and masculinity. *Gender and Society, 26*(6), 900–21. DOI: 10.1177/0891243212459074.

Wester, S. R., Vogel, D. L., Pressly, P. K., & Heesacker, M. (2002). Sex differences in emotion: A critical review of the literature and implications for counseling psychology. *The Counseling Psychologist, 30*(4), 630–52. DOI: 10.1177/00100002030004008.

Westwood, M., & Pinzon, J. (2008). Adolescent male health. *Paediatric Child Health, 13*(1), 31–36. DOI: 10.1093/pch/13.1.31.

Whitley, R. (2018). *Men's mental health on campus: Breaking the cycle.* Retrieved from https://www.psychologytoday.com/us/blog/talking-about-men/201808/mens-mental-health-campus-breaking-the-silence.

Wichard-Edds, A. (2015). *Want to help kids succeed in college? Let them take a gap year.* Retrieved from https://www.washingtonpost.com/news/parenting/wp/2015/06/23/want-to-help-kids-succeed-in-college-let-them-take-a-gap-year/?utm_term=.ac3da566222e.

Williams, J. P. (2018). *Why are black children killing themselves?* Retrieved from https://www.usnews.com/news/healthiest-communities/articles/2018-05-31/whats-behind-the-higher-suicide-rate-among-black-children.

Williams, R. A. (2009). Masculinities and fathering. *Community, Work & Family, 12*(1), 57–73. DOI: 10.1080/13668800802133784.

Willoughby, B. J., Olson, C. D., Carroll, J. S., Nelson, L. J., & Miller, R. B. (2012). Sooner or later? The marital horizons of parents and their emerging adult children. *Journal of Social and Personal Relationships, 29*(7), 967–81. DOI: 10.1177/0265407512443637.

Wingfield, N. (October 15, 2014). *Feminist critics of video games facing threats in 'GamerGate' campaign.* Retrieved from https://www.nytimes.com/2014/10/16/technology/gamergate-women-video-game-threats-anita-sarkeesian.html.

Wisner, M. (2017). *'Dirty Jobs' star Mike Rowe: Not everyone should go to college.* Retrieved from https://www.foxbusiness.com/features/dirty-jobs-star-mike-rowe-not-everyone-should-go-to-college.

Wojcik, N. (2017). *Breitbart editor's college grant for white men draws fire.* Retrieved from https://www.cnbc.com/2017/02/01/breitbarts-milo-yiannopoulos-creates-college-grant-exclusively-for-white-men.html.

Wong, A. (2018). *Boys don't read enough.* Retrieved from https://www.theatlantic.com/education/archive/2018/09/why-girls-are-better-reading-boys/571429/.

Wong, Y. J., & Rochlen, A. B. (2005). Demystifying men's emotional behavior: New directions and implications of counseling and research. *Psychology of Men and Masculinity, 6*(1), 62–72. DOI: 10.1037/1524-9220.6.1.62.

World Wide Web Foundation (2015). *Five barriers, five solutions: Closing the gender gap in ICT policy.* Retrieved from https://webfoundation.org/2015/06/five-barriers-five-solutions-closing-the-gender-gap-in-ict-policy/.

Yau, N. (2017). *Percentage of people who married, given your age.* Retrieved from https://flowingdata.com/2017/11/01/who-is-married-by-now/.

Yavorsky, J. E., Buchmann, C., & Miles, A. (2015). *High school boys, gender, and academic achievement: Does masculinity negatively impact boys' grade point averages?* Retrieved from https://paa2015.princeton.edu/papers/152814.

Yiannopoulous, M. (2014). *Feminist bullies tearing the video game industry apart.* Retrieved from https://www.breitbart.com/europe/2014/09/01/lying-greedy-promiscuous-feminist-bullies-are-tearing-the-video-game-industry-apart/.

Yogman, M. & Garfield, C.F. (2016). Fathers' roles in the care and development of their children: The role of pediatricians. *Pediatrics, 138*(1). DOI: 10.1542/peds.2016-1128.

Young, N. D., Celli, L., & Mumby, M. A. (2019). *Educating the experienced: Challenges and best practices in adult learning.* Madison, WI: Atwood Publishing.

Young, N. D. & Jean, E. (2018). Supporting struggling students on campus: An academic recipe for success. In N. D. Young, A. Fain, & T. A. Citro, *Turbulent times: Confronting challenges in emerging adulthood,* pp. 135–46. Madison, WI: Atwood Publishing.

Young, N. D., Jean, E. & Mead, A. (2019). *From cradle to classroom: A guide to special education for young children.* Lanham, MD: Rowman & Littlefield.

Young, N. D., Jean, E. & Quayson, F. O. (2017). *From lecture hall to laptop: Opportunities, challenges, and the continuing evolution of virtual learning in higher education.* Madison, WI: Atwood Publishing.

Young, N. D., Michael, C. N., & Jean (Bienia), E. (2018). *Dog tags to diploma: Understanding and addressing the educational needs of servicemembers and their families.* Madison, IL: Atwood.

Young, N. D., Michael, C. N., & Smolinski, J. A. (2018). *Captivating campuses: Proven practices that promote college student persistence, engagement, and success.* Wilmington, DE: Vernon Press.

———. (2019). *Sounding the alarm: Safety, security, and student well-being.* Lanham, MD: Rowman & Littlefield.

Zakrzewski, V. (2014). *Debunking the myths about boys and emotions.* Retrieved from https://greatergood.berkeley.edu/article/item/debunking_myths_boys_emotions.

Zanville, H. (2017). *Taking the gap year after high school as a paid service year.* Retrieved from https://www.luminafoundation.org/news-and-views/taking-the-gap-year-after-high-school-as-a-paid-service-year.

Zinzow, H. M., & Thompson, M. (2014). Factors associated with use of verbally coercive, incapacitated, and forcible sexual assault tactics in a longitudinal study of college men. *Aggressive Behavior, 41*(1), 34–43. DOI:10.1002/AB.21567.

About the Authors

Nicholas D. Young, PhD, EdD, has worked in diverse educational roles for more than thirty years, serving as a teacher, counselor, principal, special education director, graduate professor, graduate program director, graduate dean, and longtime psychologist and superintendent of schools. He was named the Massachusetts Superintendent of the Year, and he completed a distinguished Fulbright program focused on the Japanese educational system through the collegiate level. Dr. Young is the recipient of numerous other honors and recognitions including the General Douglas MacArthur Award for distinguished civilian and military leadership and the Vice Admiral John T. Hayward Award for exemplary scholarship. He holds several graduate degrees including a PhD in educational administration and an EdD in educational psychology.

Dr. Young has served in the U.S. Army and U.S. Army Reserves for over thirty-five years combined; and he graduated with distinction from the U.S. Air War College, the U.S. Army War College, and the U.S. Navy War College. After completing a series of senior leadership assignments in the U.S. Army Reserves as the commanding officer of the 287th Medical Company (DS), the 405th Area Support Company (DS), the 405th Combat Support Hospital, and the 399th Combat Support Hospital, he transitioned to his current military position as a faculty instructor at the U.S. Army War College in Carlisle, Pennsylvania. He currently holds the rank of colonel.

Dr. Young is also a regular presenter at state, national, and international conferences; and he has written many books, book chapters, and articles on various topics in education, counseling, and psychology. Some of his most recent books include *The Burden of Being a Boy: The Educational and Emotional Well-Being in Young Males* (2019); *Maximizing Mental Health*

Services: Evidenced-Based Practices that Promote Emotional Well-Being (2018); *The Special Education Toolbox: Supporting Exceptional Teachers, Students, and Families* (2019); *Sounding the Alarm in the Schoolhouse: Safety, Security and Student Well-Being* (2019); *Creating Compassionate Classrooms: Understanding the Continuum of Disabilities and Effective Educational Interventions* (2019); *Acceptance, Understanding, and the Moral Imperative of Promoting Social Justice Education in the Schoolhouse* (2019); *Empathic Teaching: Promoting Social Justice in the Contemporary Classroom* (2019); *Educating the Experienced: Challenges and Best Practices in Adult Learning* (2019); *Securing the Schoolyard: Protocols that Promote Safety and Positive Student Behaviors* (2018); *The Soul of the Schoolhouse: Cultivating Student Engagement* (2018); *Embracing and Educating the Autistic Child: Valuing Those Who Color Outside the Lines* (2018); *From Cradle to Classroom: A Guide to Special Education for Young Children* (2018); *Captivating Classrooms: Educational Strategies to Enhance Student Engagement* (2018); *Potency of the Principalship: Action-Oriented Leadership at the Heart of School Improvement* (2018); *Soothing the Soul: Pursuing a Life of Abundance Through a Practice of Gratitude* (2018); *Dog Tags to Diploma: Understanding and Addressing the Educational Needs of Veterans, Servicemembers, and their Families* (2018); *Turbulent Times: Confronting Challenges in Emerging Adulthood* (2018); *Guardians of the Next Generation: Igniting the Passion for Quality Teaching* (2018); *Achieving Results: Maximizing Success in the Schoolhouse* (2018); *From Head to Heart: High Quality Teaching Practices in the Spotlight* (2018); *Stars in the Schoolhouse: Teaching Practices and Approaches that Make a Difference* (2018); *Making the Grade: Promoting Positive Outcomes for Students with Learning Disabilities* (2018); *Paving the Pathway for Educational Success: Effective Classroom Interventions for Students with Learning Disabilities* (2018); *Wrestling with Writing: Effective Strategies for Struggling Students* (2018); *Floundering to Fluent: Reaching and Teaching the Struggling Student* (2018); *Emotions and Education: Promoting Positive Mental Health in Students with Learning* (2018); *From Lecture Hall to Laptop: Opportunities, Challenges, and the Continuing Evolution of Virtual Learning in Higher Education* (2017); *The Power of the Professoriate: Demands, Challenges, and Opportunities in 21st Century Higher Education* (2017); *To Campus with Confidence: Supporting a Successful Transition to College for Students with Learning Disabilities* (2017); *Educational Entrepreneurship: Promoting Public-Private Partnerships for the 21st Century* (2015); *Beyond the Bedtime Story: Promoting Reading Development during the Middle School Years* (2015); *Betwixt and Between: Understanding and Meeting the Social and Emotional Developmental Needs of Students During the Middle School Transition Years* (2014); *Learning Style Perspectives:*

Impact Upon the Classroom (3rd ed., 2014); *Collapsing Educational Boundaries from Preschool to PhD: Building Bridges Across the Educational Spectrum* (2013); *Transforming Special Education Practices: A Primer for School Administrators and Policy Makers* (2012); and *Powerful Partners in Student Success: Schools, Families and Communities* (2012). He also co-authored several children's books to include the popular series *I Am Full of Possibilities*. Dr. Young may be contacted directly at nyoung1191@aol.com.

Christine N. Michael, PhD, is a more than forty-year educational veteran with a variety of professional experiences. She holds degrees from Brown University, Rhode Island College, Union Institute and University, and the University of Connecticut, where she earned a PhD in education, human development, and family relations. Her previous work has included middle and high school teaching, higher education administration, college teaching, and educational consulting. She has also been involved with Head Start, Upward Bound, national nonprofits Foundation for Excellent Schools and College for Every Student, and the federal Trio programs. She is currently the program director of Low Residency Programs at American International College.

Dr. Michael has published widely on topics in education and psychology. Her most recent works include serving as a primary author on the book *The Burden of Being a Boy: The Educational and Emotional Well-Being in Young Males* (in press); *Securing the Schoolyard: Protocols that Promote Safety and Positive Student Behaviors* (in press); *Sounding the Alarm in the Schoolhouse: Safety, Security and Student Well-Being* (in press); *The Soul of the Schoolhouse: Cultivating Student Engagement* (2019); *Captivating Classrooms: Educational Strategies to Enhance Student Engagement* (2019); *Turbulent Times: Confronting Challenges in Emerging Adulthood* (2018); *To Campus with Confidence: Supporting a Successful Transition to College for Students with Learning Disabilities* (2017), *Beyond the Bedtime Story: Promoting Reading Development during the Middle School Years* (2015), *Betwixt and Between: Understanding and Meeting the Social and Emotional Development Needs of Students During the Middle School Transition Years* (2014); and *Powerful Partners in Student Success: Schools, Families and Communities* (2012). Dr. Michael may be contacted at cnevadam@gmail.com.

Elizabeth Jean, EdD, has served as an elementary school educator and administrator in various rural and urban settings in Massachusetts for more than twenty years. As a building administrator, she has fostered partnerships with staff, families, various local businesses, and higher education institutions. Further, she is currently a graduate adjunct professor at the Van Loan School of Education, Endicott College and previously taught at the College of Our

Lady of the Elms. In terms of formal education, Dr. Jean received a BS in education from Springfield College; an MEd in education with a concentration in reading from the College of Our Lady of the Elms; and an EdD in curriculum, teaching, learning, and leadership from Northeastern University.

Dr. Jean is a primary author on *The Burden of Being a Boy: The Educational and Emotional Well-Being in Young Males* (in press); *Acceptance, Understanding, and the Moral Imperative of Promoting Social Justice Education in the Schoolhouse* (2019); *The Empathic Teacher: Learning and Applying the Principles of Social Justice Education to the Classroom* (2019); *From Cradle to Classroom: A Guide to Special Education for Young Children* (2019); *The Potency of the Principalship: Action-Oriented Leadership at the Heart of School Improvement* (2018); *Dog Tags to Diploma: Understanding and Addressing the Educational Needs of Veterans, Servicemembers and their Families* (2018); *Stars in the Schoolhouse: Teaching Practices and Approaches that Make a Difference* (2018); *From Head to Heart: High Quality Teaching Practices in the Spotlight* (2018); and *From Lecture Hall to Laptop: Opportunities, Challenges and the Continuing Evolution of Virtual Learning in Higher Education* (2017). She has also written book chapters on such topics as emotional well-being for students with learning disabilities, postsecondary campus supports for emerging adults, parental supports for students with learning disabilities, home-school partnerships, virtual education, public and private partnerships in public education, professorial pursuits, technology partnerships between P–12 and higher education, developing a strategic mindset for LD students, the importance of skill and will in developing reading habits for young children, and middle school reading interventions to name a few. She has co-authored and illustrated several children's books to include *Yes, Mama* (2018), *The Adventures of Scotty the Skunk: What's that Smell?* (2014), and many of the *I Am Full of Possibilities* Series for Learning Disabilities Worldwide. She may be contacted at elizabethjean1221@gmail.com.